"Hank Shaw elevates waterfowl to its rightful place in the culinary skies. He will teach you how to turn flesh into edible works of art without sacrificing practicality. I'll be reading—and using—this book for decades to come."

—**STEVEN RINELLA**,
author of *American Buffalo* and *Meat Eater*

"You don't have to be a hunter to want to cook duck and goose. Thankfully, Hank Shaw has demystified these birds for all to enjoy!"

—**CHRIS COSENTINO**,
chef-owner of Incanto and winner of Top Chef Masters

Copyright © 2013 by Kyra Bussanich
Photographs copyright © 2013 by Leela Cyd

Published in the United States by Ten Speed Press, an imprint of the
Crown Publishing Group, a division of Random House, Inc., New York.
www.crownpublishing.com
www.tenspeed.com

Ten Speed Press and the Ten Speed Press colophon are registered trademarks of
Random House, Inc.

Library of Congress Cataloging-in-Publication Data
Bussanich, Kyra.
Sweet cravings : 50 seductive desserts for a gluten-free lifestyle / Kyra Bussanich.
    pages cm
 Includes index.
  1. Baking. 2. Desserts. 3. Gluten-free diet—Recipes. I. Title.
 TX765.B947 2013
 641.86—dc23

Hardcover ISBN: 978-1-60774-360-6
eBook ISBN: 978-1-60774-361-3

Printed in China

Design by Colleen Cain
Food styling by Adrian Hale

10 9 8 7 6 5 4 3 2 1

First Edition

Index

About the Author

KYRA BUSSANICH graduated from Le Cordon Bleu's patisserie and baking program and worked as the assistant pastry chef at clarklewis in Portland before founding her own award-winning gluten-free bakery, Kyra's Bake Shop (formerly Crave Bake Shop). She was the first gluten-free baker to appear on—and the only to win—the Food Network's *Cupcake Wars*. She was also runner-up in the all-star series *Cupcake Champions*. Kyra and her shop have been featured on the *Today* show, Fox News, the Food Network, *Food & Wine*, *Delight Gluten-Free Magazine*, *Gluten-Free Living*, the *Oregonian*, *USA Today*, *Huffington Post*, *G-Free Foodie*, *Notes from a Gluten-Free Kitchen*, *Gluten Free Portland Oregon*, and *Portland Food and Drink*. She and her husband live and eat in Portland, Oregon.

Laura Cruickshank, Jana Dieter, Jane Gjester, Nicole Grayson, Rob Miller, Jessica Mont-Eton, Heather Murphy, Susan Pater, Rachel Oedewalt, Sheila Stahl Butler, Christine Walter, and Brandy Wendler. Their comments helped me refine my recipes (and make them easier to understand).

The bake shop crew (Jackie Eizik, Carly Sullivan, Jen Petersmark, Lisa Horness, Rachel Oedewalt, Chuck Childress, Caitlin Davies, Chelsea Willis, and Stacey Roybal), who are well trained, trustworthy, and fun to work with. There were times I left them in charge of the shop so I could focus on this book—or on competing at one of the Cupcake Wars—and they kept everything running smoothly. Thank you, chickadees (and Chuck-adee)!

My inner circle, who has helped me go from a homeless (but trained) pastry chef to a successful bakery owner and author. Nikki Bircher, Laura Cruickshank, Elizabeth Hills, Amy Miller Juve, Lindsay Krall Sanders, and Beth Willis have been shoulders to cry on, ears to vent to, comediennes to crack me up, and fans to encourage me to keep going.

Michael Edward Brown, who gave me my first unofficial set of cooking lessons (in Chamonix, France, no less!).

Alissa Rozos, my first boss out of pastry school, who encouraged my creativity and taught me about plated dessert composition.

Jim Emory, for teaching me to love freshly baked homemade bread when I was six years old. I have never looked back.

Gluten-free girl Shauna James Ahern, whose journey helped me say yes to my own. It is a joy to know you!

And to my customers and readers, without whom there would be no shop and no book and I might have had to get a real job. I hope that by creating the recipes in this book, I've given you something in return.

Acknowledgments

This book did not come to fruition through my efforts alone. There are many (many!) people who encouraged, inspired, and tested recipes to help me. My thanks go out to them. In particular:

Jason, my dear husband, who has encouraged (and sometimes pushed) me to do the things I always wanted to do but was afraid to try. Without him, I would not be a pastry chef and this book would never have happened.

My parents, Robert and Susan Pater, and Jana and Chuck Dieter, who have been supportive through the years, emotionally and financially. Thank you for critiquing my writing, cheering me on, teaching me to love great food, and guiding my journey here.

My friend and mentor Laura Byrne Russell, who knows far more than I do about all things gluten-free. She has given me recipe pointers, critiques, and writing tips, and I am awed by her knowledge.

Amazing editor Lisa Westmoreland (and the rest of the talented gang at Ten Speed Press), who helped me polish and refine this piece of work and get it into your hands. I am ever grateful!

The extremely talented and artistic Leela Cyd (and design team), whose photo stylings make my desserts look as delicious as they taste. You have brought my pastries to life!

Recipe testers Victoria Andrich, Tracy Bosnian, Lilah Butler, Laura Byrne Russell,

122

DUCK, DUCK, GOOSE

Recipes and Techniques for Cooking
Ducks and Geese, both Wild and Domesticated

HANK SHAW

Photography by HOLLY A. HEYSER

TEN SPEED PRESS
Berkeley

FOR HOLLY—*my duck hunting buddy, photographer,
guinea pig, and most of all, my best friend.*

Published in the United States by Ten Speed Press, an imprint of
the Crown Publishing Group, a division of Random House, Inc., New York.
www.crownpublishing.com
www.tenspeed.com

Ten Speed Press and the Ten Speed Press colophon are
registered trademarks of Random House, Inc.

Library of Congress Cataloging-in-Publication Data
Shaw, Hank, 1970-
  Duck, duck, goose : recipes and techniques for cooking ducks and geese,
both wild and domesticated / Hank Shaw.
    pages cm
1. Cooking (Duck) 2. Cooking (Goose) 3. Cooking (Game) I. Title.
TX750.5.D82S53 2013
  641.6'91—dc23
                          2012046940

Hardcover ISBN: 978-1-60774-529-7
eBook ISBN: 978-1-60774-530-3

Printed in China

Design by Sarah Adelman
Food and prop styling by Hank Shaw and Holly A. Heyser

10 9 8 7 6 5 4 3 2 1

First Edition

CONTENTS

INTRODUCTION

Cooking a duck or a goose in today's world is an act of expression. It is a way to find that forgotten feast we Americans once enjoyed, to free ourselves from the Tyranny of the Chicken and shake our fists at the notion that fat is our enemy. Mastering these birds will make you a more competent carnivore. It will help you regain the skills we once had in our kitchens, and it will give you the knowledge needed to tackle more challenging morsels, such as giblets and wings and rendered fat. Cooking a duck or goose—a whole bird, from bill to feet—is real cooking. True, honest *cooking*.

Like pork, these birds offer an array of flavors and textures depending on which cut you choose. But unlike almost every other animal we normally consider food, ducks and geese offer a diversity of breeds and species that even a novice can detect at the table. The flavor of a Pekin duck is as far from that of a goose as a skinless chicken breast is from a rib eye. And that is just a domestic example. Throw in the world of wild ducks and geese and your experiences multiply tenfold: a roasted green-winged teal bears little resemblance to an eider, a goose, or even a cinnamon teal. The common mallard can taste markedly different depending on whether it had been eating corn, acorns, rice, or fish.

Waterfowl has a rich human history, as well. Tamed first by the ancient Egyptians, geese are one of humankind's oldest domesticated animals. Ducks, which arrived in the barnyard later, have nevertheless been domesticated for thousands of years and arose independently in two parts of the world before they spread to the rest of the globe. Cultures as far-flung as Mexico, Persia, and China have been cooking ducks and geese for more than three millennia, and nearly every cuisine in the world has found a place for duck at the table.

Perfectly cooked duck breast has the meatiness of a steak with an additional cloak of fatty, crispy skin. In fact, it is better to associate duck with beef than with other poultry: think of the breast meat as a steak and the rest of the bird as the brisket. But it is the skin that most distinguishes duck in the kitchen. Crispy duck skin is one of the greatest pleasures of the dining table. It is the reason that Peking duck has persisted as a Chinese classic for nearly seven hundred years. And crispy skin is what separates confit, a French method of lightly curing duck legs or wings and then slowly cooking them in their own fat, from any another piece of braised meat. Confit is so meaty, silky, and crispy that it has become many a chef's "death bed" meal.

I am not alone in feeling this passionate about waterfowl. Duck is experiencing a renaissance in restaurant kitchens across the continent. Seared duck breast or duck confit has become a common sight on menus. And just as with the pork revolution of the past decade, diners well outside of the nation's culinary capitals of San Francisco, New York, and Chicago are finding evidence of the trend: crispy duck tongues in Kansas City; duck skin cracklins in Toronto; duck consommé in Minneapolis; foie gras foam in Sacramento; duck legs, braised and pulled like carnitas, tucked into tacos in Austin. Diners are excited about duck. It has become the new pork.

But this renaissance need not be the province of the professionals. Restaurant cooks are not wizards. With the possible exception of Peking duck, they are not cooking duck in mystical ways that require years of apprenticeship to master. Cooking a duck properly is not rocket science, though it does require some specialized knowledge. This book's primary goal is to give you that knowledge.

I can hear some of you. You're thinking about the ducks you've eaten in the past, and the image you've conjured up is not good. Chances are the first word that popped into your head was some variant of greasy, dry, or livery. And I am certain that either you or someone you know has his or her Great Goose Disaster story. These tales of woe typically begin with visions of a Victorian Christmas and end with gallons of grease—often igniting into fireballs—dry, unhappy meat, and a lifetime of disappointment. "Oh, I tried goose once. Let me tell you about the time . . ." Even hunters who often shoot scores of ducks in a season share this fear of fowl and banish their ducks to the sausage heap.

This need not be so. With a few exceptions, the recipes in this book can be done with no special equipment from ingredients you can buy in an average supermarket. Yes, I have included a few high-wire recipes, but that is just to show you the range of dishes you can create with these remarkable animals.

In the pages that follow, you will learn how to break down a duck or goose into legs, breasts, and wings, a process not terribly different from how you handle a chicken. The hunters among you will find out how to hang, pluck, and eviscerate their birds. Throughout this book, you will discover the fundamentals of duck and goose cookery: how to cook a duck breast properly, and how to cook duck legs so that they are tender, yet still have crispy skin. I will walk you through the culinary jazz of making sausages and other charcuterie and stocks, teach you how to render duck and goose fat from both domestic and wild birds, and describe how to cook with that fat as well as with duck eggs, which may look like chicken eggs but are not.

Once you learn my method for braising duck legs, you can use it to cook not only my other braised waterfowl recipes but also to perfect your own creations. Master the task of searing a duck breast medium-rare with crispy skin and you will never be far from a memorable meal: even paired with a store-bought sauce and tater tots, a perfectly cooked duck breast never fails to impress. And after you make a few batches of sausage using my techniques, you will find yourself making links in your own personal style. Charcuterie is an addictive culinary art.

Of special importance to me is the section on giblets. Properly cooked, giblets can taste every bit as wondrous as the rest of the duck. But there is the rub: for many, "properly cooked" is an impossibility. The recipes in this book will disabuse you of that idea, and they will help you make full use of a duck's so-called fifth quarter, even if is only in gravy, sausage, or a homemade "duck burger."

But before you can cook, you must first catch your duck, be it in the market or the marsh. Thankfully, this is no longer the ordeal it once was. Ten years ago, you would be lucky to find a frozen whole duck in your supermarket. Now those same markets are starting to sell breasts and legs separately and stock fresh whole ducks at the meat counter. Farmers' markets are

"Man who stand on hill with mouth open will wait long time for roast duck to drop in."

— CONFUCIUS

increasingly offering carefully raised heritage breeds, and duck eggs are no longer a rare item. What's more, if you have an Asian market near you, you will never want for duck: Asians eat the majority of all ducks raised worldwide, and for many Chinese and Southeast Asians, duck is more common than chicken.

It is my hope that if you glean nothing else from this book, you will come away with a heaping slice of confidence in the kitchen. Waterfowl are endlessly fascinating, endlessly diverse in their forms and flavors. Get yourself some duck breasts, with a nice layer of fat and skin. Sear them in a pan until the skin crisps like a cracker and the meat is as lovely as a medium-rare rib eye. Flavor it with nothing more than sea salt, pepper, and perhaps a squeeze of lemon. Taste it. Savor it. You will see. A perfect duck breast is a revelation, a life-changing event. There will be no turning back. Ready to begin?

BASICS

FROM MARKET TO TABLE: BREEDS, BUYING, BREAKING DOWN, AND STORING

It's been a century since ducks have been this accessible in American markets, and for more than a generation the only ducks available to home cooks were wan, factory-farmed Pekin ducks shoved into a dark corner of the freezer section.

Those birds are still there, but they are increasingly being joined by ducks raised under better conditions, as well as by breeds better suited to serious cooking. And for the first time, consumers can now buy the breasts and legs of ducks, just like they do of chickens. This simple change has opened a whole new world for the American home cook.

Here's a brief guide to the kinds of ducks and geese you will find in the market, what to look for when buying, and what to do with the birds once they arrive in your kitchen.

BREEDS

PEKIN. This is the standard white-feathered duck sold in supermarkets throughout the United States. Before the Chinese domesticated it thousands of years ago, the Pekin was a mallard. The breed made its debut in the United States in 1873, and soon became known as a Long Island duck because the East End of the island was a center of duck farming. Pekins, which average three to six pounds plucked and gutted, are primarily sold whole and frozen, although they are increasingly available as breasts and legs sold separately. The meat of a typical Pekin is so pale that it cooks up very much like a chicken thigh. In fact, in old cookbooks, it's listed as "white duck." Its paleness is a function of the bird's diet and limited exercise and is a hallmark of factory-farmed ducks. Pekins raised on better diets and allowed more exercise have better color and flavor.

WHY A GOOSE IS NOT A DUCK

A whole goose will cost you at least forty-five dollars and can approach two hundred dollars in the case of special breeds. A typical domesticated goose serves only six to eight diners, which makes goose one of the more expensive options for the table. There are a variety of reasons for this, primarily to do with the fact that geese are unique among domesticated animals.

"Goose is a pain in the neck to breed," says Ariane Daguin of D'Artagnan Foods. Geese only lay eggs once a year, unlike ducks and chickens, which lay year-round. Then, once the chicks are hatched, they grow slowly. "They take six months to reach adulthood, and at any point during that time if a sickness passes by, overnight the whole flock can die."

Jim Schiltz of Schiltz Goose Farm notes that geese have one of the worst feed-to-weight ratios of all domestic animals. A goose requires close to seven pounds of feed to put on just one pound of weight, he says. A duck will gain a pound off of only two and a half pounds of feed, and a chicken's feed ratio is 1.8 to 1. The only other commonly eaten animal with a ratio similar to that of the goose is grass-fed beef.

That makes sense to Schiltz, because geese—wild and domestic—prefer a diet heavy in grass, not grain. Ducks, on the other hand, love grain. "If you fed a goose diet to a duck, it would not do well at all," he says.

Schiltz adds that geese have resisted attempts to breed them so they grow faster. "Their legs won't support it," he explains. "But honestly, growing slower is not a bad thing. Growing slower makes them more tasty."

MUSCOVY. A species native to Central and South America, Muscovy ducks were domesticated around 600 BCE by the peoples living in what is now Ecuador; the Spanish conquistadores encountered domesticated Muscovies among the Maya, Incas, and Aztecs and transported them to Spain as early as 1494. Muscovies are larger than Pekins and put on less fat.

They are an excellent eating breed for this reason, and their meat is darker and more richly flavored than that of a Pekin. In old books, you will see Muscovy ducks referred to as Brazil ducks. You will rarely see a Muscovy whole, though specialty purveyors such as D'Artagnan in New York do carry them whole. Mostly you will encounter only their breasts and legs.

MOULARD. A sterile hybrid of the Pekin and the Muscovy duck (the name means "mule" in French), this is the duck most often raised for foie gras, and its breasts are favored in the restaurant trade, where they are called *magret* breasts. Moulard breasts are twice the size of Pekin breasts, often topping one and a quarter pounds per side. One half of a Moulard breast will serve at least two diners. Moulards are also much fattier than Muscovies, so they offer the benefit of delicious fat with the larger size of the Muscovy. I have never seen Moulards sold whole, but the breasts are typically available in specialty markets or online.

ROUEN (ROHAN). A French duck bred specifically for the table (not for egg laying), the Rouen looks like a gigantic mallard. Culinarily speaking, it is a "natural" Moulard: it is large and fatty like a Moulard but is its own breed, so it will reproduce. Rouen ducks are commonly raised by artisanal breeders, so if you see ducks sold at a farmers' market, it is likely they are Rouens. D'Artagnan is selling a variant called a Rohan that is smaller but offers the same characteristics of the meatier Rouen. A half breast will feed one hungry person or two light eaters. Both Rouens and Rohans are an improvement on the Pekin, and are my favorite domestic ducks, but Rohans are available only through the D'Artagnan website.

EMBDEN GOOSE. This huge, white goose of German origin is the standard goose in barnyards across the United States. A special variant of this goose, which was developed by mixing the Embden with several other domestic goose breeds, is what the South Dakota company Schiltz sells to supermarkets all over the nation. Schiltz controls the American goose trade, so chances are if you've eaten domestic goose in the United States, it is from Schiltz. Geese are primarily sold whole and frozen in winter months, though Schiltz sells legs and breasts on its website year-round.

BUYING

In many cases, your only choice is to look in the freezer section for a frozen whole duck. This will almost always be a Pekin duck from a factory farm. Although it is not the ideal duck to work with, you can still do great things even with this sort of duck. But be careful: many of these birds are "plumped" with a salt solution the way many chickens are, and it will say so on the label. If this is the case, go easy on any salt you use with the duck, and under no circumstances should you brine it. It is already brined.

Many markets now sell ducks by the part. This is a good thing, not only because it makes it easier to cook duck on a daily basis—cooking a whole bird is more of a weekend thing, at least for me—but it's also allowed farmers to sell different breeds of duck more easily. It is not too hard to find Muscovy breasts or a packet of frozen duck legs these days. Even rarer breeds such as Moulards are finding their way into high-end supermarkets and butcher shops.

DUCK MEAT IS HORMONE- AND ANTIBIOTIC-FREE

Duck farmers in the United States are not allowed to give their birds routine doses of hormones, according to the U.S. Food and Drug Administration. Antibiotics are permitted only when a bird is sick, which means no "preventive dosing" is allowed as it is with chickens. If a bird has been given antibiotics, it must go through a "withdrawal" period before it is slaughtered, so that no residue of any medicine remains in the bird's system.

In fall and winter, markets are starting to sell fresh birds, too. A fresh duck will have a better texture than one that has been frozen, so definitely buy fresh if you can.

Also, look to your local farmers' market for high-quality ducks. Small farmers are beginning to raise ducks for meat more often, and if you can find one, cultivate a relationship. Chances are good that these will be the finest ducks around.

Finally, you can always shop online. Purveyors such as D'Artagnan sell some of the highest-quality ducks and geese in the world. They will be expensive when you factor in shipping, but they are definitely worth the cost for special occasions.

BREAKING DOWN

Perhaps the most important skill you will need to master as a waterfowl cook is how to break down a whole duck or goose. It's not terribly difficult, and if you know how to cut up a chicken, you are most of the way there. Mechanically, ducks are a little different from chickens. They tend to have a wider breastbone and a shallower keel than chickens do, and their bones are heavier. Their wings are longer, tougher, and leaner, too. They are also far fattier. That fat makes it more difficult to see the lines where you cut—between the leg and breast, the exact center of the breastbone, and so on—but once you have handled a few ducks, you will get the hang of it. Anatomically, ducks and geese are virtually identical.

To get started, you will need a fresh or thawed duck or goose. The best way to thaw the bird is to set it in the fridge for a couple of days; geese will take several days to thaw. To speed the process, you can set a wrapped bird inside a large pot and fill it with cold water. This method will thaw a duck in a few hours; a goose will take at least four to five hours.

Once your bird has thawed, set it on a large cutting board. You will need a sharp, thin-bladed knife. I use a boning knife, but a fillet knife or even a paring knife works well, too. Let me emphasize again: your knife must be as sharp as lightning. A dull knife is a lazy servant and will actually increase your chances of injuring yourself. Your other cutting tool will be heavy kitchen shears. I prefer the type that come apart for cleaning. I've used the fancier ones with springs, and I find they get gunky too easily.

Have ready a large bowl or tray for the bird pieces. When I am breaking down waterfowl, I have one small bowl for giblets; two medium bowls, one for breasts and one for legs and wings; and a large tray for the carcasses. Another good thing to have around is a towel, cloth or paper. You will want to keep your knife hand clean and dry.

STEP ONE. Start by setting the bird breast side up on a cutting surface. For a domesticated bird, reach into the cavity and pull out the neck and the giblets, which will often be packed into a little bag. Begin breaking down the bird by removing the legs. I press on the gap between the legs and breast to push as much skin toward the breast as I can (**1A**). When you make this cut, you want more skin on the breast than the legs, which will keep the breasts juicy and tender when you cook them. Slice down the gap and you will notice that you sliced skin, not muscle (**1B**). That's how you know you cut in the right spot. Continue to cut gently downward until you reach the ball-and-socket joint where the leg is attached. As you slice down to the joint, arc the knife under the tail end of the bird's back to get all of the meat off the thigh.

Snap the leg back downward to pop open the ball-and-socket joint, which frees the leg (**1C**). Tuck the knife behind the ball joint and cut the leg free (**1D**). As you cut past the socket joint toward the front of the bird, don't forget to arc the knife around the little pocket of meat known in birds as the oyster. This is my favorite part. It is small in wild ducks but is more substantial in domesticated ducks and all geese. Set aside (**1E**) then repeat with the other leg.

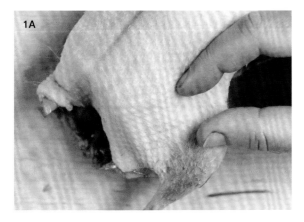

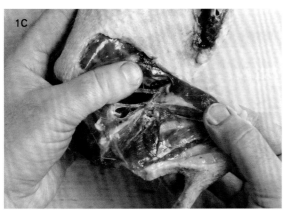

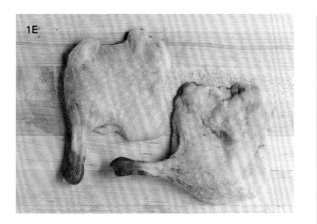

TAKING DRY AGING A STEP FURTHER

Here's a tip from executive chef Paul Virant of Vie restaurant in Chicago that can be easily translated to a home kitchen: When you buy whole ducks, cut off the breast meat still attached to the breastbones, but leave the legs and wings connected to the rest of the body.

Dry age the legs and wings uncovered in an open container in the refrigerator. Lift them off the bottom of the container by putting them on a cooling rack or even celery stalks. Leaving them for only a day will improve their flavor but you can extend the drying for as long as a week. "It develops that special dry-aged character everyone loves," Virant says.

STEP TWO. Remove the wings (if your bird still has wings; you often lose one with wild birds when wing-shooting). Turn the bird breast side down and look for the curved bone on either side of its back **(2A)**. This is the saber bone, which is the duck's shoulder blade. Using the saber bone as a guide, slice toward the neck to free the wing drumette **(2B)**. If you cut the right spot, your knife will go right through the soft cartilage that attaches the wing to the body. Don't worry if you mess it up a few times; it takes practice to know exactly where that spot is. Finish by removing the wing and cutting a little extra skin from the neck area. Repeat on the other side.

STEP THREE. Finish with the breasts. I like to take the breasts off in one piece. This lets me stuff them if I want, and it wastes less skin. Begin by making a cut along the very obvious fat pad at the center of the bird's flanks **(3A)**. Then start sliding the knife gently toward the bird's tail end along another visible fat line **(3B)**. Ducks and geese have broad breastbones, so you need to run the knife flat along this bony plate until you hit the keel bone, which divides each half of the breast.

Once you have freed the tail end of the breast, run the knife back along the breastbone toward the neck, tapping the point of the knife on the keel bone as you go. This ensures that you are cutting deep enough to get all of the meat off the bone. Continue this way

until you get to the wishbone (3C). Using the point of your knife, run it along the edge of the wishbone to free the front end of the breast near where the wing used to be. Now turn the knife upward, and with short, gentle strokes, free the breast meat from the keel bone (3D). "Freeing" the meat is how you should think of this process, rather than "slicing" or "cutting."

To repeat this on the opposite side, lay the mostly freed breast back where it was on the duck, turn the duck over, and repeat the process on the other side.

When the breast meat is almost fully freed on both sides, gently cut the skin along the top of the keel bone to separate the whole breast from the body. I

do this by turning the duck upside down and letting the mostly freed breast sides hang (3E).

When you have your breast meat on the cutting board, slice the halves apart through the skin that attaches them (3F). Now remove the tenders, which are only lightly attached to the breast. They need to be taken off, as they get in the way if you are searing the breasts by themselves. I either fry up the tenders and eat them, or throw them into the stockpot or into sausages.

Take your time at first, study the pictures, and know that each bird will be easier than the last one. Note that this technique works with any bird: pheasants, pigeon or squab, turkeys—and yes, domesticated chickens.

STORING

My first move when it's time to store ducks and geese is to get a large plastic tub and line it with paper towels. I set the birds, breast side up, in the tub, and then I set the tub uncovered in the refrigerator for a day. This dries out the ducks and finishes any aging that you may have started by hanging the birds (see page 17). No matter whether the bird is wild or domesticated, this process also will give you a crispier skin when you ultimately cook it. This works with thawed birds, too. A freshly killed duck or goose will last a week in the fridge. A store-bought bird will last closer to five days.

I always use a vacuum sealer for freezing all of my birds. So long as the seal does not break, a frozen bird will remain in good condition for a year. I cannot stress enough how useful this tool is, so buy one if at all possible.

If you don't have a vacuum sealer, pat the birds dry and wrap in plastic wrap. Then wrap again in either freezer paper (the kind with one waxy side, which you want to face inward) or aluminum foil. Wrap giblets tightly in plastic wrap, and then stuff the little packets into a heavy-duty freezer bag. Always store each type of giblet in a separate container so you can make, say, a heart dish without needing to thaw gizzards and livers.

FROM MARSH TO TABLE: WILD SPECIES, FIELD CARE, HANGING, AND PROCESSING

Hunters face a special set of challenges with the birds they bring home. A bewildering array of species fall to our guns, and even those species can vary dramatically depending on their diet. But every wild duck or goose has its place in the kitchen.

Once you have your birds home, several decisions await: Will you pluck or skin your birds? Will you hang them? Dry age them? Store them whole or break them down? I'll walk you through the process, starting with what you may find out there in the marsh.

NORTH AMERICAN WILD DUCKS

Here is a quick culinary guide to the most common species of duck you will find in Canada, the United States, and Mexico, ordered in terms of their numbers. Mallards are by far the most hunted wild duck on the continent, while canvasbacks and the species that follow it on the list are less commonly shot by hunters.

MALLARD. If you are not familiar with ducks, and can only picture in your head the white domesticated duck and that green-headed duck at the park, the mallard is the green-headed one. It is the most common wild duck in the world: mallard are highly adaptable to different environmental conditions and are found on every continent other than Antarctica. It is the stock from which all domesticated ducks, except the Muscovy, originate. An average mallard will weigh about two pounds plucked and gutted and will serve one hearty eater or two normal ones. Mallards are opportunistic eaters and will chow down on anything from rice to grass to Doritos to clams or crayfish, so they can range from wondrous to dodgy flavorwise.

TEAL. Teal is the Tinker Bell of ducks: tiny, fast, aerobatic, and pretty. The green-winged and blue-winged teal are exciting birds to hunt and are superb at the table. Both are, like the northern pintail (see opposite), primarily seed eaters, which gives them mild-tasting meat and helps them put on a thick layer of sweet fat. These are single-serving ducks, and a hearty eater can eat two whole ones at a sitting. Teal are the original duck used in the classic French dish *salmis de sarcelles*. A third teal, the cinnamon teal, is pretty but not as good at the table.

BLUEBILL (SCAUP). The most commonly hunted diver duck, the bluebill (greater and lesser) is usually strong-tasting in the West, though not always strong enough to warrant skinning. In the Midwest, however, bluebills are excellent eating: I far preferred the bluebills I shot in Manitoba to the mallards that lived alongside them. Like the teal, a bluebill is a single-serving duck. Just remember that on any diver or

Clockwise from top left: cinnamon teal, northern pintail, northern shoveler, and blue-winged teal

sea duck, beware of orange fat: that means the bird has been eating crustaceans, and it will be smelly when cooked.

GADWALL. A homely, mottled brown duck, gadwalls are smaller than mallards but are just a little too big to serve the typical eater. Two gadwalls for three people are about right. Gadwalls are a duck lover's bird: even when they are fat, they can be musky and intensely ducky. Taken to the extreme, they can be downright foul, earning the derisive name "gagwall." Gadwalls prefer to eat green things, and when they do, they tend to be skinny and smelly. But if there is grain around—rice or corn—they will fatten up and be every bit as wonderful as a pintail. Just be careful where you shoot them.

NORTHERN PINTAIL. The Prince of Ducks, the pintail is slightly smaller than the mallard, but a whole roasted one will still serve two normal eaters. They are the most highly sought-after bird in the West, because they seek out seeds over all other foods, making their meat very mild. In the Sacramento Valley where my partner Holly and I hunt, they can be so fat from gorging on rice that their livers will naturally become foie gras (see page 154), loaded with fat and growing to twice the normal size. No duck in North America can best a fat pintail at the table, with one exception: canvasback (see page 14).

NORTHERN SHOVELER (SPOONIE). Ah, the much maligned spoonie. The northern shoveler is one of the most widely distributed ducks in the world, but it is no joy at the table. It is so-called because its bill is a big, spoon-shaped filter that sucks up algae and other shrimpy, watery tidbits. Only in rice fields will spoonies put on clean fat and taste good; we call them "white spoonies" because their normally orange fat will turn white. A shoveler is a single-serving duck, but you will rarely want to roast one whole. Shovelers are best skinned and used as parts, or ground into sausage.

WIGEON. One of my favorite birds, wigeon are medium-size ducks that whistle instead of quack. They often travel in large flocks and usually decoy easier than most other ducks. Like the gadwalls, wigeon are variable. Where there is rice or other grain, they are fat, sweet, and wonderful. But wigeon will hang out at the seashore, and the ones living along the Oregon coastline are legendarily skinny and smelly. I've never encountered a fat wigeon that was stinky, however, so if you are worried, skin the skinny ones and roast the fat ones. A wigeon is a perfect single-serving duck.

REDHEAD. A large diving duck about the size of a mallard, the redhead, even though it is a diver, is generally clean-tasting because it prefers to eat seeds and plant matter over clams and crustaceans. It will eat these things, however, so watch for orange fat: if you see it, the bird will taste fishy. Most redheads are shot in the Midwest; I've only shot them in Canada, and they are rare in the West.

CANVASBACK (KING CAN). The King of Ducks, the canvasback is the most prized waterfowl in North America. It is larger than a mallard, fast, and beautiful, with a lordly nose and regal bearing that earns it its nickname. Sadly, like most monarchies, the reign of the canvasback is largely over, thanks to the decimation of its favorite foods, wild celery in the East and the roots of sago pondweed in the West. When a canvasback has been eating these starchy foods, no bird—not even the pintail—can match it at the table. But most canvasbacks live near saltwater now and dine on clams, not celery. So if you get them inland, treat them as the prize they are. On the sea, however, they are often no better than a scoter.

WOOD DUCK (WOODIES). Woodies are among the most sought-after wild ducks in America. A smallish single-serving duck, wood ducks, once known as Carolina ducks, love to eat acorns, and the nuts impart a distinctive flavor to the meat that you either love or hate. I love it. Unlike most American ducks, woodies hatch their clutch inside hollow trees and therefore depend on dead and dying riparian forests for their survival. In the past, such forested areas had been largely cleared, so wood ducks were once nearly extinct in some parts of the United States. Conservation efforts, including the placement of wood-duck boxes, have allowed populations to bounce back over the last twenty-five years. Woodies are the prettiest duck on our continent, with multicolored crests on their heads and dainty downturned bills. They are the only member of their genus in North America, although they are distantly related to Muscovies as well as and Chinese mandarin ducks, which are not found in North America.

RINGNECK. Eatingwise, the ringneck is a generally safer version of the bluebill because seeds rather than fish or crustaceans make up a much larger percentage of its diet. A ringneck looks a lot like a bluebill, but it has a ring around its bill and a fainter ring around its neck. Ringnecks are one of my favorite eating birds because they are strong tasting without being fishy. It is an intensely wild flavor similar to that of birds like snipe or woodcock—not for beginners. Ringnecks will serve one person heartily.

SURF SCOTER. A true sea duck, the scoter is a large black duck with a party on his nose: his beak looks like candy corn, with bright orange and yellow stripes on a white background. Two other scoters fly around our shores, the black scoter and the white-winged scoter, which are similar but with less entertaining beaks. All scoters are fish and clam eaters, so they must be skinned. The good news is they are big birds, so even a skinned one will serve two.

RUDDY. This little butterball is a small, stocky diving duck with a tail that sticks straight up. Like the wood duck, it is the only member of its genus in North America, and it prefers to swim around rather than fly. A century ago, in the days of commercial hunting, ruddies were called the "dollar duck" because a brace cost a full dollar—more than all other ducks save the canvasback and redhead. Ruddy ducks eat mostly plant matter, but that does not mean they are not strong tasting. I've eaten wonderful ruddy ducks inland, but near the sea they are almost invariably fishy. Like the teal, a ruddy is a single-serving duck.

A flock of mixed breeds of domesticated ducks and one goose

NORTH AMERICAN WILD GEESE

These are the most common wild geese you are likely to encounter in North America. I did not include brants or emperor geese, as I've not yet had the pleasure of eating a brant, and emperor geese are rarely shot outside Alaska.

CANADA. The Canada goose is to geese what the mallard is to ducks: the most recognized wild version of its kind in North America. Once threatened, Canada geese are now so numerous that they are pests in many places. Many subspecies of this goose exist, ranging from the little cacklers and Aleutian geese, which average only about four pounds, to the mammoth Giant Canada goose, which can top twenty-three pounds. Like mallards, Canada geese are opportunistic and will eat a variety of things. I've had many clean-tasting ones and more than a few with smelly fat. In general, the grain-eating birds are the best eating, and they are absolutely worth the effort to pluck—and let me tell you, it is an effort. It took me more than an hour to pluck a single Giant Canada I shot in Manitoba. A typical Canada weighs about ten pounds and will easily feed four to six. Incidentally, I always break down my Canada geese and cook the legs and breasts separately.

SNOW. In the Blizzard from the North, vast numbers of white snow geese fill the air on their annual migrations, with the massive waves that stream down to the Midwest from the tundra the most famous. Snow goose populations have increased so much that wildlife authorities have authorized special spring seasons on them, because the geese are destroying their delicate tundra nesting habitat in Canada. This phenomenon has extended to California and the East, too: my father, who lives on Lake Champlain in New York, wonders at the white cloud of snows that descends on the lake for a few weeks each year, stopping there to refuel on their way south. Snow geese, which average about seven pounds, tend to be skinny, and they have a weird blue skin. I skin mine, unless I get an unusually fat one. Snow geese are ideal for skinless preparations and charcuterie.

ROSS'S. Pretty much the same thing as a snow goose, only smaller (the size of a large mallard), Ross's geese are common in California. Like snows, I typically skin them and use the meat for confit or charcuterie.

SPECKLEBELLY (WHITEFRONT). The Rib Eye in the Sky, which biologists call whitefronts and hunters refer to as specks, is fatty, sweet, and superb at the table. A plump speck, as hunters call it, is essentially a giant pintail duck. Both are primarily seed eaters and will gorge on rice and other grains when they are available. Specklebelly geese average seven pounds, and a roasted one will feed four; it is the only wild goose I recommend roasting whole (see page 29).

FIELD CARE

When I am hunting, I am hunting. My focus is on finding birds, killing them cleanly and successfully, and retrieving those that I've shot. But the moment I have a duck or a goose in hand, my mind begins to break it down into food.

What species of duck is it? Mostly I know this before I've pulled the trigger. Pintail make me think of roast duck. Teal bring images of a classic French *salmis*. Scoters and shovelers, well, they go into chili or sausages. As soon as I pick it up, I feel the keel bone that separates each breast half: Is there a nice layer of fat over it? Or is this a skinny duck, a "storm bird" brought to California by a ferocious north wind and emaciated by the ordeal? Fat birds get roasted. Skinny ones get broken down.

Back in my hiding spot, which is usually a clump of reeds in the middle of the marsh, I lay my birds in the shade and above the water level. It is vital to keep your birds as cool as possible until you can get them into a refrigerator . . . within reason. I never keep my birds in a cooler, unless it is a freak day in the marsh, with temperatures over 75°F. When it gets that hot, I do bring ice. A bird left out in hot weather can rot quickly.

On the other extreme, you need to prevent your birds from freezing, too. My friend Todd Baier in Montana routinely hunts in temperatures of -10°F or colder. A duck will freeze solid if you leave it out in that weather for too long. Even tossing the birds in your truck while you hunt will help. And while an overheated duck will rot, a duck that has been frozen in the field cannot really be refrozen back home without significant loss of meat quality. Freezing damages the cell walls of the flesh, which can make any frozen meat a little mushier than fresh meat. Prefrozen meat also dries out a little faster than fresh does. None of this is terribly noticeable on a bird that's been frozen properly. But freeze it, thaw it, freeze it again, and then thaw and cook that bird and you will definitely notice it.

In warmish weather—between 60°F and 70°F— you should be fine as long as you keep your birds

DETERMINING THE AGE OF WILD DUCKS AND GEESE

This is largely a challenge for hunters, as domesticated ducks and geese are all slaughtered young, and ducklings are sent to market so young that their bones are not yet fully formed. I have sliced through the keel bone of a duckling many times without effort. Try that on an old mallard and you'll be in the market for a new knife.

Why does this matter? A young bird is a tender bird. Most wild waterfowl that hunters bring home are young (and foolish) birds. But occasionally a wise old duck or goose falls to the gun; the oldest wild duck on record was a thirty-six-year-old eider, a type of sea duck. A bird of that vintage needs to be braised, as even the breast meat will be tough.

In general, determining the age of waterfowl isn't easy. But you can look for a few things. One universal marker is the webbing on the feet: if you can tear the webbing easily, you have a young bird. The "knees" of a duck are also a decent indicator: if they are knobby, the bird is old.

A harder but effective method is to look at the covert feathers, which are the feathers on the top of the wings nearest the body. On most young birds, the tips of these feathers are buff colored. Adult birds lack this variation and instead have consistent color to the edge of the feather.

You can also check for three species-specific age markers on a goose. On a Canada goose, the cheek patch on a young bird is grayish white and on an older bird is bright white. An old specklebelly will have lots of black bars on its belly, and a young one will have only a few bars, if any. And finally, an old Ross's goose will have lots of bumpy growths on its beak.

in the shade and out of the water. When you take them home, do not stack them: lay them side by side so they can cool faster. If you stop for a beer and a burger on your way home, make sure you park in the shade and leave the windows cracked.

HANGING

For several years after I began hunting, I recoiled at the idea of hanging game birds. The idea of hanging ducks and geese ungutted and in their feathers for days and days seemed neither hygienic nor sane. Old texts wax rhapsodic about the sublime flavor of "high" game, which usually means pheasants and usually means birds that have hung for more than a week. This, I decided, was madness. I was wrong.

Nearly everyone who has ever tasted the difference will agree that dry-aged beef is a far finer thing than its pallid, wet-aged supermarket cousin. Dry aging concentrates the flavor of the meat and makes the meat more tender. It also makes it more expensive, because the layer of crusty, slightly moldy ickiness that forms on the outer edges of the meat as a result of dry aging must be cut off before the meat can be sold or served.

Hanging beef is important in part because cattle tend to be dispatched at about eighteen months to two years old, old enough to get a tad tough on the teeth. Domesticated ducks are normally slaughtered at about two months for Pekin ducks and three months for Muscovy, too young to require hanging. Domesticated geese are typically killed between three and five months of age. Most wild ducks shot in North America are about six months old, but many are older, and a few can be downright ancient, like the thirty-six-year-old eider (see the sidebar at left). Wild geese tend to be older, with average ages of two and three years old.

I normally hang my ducks for a day or two, and my geese for two to four days. Note that this is not quite as long as wild pheasants or grouse. The reason is fat. Duck fat is unusually low in saturated fats, which means that the fat can go rancid more quickly than the fat of a cow, or of a pheasant for that matter. So hang time with waterfowl is always a push-pull between tenderizing the meat and concentrating the flavor on the one hand and racing against rancidity on the other.

The process involved here is controlled rot. Enzymes and beneficial bacteria work on the carcass to our benefit, if the bird is kept in a controlled environment. Too hot and the bad bacteria take over. Too cool and you've stopped the good bugs from working, too.

So if you choose to hang your birds, hang them between 45°F and 55°F for at least a day and no longer than a week. It does not matter if you hang from the neck or feet, though I always hang from the neck.

You must hang your birds with their feathers intact. Hanging a plucked bird will dry out its skin to the point where the bird will become inedible. The oils in the feathers help keep the skin supple as the bird ages, so wait to pluck until you've hung the bird as long as you plan to.

As for gutting the bird before or after hanging, science is on the fence in terms of whether it affects the flavor of the aged bird. I always leave the guts intact. And while you might think that after aging for three days the guts would be pretty smelly and disgusting, in most cases they're not. Oddly, the cavities are typically dry inside, and the innards mostly look (and taste) fine and wholesome. There is another reason to leave the guts intact: it is much more difficult to pluck a gutted bird than a whole one. Even if you end up tossing the giblets, this reason alone is enough to keep your birds intact when you hang them.

Never hang a bird that has been shot in the guts. Feel around the vent area for wounds or blood to see if you've damaged the intestines. If you hang a bird with ruptured guts, they can ruin the whole bird. If you have a gut-shot bird, pluck and gut it as soon as possible.

You cannot hang a bird that has been frozen. Freezing kills the enzymes and bacteria that perform the magic.

PLUCKING

Plucking a bird is very much like unearthing an archaeological treasure: it is painstaking, frustrating, and messy, and yet when you are done, it is deeply rewarding. You are working hard to bring out the best in your birds.

Why pluck? Doesn't it take a long time? It's worth it. Almost all of a bird's distinctiveness resides in the skin and fat. Suffice to say that if you skin your birds, you will have an awfully hard time distinguishing a bite of coot breast from a bite of canvasback breast. Trust me, I've done blind tests, and a skinless breast loses its identity. In a different test, I served slices of pintail, canvasback, and mallard breasts, all with skin and fat. Most preferred the pintail, but the canvasback was a universal second (and my favorite). The mallard was, well, boring. None of this would be discernable without skin and fat, and you cannot keep skin and fat on a bird without plucking.

That said, sometimes it's best to skin your birds. Use this guide to determine the best option for the bird at hand.

- If the bird has been badly shot up or mauled by your dog, skin it.

- Wing-shot birds will often have pristine breasts, so always pluck them.

- Pluck "quality" ducks and geese, including mallards, pintails, canvasbacks, and teal ducks and specklebelly geese. In certain cases, also pluck wigeon, gadwall, redhead, and bluebill ducks and Canada geese.

- Skin snow geese, which have weird blue skin and almost no fat. Skin all sea ducks or divers shot near saltwater, as they will almost always taste fishy. And if you eat coots, skin them, too.

Wet Plucking Versus Dry Plucking

If you plan to pluck your birds, do it somewhere other than the kitchen. If you pluck a duck or goose in the house, you will be finding feathers forever.

Even tolerant spouses will squawk, and rightly so. I pluck the birds I bring home in the garage, away from breezes that can carry away feathers; it makes for easier clean-up afterward. I like to pluck seated on a stool wearing a long apron—the long apron hangs over my knees when I pluck, saving my jeans.

Looking at your birds, understand that the skin on ducks and geese is pretty tough, so you are less likely to tear it than you are the skin of a pheasant or quail. This is a good thing, as it means you don't need to be as delicate as you would if you were plucking a pheasant. The downside of plucking waterfowl, is, well, down. Ducks and geese have a layer of gossamer down under their regular feathers that keeps them warm and waterproof. It is not easy to get off by hand, but wax removes the down like magic.

Which is why I prefer to wet pluck my birds. Wet plucking uses scalding water and paraffin to remove the feathers. Once you get the hang of it, the result looks just like a store-bought bird. The trick is to get a giant pot of water steaming—not boiling—melt the wax in it, and dunk your birds. Then you toss the waxed birds into a big basin of ice-cold water to set the wax, let them cool a bit, and pluck away. The wax grabs the down and upper feathers, leaving you with a nice clean-plucked duck.

To get started, you will need lots of paraffin (available in the canning section of your supermarket), a good set of kitchen shears, a really big canning pot, and plenty of patience. Plucking is a messy, wet business, so be sure to wear an apron or other protective clothing.

While your pot of water is heating up, examine your ducks and geese. Chop off any badly damaged legs or wings with the kitchen shears. Next, roughly pluck your birds: pull out the tail feathers, the big wing feathers (you might need to pull them one at a time on a goose), and some of the regular feathers on the body. Be careful when you do this, anchoring the skin of the bird with one hand while you pluck with the other. Otherwise, you can tear the skin.

Put the paraffin in the water. How much? The paraffin I use comes four blocks to a box, and I find that a goose needs a full block. Big ducks need half, and on smaller ducks you can get away with two or three birds to a block.

Once you have finished the initial plucking and the wax is melted, grab the bird by the head and and feet, and swirl it around a bit on the surface (melted wax floats on water). Make sure the bird is well coated. Let it drip a little over the pot, then put the waxed bird into a basin of cold water; I use the slop sink in the garage. Let the bird chill for a few minutes, then put it somewhere to drain.

Start with the wings, as they are the hardest part. You might need to break the wax seal on parts of the bird to peel off the paraffin. Again, anchor the skin with one hand while you peel with the other. Many times you are actually keeping the wax in one place while you gently peel the skin away from it. This is especially important when working around shotgun pellet holes.

After I do the wings, I go to the tail, then the back, then the legs. Finally, I do the neck and breast. The neck skin is loose, and this is the most likely place for a tear. If I am going to save the neck for sausage (see page 189), I pluck the bird right up to its "chin." The breast is the most prized part of the bird, so it needs your full attention. Always remember to remove the wax carefully to avoid tearing the skin. Once you get the hang of it, you should be able to pluck a limit of seven ducks in a little over an hour. Geese will take a bit longer.

The only drawback with this method is the cost of the wax. You can reclaim close to half of what you use, but you will lose wax every time you pluck. I reclaim used paraffin by putting it back into the pot of hot water. I then turn up the heat until the water boils, and then skim the feathers out with a Chinese wire skimmer (often called a spider skimmer because it looks like a spiderweb). There is a trick to it: when you scoop up some feathers, rap the side of the skimmer against the side of the pot to get as much water and molten wax out of it as possible. Discard the wet feathery goop and continue until there are no more feathers in the pot. Waxing costs a little, but it is worth it for a beautifully cleaned bird.

If you decide instead to dry pluck, all you need is patience and a good set of kitchen shears. The shears are for clipping the wing tips and chopping off the head. Pluck the feathers against the grain with your thumb running across the skin. My friend Jesse Griffiths, a great wild game chef from Texas, likens the motion to dealing cards. Take your time, as this is a painstaking process, but it will work. Singe with a lighter any feathers that don't come out.

GUTTING

Gutting ducks and geese is not difficult, and there are several ways to do it. But my method is fast, and it gives you the maximum amount of potential fat to render. Once the bird has been plucked, with the head and wing tips removed, bring it to the kitchen and set it on a cutting board near the sink. Have a trash can nearby. You can wear latex gloves if you like.

FAT, FLAVOR, AND TERROIR

About a dozen of us gathered around the platter, ready to taste the sliced duck breasts. One mallard had been shot over the cornfields of the Sacramento–San Joaquin Delta, another over the rice fields of the Sacramento Valley, a third had been gorging on acorns in the Sierra Nevada foothills, and the last had been taken in the West's largest remaining natural swamp, a vast wetland in the center of California known as the Grasslands. Only I knew which bird was which. I was hosting what might be the first-ever mallard tasting, to see whether ducks of the same species, taken from different habitats, could be distinguished from one another.

The mallards had been simply seared in their own fat and then sprinkled with fine sea salt. The tasters' notes were mostly in agreement. The corn-fed Delta mallard was boring. The rice-field mallard, which had bright white fat, was clean and neutral tasting. The acorn mallard was darker in color and almost tannic in taste. Compared with the others, the Grasslands mallard, having fed on natural forage, tasted less minerally and more complex. It was the clear favorite.

In North America, only the bayous of Louisiana and Arkansas come close to Northern California in having so many waterfowl spend their winters in so many diverse habitats in such close proximity to one another. Most stay within a three-hundred-mile-wide circle centered on Sacramento. Fifteen species of duck are commonly hunted in California, not to mention seven species of goose, plus a few coots and moorhens. (The last two are gallinules, swamp-loving fowl more closely related to pheasants and chickens than to ducks, and their fishy-tasting fat makes them poor eating unless they are skinned and stewed.)

Such diversity makes hunting and eating wild ducks and geese something of a crapshoot. Each possesses its own inherent flavor, mostly due to diet and how well it can put on fat. At their best, they offer the perfect combination of dense, juicy meat and an ample layer of sweet fat topped with crispy skin. At their worst, they smell and taste like low tide on a hot day.

Hunters who return to a particular habitat year after year have definite opinions about which species taste best and which are best left alone. Nearly everyone in California agrees that the pintail, symbol of the state's waterfowl association, is a prince among ducks. Pintail are always tasty and are almost always fat—sometimes as fat as domesticated ducks, although much smaller, at an average of just under two pounds. Unfortunately, just two of a hunter's daily limit of seven ducks may be pintail, largely because of its limited breeding population.

Mallards are universally sought after because they normally taste good and can weigh nearly four pounds. But they are also opportunists in terms of habitat, and their flavor reflects where they live. We knew enough not to bother with the ones from the salty San Francisco Bay, because there they eat clams and shrimp and other invertebrates that give them a fishy flavor.

In rice country, both the wigeon, which are easily spotted by the white head of the drake (in some parts of the country, the birds are called bald pates), and the drab-looking gadwalls are excellent eating birds because they gorge themselves on rice left after harvest. Yet just one hundred miles south of the rice fields, in the Grasslands marshes, those same species are utterly rejected.

Not long after our mallard-tasting experiment, my girlfriend Holly and I finagled our way into a duck club down in the Grasslands—the territory where our winning mallard had been shot—for two days of hunting over New Year's Eve.

The clubhouse was set in what looked like a little village in the middle of a swamp. I asked my friend Pete Ottesen what sort of ducks we might find the next morning, and he suggested I look at the logbook, where each hunter records what he or she has shot that day. The latest entries showed a few gadwalls and wigeon, slightly more mallards and pintail—and several thousand green-winged teal. Far more than any other duck, teal dominate the area, and they explain why more ducks are killed in Merced County, the heart of the Grasslands, than in any other county in the United States. Teal weigh no more than a pound and are deliciously savory and fatty, with almost no fishy flavor. Other than pintail, teal are the only ducks in California that eat primarily seeds.

Looking at the club's notebook, I still thought the wigeon and gadwall we'd enjoyed so much from the Sacramento Valley might be tasty from this unspoiled marsh. So the next day Holly and I each shot a few. Pete had suggested we wait for teal, but we wanted the bigger ducks. At the plucking table, the club members all stood around pulling tail feathers and snipping off wings with shears.

"Got a gaddie, eh?" an old Portuguese farmer asked as I began plucking. I said yes, and he wanted to know if I'd made a mistake. No, I said, and he grunted and turned away. When I gutted the bird, I learned why. It stank. And it was emaciated. It was nothing at all like the well-upholstered gadwall up north. Why? When I got home and checked Frank Bellrose's *Ducks, Geese and Swans of North America,* the bible on the subject, the answer was obvious. Gadwalls prefer the stems and leaves of marsh grasses to seeds. Their rice eating in the north is the exception that proves the rule.

Seeds are the key to fine flavor in ducks and most wild birds. Pheasants, grouse, and turkeys are also big seed eaters. Even free-range chickens eat largely seeds, counting what the farmer supplies. Several biologists who study waterfowl food habits have suggested to me that humans prefer seed-eating birds because they develop more fat and fewer off flavors than birds with a more variable diet. Teal and pintail, no matter where they live, are almost exclusively seed eaters. And all waterfowl wintering in the northern rice fields eat grain left behind by the harvesting machines. Even normally sketchy-tasting scaup (also known as bluebills), a diving duck that eats lots of fish and clams, turn into delicious eating once they've been in the rice fields a few weeks.

There's a further culinary reason we hunt waterfowl when we do, and in some ways it has dictated the hunting seasons for them, as well.

At either end of their migration, waterfowl eat more animal life than plant matter. They eat lots of insects in early fall to prepare for (and recover from) the long flight south, and in spring they feast on emerging insects to recover from the rigors of courtship and egg laying, which take a harsh toll on them. For the males, courtship begins even before the season closes in late January. Ottesen's grandfather taught him always to shoot hens at the end of the season because they would still be fat while the drakes had burned off most of theirs chasing after them.

The week before I'd shot that emaciated gadwall drake in the Grasslands, all this variability came into focus in the form of an obese gadwall hen that my girlfriend Holly shot up north. It was just before Christmas, and she and I were hunting in a Sacramento Valley marsh. The wild wetlands there are surrounded by rice fields, so the birds tend to hang out in the marshes but feed on the rice. When we saw this gadwall in flight, I thought it was a mallard hen: it was gigantic for a gadwall, which is a midsize duck of about two and a half pounds, often a full pound lighter than a mallard. As soon as Holly had shot it, we knew this bird was fat. When we got it home and plucked it, under the breast we found a quarter-inch layer of white fat, a huge amount for a wild bird whose fat layer is normally less than half that thick. White fat usually means the duck has been eating seeds, probably rice.

As fate would have it, our main holiday plan fell through and on Christmas Day we found ourselves alone. We hadn't bought a turkey, but we did have this fat gadwall. It was so fat we decided to roast it slowly. I stuffed the gadwall with a cut lemon and herbs, dotted the skin with butter, and roasted it for a full hour, until the skin was completely crisp (see recipe on page 31). It reminded me of the Peking duck in New York's Chinatown: skin like cracklins, meat fully cooked but still very moist. That fat gadwall hen tells the whole story about what makes a perfect duck, and years later it remains one of the best birds I've ever eaten.

Using kitchen shears or a sharp knife, chop off the feet at the "knees." Save the feet for making stock or *glace de viande*. Unless you plan on stuffing the bird, start by chopping off the tail. Doing this gives you easier access to the innards. If you do plan to stuff the bird, the tail helps keep the stuffing inside the cavity during roasting.

Use kitchen shears to chop off the entire tail section, right behind the gizzard. You will feel the gizzard as a large, hard, round shape right behind the breastbone. When you make the cut, you will be chopping through the intestines, too. This is okay. As soon as you've removed the tail, run it under cold tap water. Remove any stray intestine bits, then turn the tail inside out to reveal the vent. Immediately clean the vent thoroughly under cold running water. This takes only a few seconds, and it is usually quite clean. Reserve the tail section if it has a layer of nice white or off-white fat. If the fat is orange, toss it. Unless the birds had been eating a lot of corn, toss any yellow fat, too. Yellow fat from corn-fed birds is delicious. Yellow fat on birds living far away from cornfields can be sketchy.

Using your first two fingers as a hook, reach around the gizzard with one hand while stabilizing the duck with the other. Pull hard to extract the gizzard, along with most (or all) of the intestines. Sometimes the liver comes with this, too.

Use the kitchen shears or a knife to free the gizzard from the intestines. Discard the intestines. If the gizzard is encased in white fat, remove the fat and save it. Toss the gizzard into a bowl reserved for giblets.

If the liver has come with the gizzard, gently remove it from the intestines. Look at it. You will notice a small ovoid gland the deep green of a NyQuil gel cap: that's the gallbladder. You can remove it by carefully cutting around it with a sharp knife. Or, you can do as I do: hold the liver under cold, running water, pinch around the gallbladder with one hand while holding the liver with the other, and pull the gallbladder away. You need to do this under running water because the bile from the gallbladder is very bitter and can ruin the duck's liver. Rinse the liver and put it into the giblet bowl.

The heart and lungs will still be inside the duck. Reach into the cavity and locate the heart, which will feel like the firm little lump of meat it is. Pull it out. Slice off the top of the heart just above the fat ring to remove any stray veins and arteries. Rinse it well and put it into the giblet bowl.

Use your fingernails to scrape out the lungs, which will be lurid pink, and the kidneys, which are burgundy spots buried in the backbone of the duck near where you cut off the tail. Discard. Rinse the bird well under cold, running water and let it drain.

I always use kitchen shears to remove the second digit of each wing, even if I am going to cook these digits later. They are very tough and must cook longer than the rest of the bird, which means they need special treatment. I leave the drumette on the wings with the body if I am going to roast the bird whole, however.

Using kitchen shears, remove the neck about an inch away from the body: you don't want to cut too close to the body because the skin will retract and expose some of the breast, and you need the breast fully protected with skin. After you've done this, remove the stump of the neck with shears, leaving the skin intact. If you want to save the rest of the neck, push the neck meat through the neck skin, using your fingers to break any bits of connective tissue. Use the neck skin as a sausage casing, or chop it and render it for fat. Save the feet, wing tips, and neck meat for stock.

COOKING WITH DUCK: FLAVORS AND WINE AND BEER PAIRINGS

The most fundamental differences between waterfowl such as ducks and geese and gallinules like chicken, turkey, pheasant, and quail are the meat and fat. For one, waterfowl are almost always fatter, and ducks and geese are entirely made up of red meat. Think of ducks and geese as beef with an overcoat of fat and crispy skin. Breasts should always be served pink, and legs and wings should be slowly cooked, like beef brisket.

The reason waterfowl are all-red meat birds is because they are marathon flyers. Gallinules like chickens are walking birds that fly in short bursts to escape predators, or to roost in trees at night. Ducks and geese fly as a matter of course during most of their lives, from loafing areas where they hang out and preen to marshes or farm fields where they eat, some of which can be miles from where they sleep at night. For example, in California it is not uncommon for a duck to sleep in Tule Lake and eat in the Sacramento Valley, 225 miles away. Red, slow-twitch muscle tissue is what animals build to move long distances. White fast-twitch muscle is what animals use for sprinting. Ducks are distance flyers, and chickens are sprinters.

One of the most striking things I've discovered over the years is that virtually everything works well with duck. "Ducks are incredibly versatile," says chef Tony Maws of Craigie On Main in Cambridge, Massachusetts. "Fruits are not a problem, vegetables are not a problem. It can take spice and heat. Duck is almost like pork belly, which is why cooks are so excited to work with it."

Maws's association between duck and pork belly is apt. I am betting that the first thing you think of when you conjure up an image of duck is fat. Duck—at least domesticated duck—is unquestionably fatty. A good portion of all duck and goose cookery is dedicated to dealing with that fat. If you fail, you can wind up with a greasy mess. But just the right amount of duck fat, served alongside skin so crispy it crackles, makes duck exciting. As any chef will tell you, fat equals flavor.

The most traditional and best way to manage the richness of duck is to invite mustard, horseradish, vinegar, or pickles to the party. You need something sharp for balance. Think about the combination of a hot dog with mustard or a fatty prime rib with horseradish and you get the idea. Fruit adds another element

DUCK CAMP SURVIVAL KIT

I get asked a lot about duck recipes that can be done in a rough kitchen, either in the field or at the duck club. My advice is always the same: so long as you have a few staples on hand, you can always make a great meal after a long day in the marsh. Here's what I'd want to see in the cupboards of every duck club:

- **Salt and pepper.** Sounds like a no-brainer, but you'd be surprised how many times I've seen people forget these most basic ingredients.

- **Onions and garlic.** These staples keep for a long time in the pantry and form the basis for almost every recipe in this book.

- **Stocks.** Yes, homemade stock is better, and you can make shelf-stable stock if you pressure can it (see page 221). But having a few boxes of store-bought broth around will greatly improve your camp cooking.

- **Wine, port, and brandy.** For obvious reasons, but also to add flavor to sauces and stews.

- **Jelly, honey, syrup, or molasses.** Duck really benefits from some sweetness.

- **Vinegar.** Any kind but distilled. A splash brightens any dish and cuts the fattiness of the bird.

to duck: sweetness. A tart fruit such as cherry or black currants, blueberries, or stone fruits can almost single-handedly achieve that perfect balance of flavor so canonized in Asian cuisine: sweet, sour, savory, salty, and spicy.

"There is a reason that *canard a l'orange* is such a classic dish," says Ariane Daguin of D'Artagnan Foods, one of the world's leading authorities on duck cookery. "Everything happens for a reason. Duck needs something to cut it a little bit, and sweetness and acidity work."

Vinegar and citrus go a long way toward doing this. In most cases, which vinegar is your choice, but many cooks, including myself, prefer sherry vinegar for duck. "It has an almost oxidized aroma and almondy smell that really works with duck," says chef Brad Farmerie of Public restaurant.

I also tend to salt my duck a little heavier than I would a comparable piece of chicken. A little extra saltiness highlights the flavor of the meat and cuts the fattiness of the bird.

So long as you remember that the salty-savory-rich part of your meal is covered nicely by the duck, you can design your own recipes from there.

WINE PAIRINGS

Matching wine with waterfowl is not difficult—red wine with duck is one of the easier pairings to understand—but nuances exist that will help you better match the wine to the dish. And don't forget rosés and whites, either: each has its place with ducks and geese, depending on the preparation.

Wild ducks and geese are stronger flavored than their domesticated cousins, so choose your wine accordingly. And even within those categories, the meat of a heritage breed Muscovy will be redder and stronger than that of a supermarket Pekin. A ringneck or bluebill breast will have darker meat than a pintail or green-winged teal breast. A domesticated goose will be milder than a snow goose.

If I had to choose only one wine to go with all my ducks or geese, it would be a French Châteauneuf-du-Pape, a complex blend of varietals native to the Côtes du Rhône region of France. It is big but not burly like a Cabernet, and it plays alongside the duck without overpowering it. A California Cabernet is just too much for even a strong-flavored duck.

In general, go for a lighter red. Pinot Noir, whether from Burgundy, Oregon, or California, is the classic pairing for duck, and it is so for a reason. But a Grenache, Chianti, Barbera, or Merlot would all work well. If you want to drink Zinfandel with your duck, be sure it is a drier, more austere wine, such as one from Italy or from California's Alexander Valley or Amador County.

A dry rosé is a good idea in hot weather, as is one of those tropical-smelling white varietals that originated in the Côtes du Rhône, like a Viognier or a Roussanne made in California. Whites are classic with duck confit. I'd suggest an unoaked Chardonnay, a Chenin Blanc, or an honest-to-goodness Chablis. If you are eating foie gras, sweet whites such as Sauternes or Beaumes de Venise are traditional.

Going spicy? Try an off-dry German Riesling or Gewürztraminer. It really works. Try one of these wines with Laotian Duck Salad (page 72) or Buffalo Duck Wings (page 141).

Two things to avoid are acidic or overly tannic wines. While you'd think a tart, felty red would play off fatty duck, for some reason it just doesn't work. Ditto for the hedonistic fruit bombs made in many parts of California and Australia. A hot, alcoholic, jammy red wine is a terrible choice.

BEER PAIRINGS

Beer and waterfowl are just as good a combination as wine and waterfowl. If you are making a rich, fatty dish such as Cassoulet (page 130), an acidic, hoppy, or sour beer is the right choice. If you have a more delicate dish, think lighter and more floral. Spicy foods like hoppy or sweet beers. After talking to a number of beer experts, the universal choice for a go-to beer with duck is a Belgian. "Duck practically cries out for Flanders Red, a tart-sweet style of beer with cherry and almond notes," says Kevin Pratt, brewmaster of the Santa Monica Brewing Company in California.

Rick Sellers, former beer director at *Draft* magazine, adds, "Belgian dubbels pair great with duck, especially bottled versions with their higher carbonation levels—toffee sweet, slightly peppery, and fairly robust. Flanders reds are also lovely, like Duchesse de Bourgogne, with a slightly sour and sweet cherry flavor. For fattier dishes look for a saison, quite possibly the best beer style to pair with food; super dry, effervescent with great pear notes." Here are some other tips to help you choose the best beers for your birds:

- Scottish ales, like McEwan's, are malt-driven beers, which work well with savory, smoked, and grilled dishes that are light on fat. I am partial to a Scottish ale with Smoked Duck (page 41).

- If you are barbecuing duck and have lots of crispy skin and fat, go for a lager or pilsner. This is where you want that ice-cold macrobrew. My choice? The High Life, served ice-cold. But you can go fancy with any good lager or pils.

- Braises and heavy stews work best with the Belgian beers (think dark ales or Chimay) or a German Doppelbock. I find that malty beers like brown ales and Marzen work well, too.

- If you are cooking with beer, avoid hoppy beers. Their bitterness will wreck your dish. Go for a simple macrobrew or a malty beer. I especially like to cook with Guinness. A Belgian saison is a good choice, too.

- Spicy dishes work very well with India pale ales, or really any pale ales, as they all tend to be hoppy. That bitterness really plays well against the heat of a dish like Laotian Duck Salad (page 72) or Duck Bulgogi (page 71).

I've included a rough guide to the difficulty of each recipe in this book based on the time and skill required to pull it off. In general, one-star recipes are those easy enough to do after work on a weeknight. Two-star recipes are still easy, but might require a few hours' cook time, or some of your attention in preparation. Three-star recipes are either time-consuming or need a bit of kitchen skill. The four- and five-star recipes are either all-day affairs, or they demand some significant knife skills or special equipment. For example, many of the charcuterie recipes in this book—most of which are four-star—are not terribly difficult, but you need some special equipment and you must slow down and pay attention to detail in order to succeed with them.

WHOLE BIRDS

A whole roasted goose, skin golden brown and crispy, is a holiday icon. And those lacquered barbecued ducks in Asian markets are one of the first things you think about when you picture your nearest Chinatown. Whole birds stir something inside us, something ancient. But sadly, with a few exceptions, a whole roasted duck or goose is not the best way to enjoy these birds. "The worst thing you can do to a [domesticated] duck is roast it like a chicken," says chef Sheamus Feeley of the Hillstone Restaurant Group in Colorado.

That's because the ideal cooking temperatures for duck breasts and duck legs are more than forty degrees apart. You can roast a whole chicken because the difference in ideal temperature between its breast meat and its legs is less than twenty degrees. But this doesn't mean you should never cook a whole duck or goose; it just takes a little more finesse. This chapter is all about tricks and tips to getting you there easily.

Let me start by saying that there is no bigger difference between a wild bird and a domesticated one than when you cook it whole. Wild ducks and geese are smaller, leaner, and tougher than domesticated waterfowl, which are often so fat you need to pour off excess fat several times during roasting. The only time the two birds come close is when you have a plump wild duck, such as a pintail, and a lean domesticated one, such as a Muscovy.

HOW MANY DUCKS, HOW MANY PEOPLE?

Here is a general guide for whichever bird you might find in your kitchen. These numbers assume you are also serving some sort of starch and vegetable with your duck or goose. If you are a hearty eater, or if there is little else on the dinner table, you might need to adjust this downward.

Domesticated
3- to 6-pound Pekin duck or Muscovy hen: serves 2 to 4
5- to 10-pound Muscovy drake, Rouen, or Moulard duck: serves 4 to 6
8- to 10-pound goose: serves 5 or 6
11- to 12-pound goose: serves 6 to 8

Wild
Teal or ruddy duck: just about serves 1
Wigeon, wood duck, shoveler, bluebill, or ringneck duck: serves 1 nicely
Mallard, pintail, canvasback, gadwall, redhead, or black duck or
    Ross's or Aleutian goose: serves 1 or 2
Canada or specklebelly goose: serves 4 to 6

ROASTING A PERFECT DUCK OR GOOSE

You can roast a whole domesticated duck or goose with perfect success. The key to getting medium-rare breast meat and tender fully done legs and wings is to take the bird apart midstream. You roast the whole bird for a while, then you slice off the breast meat and finish it in a pan once the legs are done. It's really a more civilized way to eat. And because you are cooking at a relatively low temperature, you won't smoke up your kitchen.

Since the ducks and geese you buy in the store come with giblets, I've also included a recipe for traditional holiday gravy. If you don't want to use your giblets for gravy, make the German giblet soup *Gänseklein* with them (page 159).

This recipe is specifically designed for fat domesticated ducks and geese. Try this method with a wild bird only if it is large and very fatty, such as a big mallard or pintail duck or a specklebelly goose.

You will get lots of extra goose fat from this. Save it. Duck fat and goose fat are God's gift to potatoes, plus they are a spectacular medium for cooking winter greens such as kale, spinach, or chard.

DIFFICULTY: ✳ ✳

SERVES 2 TO 8
(SEE CHART AT LEFT)

PREP TIME: 35 MINUTES

COOK TIME: 1 ½ HOURS

1 domesticated duck or goose

1 lemon, halved

Kosher salt and freshly ground pepper

½ yellow onion, chopped

1 head garlic

1 tablespoon duck or goose fat or unsalted butter

GRAVY

**Giblets (except liver), neck, and wing tips
   from duck or goose**

1 tablespoon duck or goose fat or unsalted butter

½ cup chopped onion

2 tablespoons all-purpose flour

½ cup Madeira or sherry

2 cups Basic Duck Stock (page 222) or chicken stock

1 teaspoon dried thyme

If the duck or goose has been refrigerated, bring it to room temperature before cooking. Keep it in its plastic wrapping resting in a pan until you are ready to cook it, so that if the covering leaks for any reason, the juices will be confined to the pan. If the bird is frozen, you will need to thaw it in the refrigerator for at least 24 hours; geese will need a full 48 hours.

Remove the neck and giblets (heart, gizzard, liver) and reserve all but the liver for the gravy; use the liver for another recipe. You want to reserve the last two joints of the wings for the gravy, as well. To do this, use kitchen shears—or a small, sharp knife—and cut across the side of the joint, severing the tendons. Bend the joint backward to break it, and cut the remaining skin and tendons. You should not need to cut bone at all. Next, cut off the neck skin about ½ inch away from the body.

To remove excess fat (save it for use as cooking fat; see pages 146 and 203), grasp the fat inside the body cavity, pull it free, and put it in a bowl. Now slice off the wide belly flaps covering the body cavity, and then remove the tail, also called the pope's nose. To ensure crisp skin, pierce the skin all over with a clean needle or the tip of a sharp knife, positioning the tool at an angle so that you are piercing just the skin and not the meat.

Preheat the oven to 325°F. Have ready a roasting pan with a rack. Rub the duck or goose all over with the cut sides of the lemon. Use both halves to coat it thoroughly. Put the halves inside the cavity. Sprinkle salt liberally all over the bird. Use more salt than you think you need;

continued

it helps crisp the skin and adds a lot of flavor. Slice off the top ½ inch or so of the garlic head, and place the head inside the cavity. Place the bird, breast side up, on the rack in the pan and slide the pan into the oven.

When the bird goes in the oven, start the gravy. Chop the giblets, wing tips, and neck and put them in a large pan with the goose fat. Sprinkle with salt, place over medium-high heat, and cook, stirring as needed to prevent scorching, until the pieces are browned. Add the onion and stir to combine. When the onion is slightly browned, sprinkle in the flour and again stir to combine. Cook over medium heat, stirring often, for 5 to 10 minutes, until the mixture smells nutty. Turn the heat to high and add the Madeira. Let the liquid boil furiously for a minute or two, then add the stock and stir to combine. Add the thyme, turn down the heat so the gravy is at a bare simmer, and leave to cook, stirring occasionally and checking every now and again that it is not cooking too fast.

After the bird has cooked for 25 minutes, spoon out some of the fat from the roasting pan; discard it or use it for roasting potatoes later. Test the temperature of the breast with an instant-read thermometer. For a smallish duck, the temperature should register between 130°F and 140°F. Large ducks and geese may need up to 45 minutes to get this warm. When the breast has reached this point, remove the bird from the oven but keep the oven on.

Carve off the breasts (see page 10) and put them on a platter, skin side up. Tent the breasts with aluminum foil. Put the bird (minus the breasts) back into the oven and cook for another 45 minutes. Meanwhile, continue to watch the gravy. If it gets too thick, add a little water or stock.

After the additional 45 minutes have passed, probe the thickest part of the bird's thigh with the thermometer. It should register at least 165°F. If it is higher, that's fine, as the legs of waterfowl are very forgiving. If it is lower,

keep roasting it. Remove the garlic from the cavity. Once the legs hit their target temperature, remove the bird from the oven, tent it with foil, and set aside.

Remove the garlic cloves from their skins, add to the gravy, and cook for 5 minutes. Fish out the neck and wing pieces and pick off any bits of meat and toss them into the gravy. Pour the gravy into a blender and blend until very smooth. You might have to do this in batches to avoid it spurting out of your blender. You want the gravy to be thick but not gloppy. If it is too thick, add water to thin to a good consistency. Return the gravy to the pan and put over very low heat. Simmer it if it is too thin. (Note: If you like chunky gravy, by all means skip the blender step.)

Heat a large sauté pan over medium-high heat and add the duck or goose fat. Meanwhile, lift the breasts, which should be a lovely pink on the meat side, and pat them dry. Pour any accumulated juices into the gravy.

When the fat is hot, place the breasts, skin side down, in the pan and sear the skin hard. You might need to press down on the breasts a little to get good contact. Check after 2 to 4 minutes. You want a rich brown. When the color is good, remove the breasts and immediately salt the skin. Set aside, skin side up. Move the pan off the heat.

Carve off the legs and wings of the bird. Get the sauté pan hot again and sear the skin surfaces of the legs and wings. While they are searing, slice the breast at an angle to ensure you get a good amount of skin with each slice. Salt the legs and wings and serve. You have worked hard to get a good sear on the skin, so put your lovely gravy underneath the meat or on the side, not on top of the skin. Be sure to save the bones from the carcass to make stock (page 222).

SLOW-ROASTED DUCK

This is an easier way to roast a duck that does not involve cutting off the breast midstream. It is a European method that results in a thoroughly cooked bird with no pink breast meat. You start the duck in a low oven and finish on high to crisp the skin. This method works with domesticated ducks and very fatty wild ones.

DIFFICULTY: *

SERVES 2 TO 4, DEPENDING ON THE DUCK

PREP TIME: 15 MINUTES

COOK TIME: 35 MINUTES TO 1 HOUR

1 domesticated duck, or 2 very fat wild ducks

1 lemon, halved

1 tablespoon kosher salt

4 sprigs sage, rosemary, flat-leaf parsley, or thyme, or a mixture

Preheat the oven to 300°F. To ensure crisp skin, pierce the skin all over with a clean needle or the tip of a sharp knife, positioning the tool at an angle so that you are piercing just the skin and not the meat. Another option that works very well comes from chef Eddy Leroux of Restaurant Daniel in New York City: score the skin of the whole duck with a sharp knife in the same sort of cross-hatch pattern you would use if you were cooking just the breast. Leroux's method looks odd but results in a crispier skin. Whichever you choose, opening up the skin helps render the fat underneath, making it crispier.

Rub the duck all over with the cut sides of the lemon. Use both halves to coat it thoroughly. Put the spent halves inside the cavity. Liberally salt the bird; use a little more salt than you think you need. Stuff the cavity with the herbs.

Put the duck in a cast-iron frying pan or other heavy, ovenproof pan and roast for 45 minutes. If you are roasting small wild ducks (wigeon, teal, wood duck, or the like), roast for 30 minutes. Check the fat accumulating in the pan and pour some off as you go. Save this fat to cook with later.

Remove the pan from the oven and turn the heat up to 500°F. When it reaches this temperature, roast for 5 to 15 minutes longer. Small birds such as teal or wigeon will need only 5 minutes, and large birds such as Muscovy or Rouen will need the full 15 minutes; a mallard will need 10 minutes.

Remove from the oven and let the bird rest before carving or serving. You'll only need 5 minutes resting time for small birds, 10 minutes for other ducks. Carve as directed on page 32.

A WORD ON SALT

All salts are not alike. For this book, I use Morton's kosher salt, the kind that comes in the big blue box. The other common household brand, Diamond Crystal, is ground finer than Morton's. This means that if you are a Diamond Crystal user, you will need less salt than what I call for in my recipes. This is why in my salami, baking, and curing recipes, I also provide salt (and curing salt) measures by weight in addition to volume.

I prefer to use bulk sea salt in my kitchen—I make my own from the Pacific Ocean—and I also use a variety of finishing salts, such as French *fleur de sel, sel gris,* flaked salt, and smoked salt. The best place to get your hands on quality salts is The Meadow, which has shops in Portland, Oregon, and in New York City. They sell online at www.atthemeadow.com.

HOW TO CARVE DUCKS AND GEESE

Carving a duck is pretty much the same as carving a chicken or turkey. There are lots of ways to go about it, but this is what I do.

With the bird breast up, take off the legs and wings the same way you would when breaking down a whole duck (see page 8), slicing the skin between the breast and leg into the open area beneath. Use the point of the knife to locate the ball-and-socket joint that holds the leg to the body. Pop the joint by moving the leg downward. Slip the knife around the joint from the tail end of the bird. Once the leg is free from its socket, use the point of the knife to free it from the body, making sure to cut out the "oyster," the oval knob of meat in front of the ball joint. Do this for both legs.

To remove the wings (usually just the drumette), turn the duck over to reveal the curved saber bone along its back; this is the equivalent of its shoulder blade. Slice along this bone toward the neck of the duck, feeling with the point of your knife for the joint that attaches the wing to the body. Use the point of your knife to separate the wing from the joint, taking care to cut out as little of the breast meat as possible. Do this for both wings.

For the breast, take the whole breast off first and then slice it. Start by cutting each half free. Begin at the keel bone, which separates the breast halves, and slice down along the keel bone, tapping the point of your knife against the breastbone. Start in the middle of the breast and work toward the tail end, then work the other way, toward the wishbone. When you get to the wishbone, use the knife point to cut around it and then down to where the wing was. Free the breast from the carcass with short strokes of the knife. Once it's free, peel off the tender. Eat it, as it is the cook's treat. Slice the rest of the breast on the diagonal, to get the best ratio of skin to meat.

Once you're finished, don't forget to save the carcass for stock!

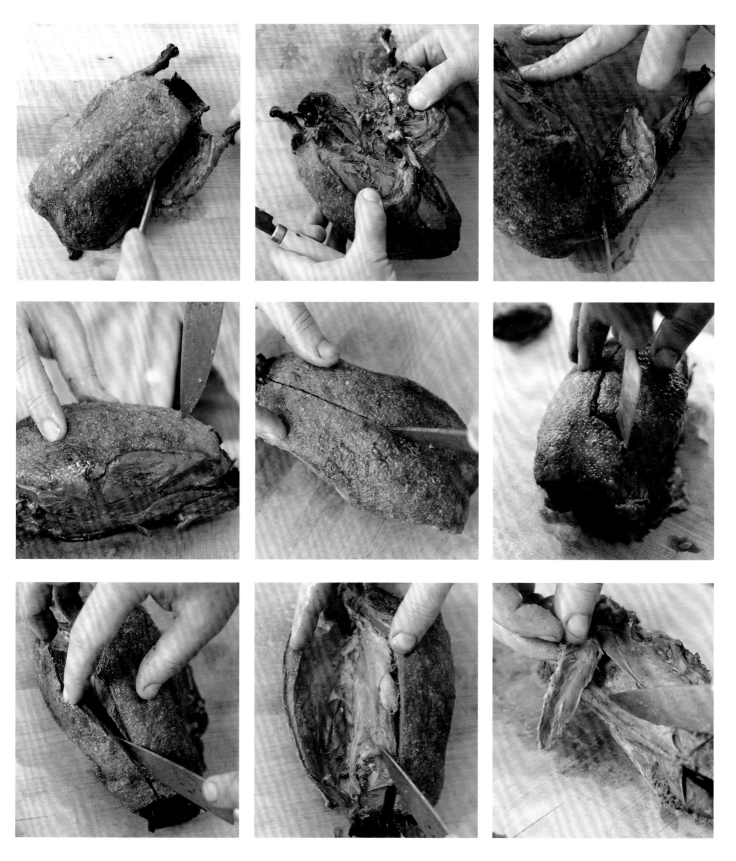

CANVASBACK, KING OF DUCKS

"Get ready, here they come!" My friend R. J. hissed as two ducks came roaring in over our flooded rice field, right over our decoys. I saw them just in time. Two big ducks, flying in fast, coming right to left. I focused on the trailing bird. "Now!" R. J. shouted, and we let fly. I dropped the trailing bird, while our friend Jim dropped the lead bird.

Riley the dog leapt from the duck blind into the water and soon returned with my bird, which I'd thought was a hen mallard. But as Riley swam closer, I saw the unmistakable aristocratic bill of a hen canvasback. "Canvasbacks!" I was beaming from ear to ear. Even though I'd shot my first specklebelly goose of the year, a mallard, and two teal that day, it is the canvasback that lingers largest in my mind.

Canvasback, King of Ducks—or in this case, Queen of Ducks. *Aythya vallisneria*. Where others dream about green-headed mallard drakes or fat pintail, I dream of King Can. It's the historian in me. No duck has risen to a higher plane at the table than the canvasback. George Washington prized it, as did the robber barons of the Gilded Age and the rough-hewn voyageurs of the Canadian frontier, who traded beaver pelts so they could feast on canvasbacks. It was, for a while, the most prestigious item anyone could put on a menu.

Weighing in at up to 3½ pounds for a big drake, the canvasback is among North America's largest wild ducks. It's larger than a mallard or a pintail, and can easily feed two for dinner. Size was only a minor factor during the canvasback craze of the late 1800s, however. Flavor was the real reason. Canvasbacks prefer to eat the starchy roots of vallisneria, or wild celery, so much that they were named for the plant. Where vallisneria lives, you will find canvasbacks. And a can that has been eating wild celery will be one of the sweetest, fattest ducks in the world. It's a flavor finer than the best rib eye. And back in the day, everyone who was anyone wanted it.

A look at the century-old menus of such swanky establishments as the Waldorf Hotel in New York City shows that an order of canvasback duck was priced at $4.50 in 1907. Do a little math and that's the equivalent of about $115.00 in today's dollars. Even at a market, a canvasback might cost $1.25, or the equivalent of about $38.00 in today's dollars. Consider for a moment that the average worker in the United States in 1907 earned $0.19 an hour, and you realize that it would take nearly three days' pay for that person to earn enough to order canvasback at a restaurant.

So how was canvasback served at the Waldorf? Only one way. In nearly forty recipes or mentions of canvasback being served dating from 1877 to 1907, all are roasted rare, carved, and served with a red currant sauce (or jelly) and a side of "fried hominy." Even the rich knew that this was a dish best served simply.

All this prestige came at a terrible price. Pollution from the emerging Industrial Revolution and silt from a United States increasingly yoked under the plow laid waste to the submerged gardens of wild celery, sago pondweed, wapato, and widgeon grass that the canvasback traditionally relied on. This weakened the population, and the commercial hunting boom of the late 1800s drove the birds to the brink of extinction.

The canvasback became the poster child for the movement to ban market hunting in the early 1900s. But it was already too late. For decades after commercial hunting ceased, canvasbacks remained rare. Never an overly abundant duck to begin with, there are still only about 760,000 canvasbacks in North America; compare this to the 10.6 million mallards living across this continent. Hunters have only been allowed to take one canvasback per day for decades, and in some cases—2010 to 2011 being the most recent—the season on canvasbacks is closed altogether. Every canvasback we get is a trophy. And while a mounted can is a beautiful thing, my trophies are at the table.

Most canvasbacks in California spend their winters around the San Francisco Bay. But we do see them inland with some frequency, roaring over big water at the Delevan National Wildlife Refuge and, occasionally, in rice fields. That's where R. J. had invited me to hunt that day.

The hen canvasback I'd shot was pretty skinny. We'd had several days of tremendous north winds, which forces the ducks to expend far more energy just to get from place to place than they normally would. We suspected that these cans were in the rice to recover. And we were right. Her crop was full of unhulled rice, and her liver was so engorged with fat that it had become wild foie gras—an even rarer treat.

A century later, there is still really only one way to cook a canvasback. So I re-created the venerable recipe from the Gilded Age. The recipe for roast canvasback on page 49 is a masterpiece, a perfect harmony of rich and savory, acidic and sweet. It is history on a plate.

GRILL-ROASTED DUCK

Grill roasting—cooking a whole duck in a scorching-hot, closed grill—is my favorite way to cook a whole wild duck. It's even better than the slow-roasted method on page 31, so I do this in the winter, too. The reason is heat. You can get your grill far hotter than any oven, and the higher the heat, the better a wild duck cooks. This method will work with a lean domesticated duck such as a Muscovy, too. But do not try it with a regular supermarket Pekin, as they are too fatty. Better to barbecue your fatty ducks (see page 38).

A general rule in roasting birds—all birds, not just waterfowl—is the smaller the bird, the higher the heat. So roasting a teal requires more heat than roasting a goose. This is because you want to crisp the skin without overcooking the meat. To do this with a small bird requires speed, and higher heat gives you that.

DIFFICULTY: *

SERVES 2 TO 4, DEPENDING ON THE DUCK

PREP TIME: 30 MINUTES

COOK TIME: 10 TO 22 MINUTES

2 wild ducks, 1 Muscovy duck, or 4 teal ducks

2 tablespoons vegetable oil

1 tablespoon kosher salt

Freshly ground pepper

1 lemon, cut into wedges

Start with a room-temperature bird by setting it out on the counter for 30 minutes or so. Fashion a drip pan for your grill out of aluminum foil, or use a cheap foil roasting pan from the supermarket, and pour water into it to a depth of ¼ inch. This will catch any dripping fat and prevent it from igniting.

Set up your grill with an open space to one side. This means leaving off one of the three burners on a gas grill, or keeping a spot open on a charcoal- or wood-fired grill. The drip pan goes in the open space or on the unused burner. Get the grill, with its cover down, really hot, at least 500°F; even 600°F is not too hot. Watch it if your temperature gets any higher, however, because duck fat can catch fire when the temperature climbs above 700°F.

Coat your ducks with the oil and then season them well with the salt. Quickly open the cover of the grill and put the ducks, breast side up, on the open spot, over the drip pan. Re-cover the grill.

A small teal can be fully roasted in 10 minutes. A large duck, such as a canvasback or mallard, will take about 15 minutes at 600°F, but never more than 22 minutes, as long as the heat is 500°F or higher.

Take the ducks out and set them on a cutting board. Tent them loosely with foil and let them rest for as little as 5 minutes for a teal to as long as 15 minutes for a canvasback. Carve (see page 32) and serve with pepper and lemon wedges on the side. Simple—and perfect.

BARBECUED DUCK

If you are not concerned with having the breast meat of a duck medium to rare, barbecuing is a great option. Domesticated ducks are the primary candidate for the barbecue, but a fat wild bird works, too. If you are working with wild birds, brining them will keep them moist during the long cooking time. I prefer a brine of ¼ cup kosher salt to 4 cups water. Mix well to dissolve the salt, then brine the legs and wings for at least 2 to 3 hours or up to overnight. Domesticated ducks have so much fat that they don't need a brine to help them.

Hold off on applying any sauce until the duck is at least half-cooked. When it is time, paint on the barbecue sauce and cook for 10 minutes. Flip, paint, and cook for another 10 minutes. Barbecuing is forgiving, so you can repeat this process a couple of times before the meat begins to dry out too much.

Below is one of my favorite barbecue sauces. Other great sauces with barbecued duck are the Chinese *char siu* and South Carolina mustard sauces on pages 137 and 138.

DIFFICULTY: ∗

SERVES 2 TO 4

PREP TIME: 10 MINUTES

COOK TIME: 3 HOURS

1 domesticated duck, or 2 very fat wild ducks

Kosher salt

SAUCE

1 yellow or white onion

¼ cup vegetable oil (such as canola or peanut)

4 tablespoons unsalted butter

1 fresh hot chile (such as serrano or jalapeño), chopped

1 cup bourbon

½ cup ketchup or tomato sauce

½ cup freshly squeezed lemon juice

½ cup cider vinegar

⅓ cup dark molasses

⅓ cup Worcestershire sauce

2 to 3 tablespoons brown sugar

Kosher salt

Cayenne pepper, for seasoning

Remove any excess fat from the cavity of the duck. Trim off the fatty belly flaps covering the body cavity, and then cut off the tail section. Next, cut off the neck skin about 1 inch away from the body. This protects the breast meat from drying out. Reserve the fat and skin pieces to render for cooking fat (see page 203).

To ensure crisp skin, whether using a domesticated duck or fatty wild ducks, pierce the skin all over with a clean needle or the tip of a sharp knife, positioning the tool at an angle so that you are piercing just the skin and not the meat. Salt the duck well inside and out.

Your grill setup should be something like this: Make an open space for your bird to cook away from direct heat. In a gas grill, this means leaving two of the three burners off. With a charcoal- or wood-fired grill, put the fuel on one-half of the grill floor and leave the other half open. A domestic duck or a fatty wild one will drip a lot of fat as it cooks, so you'll want to put a disposable foil pan below the grate where the duck is resting to catch the drips. Pour water into the pan to a depth of about ¼ inch; this prevents the dripping fat from igniting. In a charcoal or wood-fired grill, put the pan in the open space on the grill floor. If using a gas grill, place the pan on one of the unused burners.

When you have your setup, fire up the grill. When it is hot, place the duck in the grill over the drip pan, close the lid, and let it cook. Watch the temperature closely for the first 20 minutes or so, and, using a thermometer, make sure it does not go above 300°F. Stabilize the temperature by adjusting the burner on a gas grill (using a second burner on low heat if it is cold out or a windy day) or by adjusting the vents on a charcoal grill (the narrower the vents are opened, the cooler your interior temperature will be). You want the temperature between 225°F and 280°F. Let the duck cook, undisturbed, for 1 hour.

Meanwhile, make the barbecue sauce. Grate the onion on the large holes of a box grater-shredder. Or, if you don't have a grater, finely mince the onion. In a saucepan, combine the oil and butter over medium-high heat. Add the onion and chile, lower the heat to medium, and cook, stirring occasionally, for 3 to 4 minutes, until the onion is translucent. You do not want the onion to color. Take the pan off the heat and add the bourbon. Return the pan to the stove, turn up the heat to medium-high again, and boil the bourbon for 5 minutes. Add the ketchup, lemon juice, vinegar, molasses, Worcestershire sauce, and sugar, mix well, and bring the mixture to a

simmer. Cook the sauce, stirring occasionally, for a few minutes to blend the flavors, then taste it. Adjust the seasoning with salt, cayenne, and molasses. Let the sauce simmer gently until it thickens, about 20 minutes. Keep warm over very low heat. If you want, you can puree it in a blender.

After an hour, check the duck and the drip pan. If the pan looks like it is filling up, drain it into a heatproof container. Paint the duck with the barbecue sauce, cover the grill again, and let it cook for another 1 to 2 hours, painting on barbecue sauce every 20 to 30 minutes. Make sure you let the duck cook for at least 10 minutes after your last application of the sauce; this lets it caramelize a bit on the bird.

The duck is ready when the drumstick registers at least 170°F on an instant-read thermometer, or when the leg begins to fall away from the rest of the carcass. Carve (see page 32) and serve.

SUMMERTIME FARE

Normally you'd associate such a powerfully flavored red meat with cooler weather, but duck works well when the mercury rises, too. Think about using duck whenever you would use beef, pork, or lamb in the summer: grilled medium-rare and served simply with seasonal vegetables, or slowly barbecued with your favorite sauce.

"A wise duck takes care of his bill."

—AMERICAN PROVERB

SMOKED DUCK

Those who know their way around a smoker know that fat is a critical element in this process. Fat absorbs the flavor of the smoke better than the meat itself. This is why you see lots of recipes for smoked pork and salmon; both are fatty animals. So are waterfowl.

You need to decide whether to brine or not. Both methods work. Brining a duck, especially if you use curing salt (a mixture of salt and sodium nitrite), will help preserve the bird longer in the fridge and will let you smoke it longer and cooler without drying out the meat. If you are skipping the brine, simply salt the duck or goose well, let it rest at room temperature for a few hours before smoking, and pat it dry before you put it in the smoker. It's vital that you start with a room-temperature duck.

As for flavors, I am in love with the combination of smoke, duck, salt, and maple. I need no other flavors in my life, but honey would be good, as would a Cajun rub, something vaguely Indian, chiles, French *quatre épices*, and so on. Use your imagination. As for wood, I am a big fan of fruit or nut woods, like apple, pecan, hickory, or walnut. Oak and beech are fine, but mesquite is too strong for duck.

If you have a smoker, just follow the directions that came with it to set it up and smoke your duck. If you have only a kettle grill, you can turn it into a smoker following a handful of relatively simple steps (page 43).

Thinly sliced on the diagonal, smoked duck is fantastic as part of an appetizer plate or in a sandwich. You can also carve a whole breast, sear the skin side in a frying pan until it crisps again, and serve it with polenta or lentils (page 44).

Beware: If you are buying a domestic duck, read the package. Some are "plumped" with a salt solution of up to 12 percent, so they are essentially prebrined. Do not brine these birds a second time. Prebrined domestic birds also need longer drying time.

DIFFICULTY: ✱ ✱ ✱

SERVES 4

PREP TIME: 6 TO 14 HOURS, PRIMARILY BRINING AND DRYING TIME

COOK TIME: 4 TO 7 HOURS

1 domesticated duck or wild goose, or 2 fat wild ducks

BRINE
¼ cup kosher salt
1 teaspoon Insta Cure No. 1 (see page 196), optional
4 cups water
1 cup maple syrup

If you are using a domesticated duck or goose, remove as much of the fat from inside the body cavity and around the neck as possible. Set the fat aside to use later. Whether using a domesticated duck or fatty wild ducks, pierce the skin all over with a clean needle or the tip of a sharp knife, positioning the tool at an angle so that you are piercing just the skin and not the meat. This helps the rendered fat to escape. Cut off the neck skin about 1 inch from the breast meat.

To make the brine, in a container just large enough to hold the duck, stir together the kosher salt, curing salt, and water until the salts dissolve. Place the duck in the brine, cover the container, and brine in the refrigerator for 4 to 12 hours. You may need to top it with a weight to keep it submerged.

Remove the duck from the brine, pat it dry with paper towels, and set it on a cooling rack under a fan or in a cool, breezy place. Let the duck air-dry for 2 to 3 hours. Don't skip this step, or the smoke will not adhere to the duck well.

continued

While the bird is air-drying, pour the maple syrup into a small, heavy saucepan, place over medium-high heat, bring to a boil, and boil until reduced by half. This should take about 8 to 12 minutes. Let cool to room temperature.

When the duck is dry, paint the exterior of the bird with some of the maple syrup. Set the remainder of the syrup aside to use later. Set up your smoker with a drip pan, then set the bird in the smoker with the drip pan beneath it. Put the excess fat from the body cavity into the drip pan. This will render as you smoke the duck, yielding smoked duck fat mixed with maple drippings, which may just be the greatest substance known to man.

Smoke the duck between 200°F and 275°F for 4 to 7 hours, depending on how smoky you want your bird. Baste the duck with the maple syrup every 45 minutes to an hour. If you smoke at the low end of the spectrum, the skin will not be crispy but the meat will be more tender; you can crisp the skin in a sauté pan before serving. You will know the duck is done when a thermometer stuck in the thigh reads 170°F to 175°F, or when the leg meat begins to come away from the bone.

Allow the duck to cool before carving (see page 32).

TIPS FOR SMOKING WILD BIRDS

Any domestic duck can be smoked with success. If you are using wild birds, here are some guidelines:

- Don't smoke sea ducks, divers, or shovelers you think might be fishy. Smoking will not help you. Skin these birds and do something else with them.

- Avoid smoking snow geese or any other wild bird that is über-lean. You need some fat to make smoking work. Even a little is okay.

- Never smoke a skinned duck. Remember, the smoky flavor lingers in skin and fat far more than it does in meat. If you smoke a skinned duck, it will be more like jerky and less like a proper smoked duck.

- Smoking whole birds gives you better results than pieces, so I generally smoke only whole birds; goose legs are an exception. You can carve whole birds afterward.

- Big ducks smoke better than small ducks, although there is no reason you can't smoke a teal.

HOW TO TURN YOUR KETTLE GRILL INTO A SMOKER

Not everyone has a smoker, but you can still make excellent barbecued or smoked foods with a simple kettle grill, if you know how to modify it correctly. I used this arrangement for years before I bought a dedicated smoker:

- Soak wood chips in water to cover for at least 2 hours. Overnight is better.

- Place water pans in the grill. Disposable foil roasting pans from the supermarket are great for this, and you do not have to toss them after each use. Fill these pans halfway with water and place them beneath the duck or goose. This lets sauce and fat drip into something that will not wreck the bottom of your grill or cause flare-ups. Second, it helps keep the meat moist. Third, it moderates the temperature around the meat, which is vital in such a small space.

- Get the coals hot. A chimney starter is the easiest way to ready lighted coals for the grill. I am especially fond of lump charcoal because I get a better flavor and a cleaner smoke. Could you go all wood? Sure, but it needs to be something like oak or hickory, which burns steadily and slowly.

- Once the coals are good and hot, put a couple of handfuls of the soaked wood on the coals. Place the top grill grate on the grill. Position the grate in a way that if you are using a hinged grate, one of the hinged areas lifts up over the coals so you can easily get to them. Put the duck on the grill away from the coals over the water pans. Under no circumstances should you let the meat rest directly over the coals.

- Cover the grill, positioning the vent on the cover directly over the meat. This helps direct the smoke over the meat. Close all vents (bottom one, too) to keep the temperature as low as you can go; if you have an especially tight lid, keep the vents open just a little. You are now smoking.

- Watch the temperature. This would be a good time to open a beer or drink some lemonade and sit back. Keep one eye on the grill to make sure you see some smoke coming out of it. Check the temperature if your grill lid has a thermometer. It should read no higher than 300°F, and ideally around 225°F to 250°F. If your kettle grill does not have a built-in thermometer (most don't), put a meat thermometer into the cover vent and check it from time to time. If your temperature starts to soar, open the lid and let the coals burn down. Then add more soaked wood and close the lid again; you should be okay. If your temperature drops below 225°F, open the vents. If that doesn't work, open the lid and add more coals and soaked wood.

- Every 1 to 1½ hours, check the coals and rotate the meat. You may need to add coals and wood chips.

SMOKED DUCK WITH LENTILS

This is an elegant way to serve slices of smoked duck. Chanterelles are a winter mushroom on the West Coast, so it is a natural pairing here. In other parts of the country, I'd suggest shiitake mushrooms, which are available year-round. Regular button mushrooms will do in a pinch.

Beluga lentils, which are tiny and black, are my favorite: they are prettier, firmer, and nuttier than regular green lentils. You can substitute green lentils if you like, but yellow or red lentils will dissolve.

DIFFICULTY: ✳ ✳ ✳

SERVES 4

PREP TIME: 10 MINUTES

COOK TIME: 35 MINUTES

3 cups Basic Duck Stock (page 222) or chicken stock

Kosher salt

1 cup beluga lentils

8 ounces chanterelle mushrooms, coarsely chopped

3 tablespoons duck fat or olive oil

1 Smoked Duck (page 41), carved

1 tablespoon minced garlic

1 tablespoon cider vinegar

½ cup Duck Glace de Viande (page 226), or 1 cup
   Basic Duck Stock (page 222) reduced to ½ cup

1 teaspoon prepared mustard

1 teaspoon Worcestershire sauce

Minced fresh chives, for garnish

In a saucepan, bring the stock to a simmer and taste for salt. If you are using store-bought chicken stock, you won't need to add salt. Add the lentils and adjust the temperature so the stock is just steaming, not simmering. Cover the pan and let the lentils cook for about 30 minutes, until they are tender but still hold their shape.

Meanwhile, place a large sauté pan over medium-high heat. When it is hot, add the chanterelles, shaking the pan as they go in. Let the mushrooms sear in the dry pan for 2 to 3 minutes, until they give off their water, then sprinkle with salt. Bring to a boil and boil for 2 to 5 minutes, until most of the water evaporates. Add 2 tablespoons of the duck fat and toss to coat the mushrooms. Sear until they begin to brown, then remove with a slotted spoon.

Add the remaining 1 tablespoon duck fat to the pan and lay the smoked duck pieces, skin side down, in the hot pan. Sear until the skin crisps, about 3 minutes. Transfer the duck, skin side up, to a cutting board.

Add the garlic to the pan and sauté for 1 minute. Mix in the vinegar, *glace de viande*, mustard, and Worcestershire sauce and boil down by half. Turn off the heat.

Drain the lentils and put them in a bowl. Mix in the chanterelles to half of the sauce in the sauté pan. Spoon some lentils onto each plate, arrange some of the duck pieces on the lentils, then top with the chives. Drizzle the remaining sauce around everything and serve.

CLASSIC SALMIS OF DUCK

Salmis (pronounced sal-me) is an ancient French dish that calls for roasting a wild duck (or a lean domesticated one, such as a Muscovy) in a very hot oven, carving it, and then making a rich sauce with the carcass. (If your oven does not get superhot, you can grill-roast your duck as described on page 36.) You let the legs finish cooking in the cooling oven while you make the sauce, and then only "nap" the breast meat in the sauce to reheat it. If I had my choice of ducks to make this recipe with, I'd choose a fat wigeon, teal, or wood duck. It is a perfect single serving. *Salmis* is historically served with big croutons—think Texas toast—and sautéed mushrooms. A bold French red wine, such as a Bordeaux, Côtes du Rhône, or Châteauneuf-du-Pape, is a must with this recipe.

DIFFICULTY: ✳ ✳ ✳

SERVES 4

PREP TIME: 35 MINUTES

COOK TIME: 1⅓ HOURS

1 Muscovy duck, or 2 to 4 wild ducks

Kosher salt and freshly ground pepper

½ ounce (about 1 handful) dried mushrooms, such as porcini, shiitake, or black trumpets

2 cups hot water

1 tablespoon duck fat or unsalted butter per duck plus 4 tablespoons

Small handful of celery sticks, plus 1 celery stalk, chopped

½ cup chopped shallot

1 carrot, peeled and chopped

2 bay leaves

1 teaspoon dried thyme

¼ cup brandy

1½ cups dry red wine

1 cup Basic Duck Stock (page 222) or beef stock

1 pound fresh mushrooms (such as button or cremini), coarsely chopped

½ cup chopped yellow onion

1 crusty baguette, cut into slices on the diagonal about 1½ inches thick

2 tablespoons unsalted butter, for finishing the sauce

Duck liver pâté (page 179), optional

Minced fresh flat-leaf parsley, for garnish

Turn on the oven to 500°F or its highest setting. Let it preheat for a full 30 minutes. Pat the duck(s) dry with a paper towel, salt well inside and out, and then let sit at room temperature while the oven heats.

Also while the oven is heating, in a small bowl, soak the dried mushrooms in the hot water to reconstitute them. When they are soft, lift them out of the water, squeeze them dry, chop, and reserve. Line a fine-mesh sieve with a plain paper towel, and pour the soaking water through it into a measuring cup. Reserve 1 cup of the soaking water.

When the oven is ready, pat the duck(s) dry again with a paper towel, then smear the outside with the duck fat or butter; you will need about 1 tablespoon per duck. Put the celery sticks in the bottom of a cast-iron frying pan or other heavy ovenproof pan to serve as a rack for the duck(s), then pour just enough water into the pan to cover the bottom, ¼ cup at most. Place the duck(s), breast side up, on the celery sticks.

Slip the duck(s) into the hot oven and set the timer for 15 minutes. At the 10-minute mark of roasting, baste the duck(s) with the juices that have collected at the bottom of the pan. If you are roasting wild ducks, after 15 minutes have elapsed, take the pan out of the oven, remove the ducks from the pan, and let the birds rest on a cutting board. (If you are roasting teal, they will need to be basted after 5 minutes, and will need only about 10 minutes in the oven.) If you are roasting a Muscovy

continued

continued from previous page

duck, transfer it to the cutting board after 22 to 25 minutes have elapsed. You want the breast meat to be quite rare and the legs a little undercooked.

Let the duck(s) rest for 10 minutes before carving (see page 32). Turn off the oven. Pour off most of the juices from the pan; set the legs and wings, skin side up, in the pan and put the pan back in the oven. The carryover heat in the oven should be hot enough to finish cooking the legs and wings while you make the sauce. (If you used your grill rather than your oven, put the legs and wings in a pan in the oven and turn the oven on to the warm setting.) Set the breasts, skin side up, on the cutting board for now.

Cut the carcass(es) into small pieces with heavy kitchen shears or chop with a cleaver and put the pieces in a Dutch oven or other heavy pot with 2 tablespoons of the duck fat or butter. Place over medium-high heat and brown the carcass pieces. Add the shallot, chopped celery, carrot, and rehydrated mushrooms and cook, stirring occasionally, for 8 to 10 minutes, until the vegetables begin to brown. Mix in the bay leaves, thyme, and brandy and cook until almost all of the brandy boils away. Stir in the wine, stock, and the reserved mushroom water, increase the heat to high, and bring to a boil.

While the sauce is boiling, place a sauté pan over high heat. When it is hot, add the fresh mushrooms, shaking the pan as they go in. Let the mushrooms sear in the dry pan for about 4 minutes, until they give off their water. Let almost all the water evaporate before adding the remaining 2 tablespoons duck fat or butter, a little salt, and the onion and sauté over medium-high heat for about 6 to 8 minutes, or until nicely browned. Remove from the heat and reserve.

Toast the bread slices (or fry them in duck fat or butter) and set aside.

The sauce, which has been boiling, will have reduced considerably. Strain it through a fine-mesh sieve into a small saucepan, place over high heat, and boil until reduced by half.

While the sauce is reducing, set the duck breasts, skin side down, in the pan in the oven. This will help crisp the skin a little. If you cooked the duck on the grill, you will need to quickly sear the duck breasts over high heat in the pan you cooked the mushrooms in.

When the sauce is ready, remove from the heat and swirl in the 2 tablespoons butter. The sauce should have the consistency of thin gravy. Season the sauce with salt and pepper.

To finish the dish, give the legs a quick dip in the hot sauce, then arrange on individual plates. Dip the breasts into the sauce and arrange them, skin side up, on the plates. Spread the pâté on the toasted bread slices and give everyone some mushrooms. Pour a little extra sauce over the duck and garnish with parsley.

ROAST WILD DUCK WITH FRIED HOMINY

This is a recipe specifically for larger wild ducks that have a moderate amount of fat—preferably canvasbacks, if you can get them. It will not work well with hugely fat ducks or domesticated ducks. The sauce and the fried hominy cake were classic accompaniments to roast canvasback at the turn of the twentieth century, when commercial hunting still allowed the wealthy to dine on waterfowl's royalty. To eat a duck cooked this way is to enjoy a slice of the Gilded Age.

White hominy grits are easily bought in much of this country, but fine-grind white polenta or white cornmeal is a good substitute. If you want to be authentic, fry the little cakes in lard, but only if you have freshly rendered lard. Otherwise, use duck fat or butter. Keep in mind you need to make the hominy a few hours ahead to let it cool. Red currant jelly is sold in many supermarkets, but you can really use any red fruit jelly. You are looking for red and tart.

Serve the duck and hominy with a bitter green salad and a big, burly red wine. This is the time to break out the Châteauneuf-du-Pape.

DIFFICULTY: ✳ ✳

SERVES 4

PREP TIME: 1½ HOURS, INCLUDING COOLING TIME FOR THE HOMINY

COOK TIME: 18 TO 22 MINUTES

FRIED HOMINY

10 cups water

Kosher salt

2 cups grits

2 eggs

1½ cups dried bread crumbs

3 tablespoons duck fat or unsalted butter

2 canvasback or other large wild ducks

2 tablespoons duck fat or unsalted butter, softened

Kosher salt

1 large shallot, minced (about ¼ cup)

½ cup red currant jelly or syrup

2 tablespoons Worcestershire sauce

½ cup Duck Glace de Viande (page 226), or 1½ cups Basic Duck Stock (page 222) reduced to ½ cup

Dash of hot-pepper sauce

To cook the hominy, in a saucepan, combine the water and about 1 tablespoon salt and bring to a boil over high heat. Start stirring the water with a wooden spoon and then pour in the grits in a slow, steady stream, continuing to stir to prevent lumps. Turn the heat to low and cook, uncovered, stirring often, for at least 20 minutes or up to 1 hour, until the grits have thickened and the water is absorbed. The longer you cook the grits, the smoother and softer they will get. Taste for salt midway through the cooking to be sure the seasoning is to your liking and adjust if needed. Turn out the grits into a loaf pan or other small, deep container and let cool for at least 1 hour.

Turn on the oven to 500°F or its highest setting. Let it preheat for a full 30 minutes. Pat the ducks dry with a paper towel. Smear the duck fat evenly over the outside of the birds, then salt them well inside and out. Let the birds sit at room temperature while the oven heats.

Meanwhile, turn the cooled hominy out onto a cutting board and slice off the side that was exposed to the air (the breading will not stick to any part of the hominy exposed to air). Cut the rest of the hominy into shapes

continued

continued from previous page

of your choice; I like to use a 4-inch circle mold or biscuit cutter. In a shallow bowl, beat the eggs until blended. Put the bread crumbs in a second shallow bowl.

Put the ducks in a cast-iron frying pan or other heavy, ovenproof pan and slip them into the hot oven. Set the timer for 18 minutes.

To fry the hominy, put the duck fat in a large frying pan and place over medium-high heat. As soon as the fat is hot, one at a time, dip the hominy pieces in the eggs and then in the bread crumbs and add to the pan. Fry, turning once, for about 3 minutes on each side, until golden. Set aside on a cooling rack or paper towels to drain.

At the 10-minute mark of roasting, baste the ducks with any duck fat that has rendered off the birds. When the ducks are done to your liking, take the pan out of the oven, immediately transfer the ducks to a cutting board, and tent them loosely with aluminum foil. A medium-rare duck will be done in about 18 minutes and a medium duck in 20 to 22 minutes. Do not go past 25 minutes, unless the duck is really fatty. Look for an internal temperature in the breast of 135°F to 140°F.

As the duck rests, make sure you have at least 2 tablespoons of fat in the pan you roasted the birds in. If you have more, spoon it off. Set this on the stove top over medium heat. Be careful, as the pan will be hot. Add the shallot and sauté for 2 minutes, until it begins to brown. Add the jelly, Worcestershire sauce, *glace de viande*, and hot-pepper sauce and bring to a rolling boil. Let the mixture cook down until a wooden spoon dragged through it leaves a noticeable trail. You want a thick consistency but not as thick as a syrup or gravy. Taste and season with salt.

Carve the ducks (see page 32) and stir any juices from the cutting board into the sauce. Pour some sauce on each dinner plate, add a hominy cake or two, and top with a portion of duck. Serve at once.

"No goose has ever voted for an early Christmas."

—IRISH PROVERB

CHINESE DRUNKEN ROAST DUCK SOUP

This is my version of a Chinese tonic soup often given to new mothers in the days just after they give birth. There are many variations on it, and mine is inspired by a soup I ate at a local Sacramento institution, Frank Fat's Chinese restaurant. Fat's has been cooking hunters' ducks for generations, but this soup isn't normally on its hunters' menu. I had asked for a "real Chinese" menu for our dinner, and we were served a soup like this one. The depth of flavor in the stock knocked us all back in our seats. Especially intriguing were a slight bitterness from the stewed burdock root and a warm earthiness from lots of shiitake mushrooms.

Fat's never gave me its recipe for this soup, but another excellent Chinese chef, David Soohoo, helped me develop this version.

Burdock, a long, slender root with ivory flesh and rough brown skin, can be found in high-end supermarkets and Asian markets, and flavorwise there is no substitute. But if you cannot find burdock, you can use turnips or carrots. If you happen to have master stock (page 225) and flavored fat (see page 107) on hand, this soup will be even richer.

DIFFICULTY: ✱ ✱

SERVES 4

PREP TIME: 20 MINUTES

COOK TIME: 1½ HOURS, PLUS DUCK ROASTING TIME

2 wild ducks, or 1 domesticated duck, preferably a Pekin or Muscovy hen

3 tablespoons duck fat, lard, or vegetable oil

8 ounces shiitake or button mushrooms, sliced

3 tablespoons peeled and minced fresh ginger

3 large cloves garlic, thinly sliced

1 or 2 small dried chiles, broken into pieces

1 cup Shaoxing wine or dry sherry

4 cups Chinese Duck Stock (page 225)

12 ounces burdock root, sliced into ¼-inch-thick coins

5 green onions, white and green parts, thickly sliced

Soy sauce, for seasoning

Start by either grill roasting the wild ducks (see page 36) or slow roasting the domesticated duck (see page 31). Set the cooked duck(s) aside on a cutting board to cool. When cool enough to handle, remove the breasts, wings, and legs. Use a cleaver or heavy kitchen knife to chop the legs and wings into 2 or 3 large pieces and cut the breast into thin slices. Set aside.

In a large wok, Dutch oven, or other heavy pot, heat 2 tablespoons of the duck fat over high heat. The moment the fat begins to smoke, toss in the mushrooms and stir-fry for 3 minutes, until they begin to brown. Add the remaining 1 tablespoon duck fat to the pan and then add the ginger, garlic, and chiles and stir-fry for another minute, until fragrant.

Add the wine, stock, duck legs and wings, and burdock and bring to a simmer. Adjust the heat to maintain a simmer, cover, and cook for 1 hour, until the burdock is tender. Add the sliced duck breast, the green onions, and soy sauce to taste and cook for 2 minutes, just to heat them through. Serve at once.

PEKING DUCK

This is the Mother of All Duck Recipes. And to be honest, the only recipe in this book I was actually scared to try. Everything I'd heard about cooking a Peking duck was that it was impossibly hard to do—that even many Chinese restaurants never made it in-house, preferring instead to have premade ducks trucked in during the dead of night from some shadowy Peking duck chop shop far, far away. (This is true, actually.)

The truth is, Peking duck *is* hard. What's more, the process can make the breast meat gray and dry until you get the hang of it. But Peking duck isn't about the meat: the Pekin breed of duck used for Peking duck doesn't have a ton of meat on it compared to, say, a Muscovy, and in many high-end Chinese restaurants, they barely give you any meat at all. This recipe is all about the skin: crispy, lacquered, crunchy skin. Honestly, you might as well do as some Chinese restaurants do and use the rest of the duck for a wonderful soup and just eat the skin. It's worth it. Do not try this recipe with a wild duck unless it is very fatty.

DIFFICULTY: ★ ★ ★ ★ ★

SERVES 4

PREP TIME: 36 HOURS

COOK TIME: 1¾ HOURS

1 whole duck, ideally a Pekin or a very fat mallard
   or pintail

4 quarts plus 1 tablespoon water

2 cups vinegar (distilled is fine)

¼ cup honey

2 teaspoons soy sauce

2 tablespoons kosher salt

2 teaspoons baking soda

Hoisin sauce, for serving

Pancakes for Peking Duck (recipe follows), for serving

6 green onions, white and green parts, thinly sliced
   on the diagonal

1 cucumber, halved, seeded, and cut into matchsticks

Dry the duck inside and out with paper towels. Remove all excess fat from the body cavity. Using your fingers, and starting with the breast, loosen the skin and separate it from the meat. Be careful not to tear the skin. (I start this from the neck side, wriggling my fingers under the skin to break the weak connective tissue that keeps the skin on the meat.) When you get your fingers to the area around the thigh, work downward to loosen the flanks. Don't bother with the back of the bird, as that skin is very tightly attached.

In a large saucepan or kettle, bring the 4 quarts water and 2 cups vinegar to a boil.

Set a cooling rack on a baking sheet and put the duck on the rack. Move the duck—still on the rack in the pan—to the sink. Slowly pour half of the boiling water over the duck, then flip the bird and pour the rest of the boiling water over it. Let the duck drip-dry for 10 minutes.

In a small bowl, combine the honey, soy sauce, and remaining 1 tablespoon water and stir until smooth. (If you cannot get everything to mix smoothly, heat the mixture in a microwave or in a small pot on the stove top.) Work the mixture all over the skin, coating the whole duck. In a second small bowl, stir together the salt and baking soda. Sprinkle the mixture evenly over the entire duck.

Put the duck—breast side up and still on the rack—in the refrigerator, uncovered, for at least 12 or up to 36 hours. Or set the duck in front of an electric fan for a couple of hours, rotating frequently. You want the skin to dry completely.

Preheat the oven to 350°F.

Put the duck, breast side up, on the rack, and put the rack in a large roasting pan. If you don't have a roasting pan large enough, set the duck right on the rack in the oven and put a rimmed baking sheet beneath it to catch the dripping juices and fat. Roast the duck for 1½ hours. You may need to rotate the duck during this time so it browns evenly. The duck is done when it is a pretty mahogany brown. Move the duck to a cutting board and let it rest for 10 minutes.

To serve, carve the duck. Start in the usual way (see page 32), taking care to lift off the skin as it comes free. Set the skin on the cutting board apart from the meat. You can now eat the duck any way you want. Traditionally, the breast meat and skin are cut into 2-inch squares and served with the skin placed on top of the pieces of breast meat. For the legs, you can either leave them whole for people to eat by hand, or carve the meat from the bone and place it on a large platter with the squares of breast meat and skin. To eat the duck, each diner spreads a little hoisin sauce on a warm pancake, tops the sauce with some green onion and cucumber, then with a little duck meat and skin, and rolls the pancake loosely around the filling.

PANCAKES FOR PEKING DUCK

DIFFICULTY: *

MAKES 8 PANCAKES

PREP TIME: 45 MINUTES

COOK TIME: 10 MINUTES

2 cups all-purpose flour

Pinch of salt

¾ cup boiling water

2 tablespoons toasted sesame oil,
   plus more for kneading and frying

2 tablespoons peanut oil or other vegetable oil

Put the flour and salt in a large bowl and make a well in the center. Pour the boiling water into the well and mix together with a fork until you get a shaggy mass. Wipe all the dough off the fork and continue with your hands. Turn the dough out onto a work surface and knead for about 5 minutes, until the dough is smooth. If the dough sticks to the work surface, lightly oil the surface. Put the dough in a plastic bag and let stand at room temperature for at least 30 minutes; it should be refrigerated if held beyond 2 hours.

Cut the dough into 4 pieces. Keep the unused dough in the plastic bag while you work in batches. Take 1 piece of dough and, using your palms, roll the dough back and forth on the work surface into a log about 1½ inches thick. Cut the log crosswise into 4 equal pieces. Using a rolling pin, roll each piece into a pancake about 3 inches across. Lightly paint the surface of 1 pancake with a little of the sesame oil, then top with a second pancake. Gently press the pancakes together, then roll them out to make a new pancake about 6 inches in diameter. Repeat this process with the rest of the dough until you have 8 doubled pancakes each 6 inches in diameter. They should not be more than ¼ inch thick.

Place a nonstick frying pan over medium-high heat. When it is hot, add the peanut oil and a little sesame oil and cook for about 30 seconds to 1 minute, until the underside begins to bubble a little and brown. Flip and cook the second side the same way (it will take a little less time), then transfer to a work surface. Stack the doubled pancakes and cover them with a tea towel while you cook the rest. When you are ready to eat them, carefully separate the paired pancakes and serve warm.

PIECES

BREASTS

The amount of fat on duck breasts confounds many beginning cooks. We all enjoy a bit of luxurious fat now and again, but few of us like a big glob of gooey suet in our mouths. The best way to meet this challenge is first to stop thinking of a duck breast as poultry. It's essentially a steak, and should be cooked like a steak. Your task is to render that fat and crisp that skin, all the while preventing the meat from overcooking. It's a lot easier than it sounds.

Duck and goose breast can also be served skinless, ground up like hamburger, poached gently, or cooked over an open fire. It is the most versatile part of the bird.

HOW TO PAN SEAR A DUCK BREAST

This is my basic method for pan searing a duck breast. This is the starting point for many of the other recipes in this chapter, but beyond that, this is a core skill you need to know to be a good duck cook. Follow this method and you will have crispy skin, most of the fat under that skin will be rendered away, and the meat itself will be a perfect medium to medium-rare. When I am tired or don't feel like cooking anything grandiose, I will pull out a couple of duck breasts and cook them this way. No matter how wound up or stressed I am from the day, a perfectly seared duck breast on a dinner plate always makes me happy. It's my comfort food.

This technique is geared to most duck breasts, but for very large duck breasts, such as Moulard, or goose breasts, follow the directions in Pan-Roasted Goose Breasts with Orange and Ouzo on page 80. Keep in mind that these instructions are for skin-on breasts. Cooking a skinless duck breast requires a slightly different technique (see page 61).

DECODING DUCK AND GOOSE BREASTS

The breasts of ducks and geese can weigh anything from a few ounces, in the case of a wild teal, to more than two pounds in the case of a Canada goose. Here is an idea about what to expect for skin-on breasts.

Teal or other small wild duck: 2 to 3 ounces
Wigeon or other medium duck: 3 to 6 ounces
Domestic Pekin or mallard or other large wild duck: 6 to 9 ounces
Muscovy (hen): 6 to 10 ounces
Muscovy (drake): 8 to 12 ounces
Rouen, small Canada, or specklebelly goose: 11 ounces to 1 pound
Moulard (magret): 1 to 1¼ pounds
Large Canada or domestic goose: 1 to 2 pounds

STEP ONE. If you are using a domesticated duck or a very fat wild duck, use a sharp knife to score the skin (but not the meat) in a crosshatch pattern, making the slashes about 1 inch across. This helps the fat render and will give you a crispier skin. Salt the breast well on both sides, then let it stand on a cutting board for at least 15 minutes or up to 1 hour. This does two things: first, it lets the duck come to room temperature before it is seared, and second, it allows the salt to penetrate the meat, which both seasons it and pulls some water out of it—water that would prevent the skin from crisping up.

Right before you plan on cooking the duck breasts, dry the skin. If you have not scored the duck breast, use the back of a chef's knife (or a butter knife) to scrape the skin side of the breast. This removes a lot of excess moisture. Don't try this if you've scored the breast or you might rip all of that delicious skin. In either case, pat the breasts dry.

STEP TWO. If you are cooking duck with a lot of fat, lay the breasts, skin side down, in a large, cold sauté pan, place on the stove top, and turn on the heat to medium. For leaner ducks like Muscovy or wild duck breasts, heat the pan over high heat for 1 minute, then add 1 tablespoon duck fat, unsalted butter, or other fat. Let the fat heat for another minute. Do not let it

smoke. Then, lay the duck breasts, skin side down, in the pan.

Use the flat of your tongs or a spatula to press down on the breasts for the first 30 seconds to a minute to get good contact between the skin and the pan. Otherwise, you might have a spot in the center of the breast that is not as evenly browned.

STEP THREE. Cook at a jocular sizzle—not an inferno, not a gurgle. You will need to adjust the heat for this. I cook most of my duck breasts at medium heat. How long? It depends. I like my duck medium to medium-rare. Regular domestic ducks (Pekin), Muscovy ducks, mallards, pintail, and canvasbacks need 6 to 8 minutes. Medium-size ducks like wigeon, gadwalls, or shovelers need 3 to 5 minutes. For small wild ducks such as a teal or a ruddy, you need only about 3 minutes on the skin side, and you might want to keep the heat higher. If you are cooking ultrafat Moulard ducks or a goose breast, you will want the heat on medium-low and you'll need to cook the skin side for a solid 8 to 10 minutes. In all cases, you are looking for a golden, crispy brown.

The key is to let the breast do most of its cooking on this side. It's the flattest side, and it will give you that fabulously crispy skin we all know and love.

STEP FOUR. Once the skin is golden brown and the sizzling dies down a bit, flip the breasts over. Lightly salt the now-exposed skin immediately. Doing this will absorb any extra oil and definitely gives you an even yummier, crispier skin. Cook until the meat feels slightly firm to the touch (see sidebar opposite). This will take 1 to 2 minutes for small ducks, 3 to 5 minutes for domesticated ducks and medium or large wild ducks, and 4 to 6 minutes for large domesticated ducks or geese.

STEP FIVE. Stand the two breast halves next to each other, thick edge down, for 30 to 90 seconds, just to get some good color. If you only have one duck breast, lean it against the side of the sauté pan and move the pan so the duck is right above the burner.

STEP SIX. Take the pan off the heat; transfer the duck, skin side up, to a cutting board; and tent loosely with aluminum foil. The breasts of small wild ducks like teal need only a couple of minutes to rest. A large duck or goose breast will need 10 minutes. Everything else benefits from a rest of about 5 minutes.

You can slice the breast from either end, either side up. You can get thinner slices by cutting with the skin side down, but you'll lose a little of the crispiness of the skin. If you are serving a whole breast, always serve it skin side up, with its sauce underneath.

THE FINGER TEST FOR DONENESS

The fastest and most effective way to test for doneness is the finger test.

Open your right hand loosely. Take the tip of the index finger of your left hand and press down on the fleshy area of your right hand where your thumb connects with the rest of your palm, making sure your right hand is relaxed. That's what raw meat feels like.

Now touch the tip of the index finger of your right hand to the end of your thumb. With your left hand, press that fleshy part at the base of the thumb: it should feel a little less squishy. That's how medium-rare meat feels.

Move back one finger on your right hand, so you are now touching the tip of your middle finger to your thumb. With your left hand, touch the fleshy part of your thumb again: this is medium.

One more finger back (to the ring finger on your left hand) and you get to medium-well. Not so good for any red meat, and terrible for duck. Finally, touch your pinky to your thumb and feel the base. Rock hard, right? That's well-done, which means you just made cat food from your duck breast.

Remember, once the duck or goose breast is resting, carryover heat will continue to cook it. So I always take the breasts off the heat a little before they are where I want them, which is on the rare side of medium. Once they have finished resting, the breasts are perfectly cooked.

COOKING A SKINLESS DUCK BREAST

For the most part, it is a sin against God and nature to waste the skin of a duck. But skinless duck breasts do have their place in the kitchen. For stinky wild ducks like scoters, skinless is the way to go for the health-conscious or anyone who cannot have much fat in their diets. And as much as it pains me to note, many hunters skin all their ducks, leaving them with piles of skinless breasts.

Even I skin some of the wild birds I bring home. Sea ducks, many divers, mallards, and wigeon that have been living in saltwater, snow geese, coots, and shovelers are all candidates for skinning. That's because their diet makes their fat fishy or otherwise smelly. Roast a whole scoter, eider, or other sea duck and it will smell like the garbage bin outside a fish market. But if you remove all the skin and fat, these birds are perfectly fine.

In the realm of domesticated birds, you will have to remove the skin from your ducks yourself; I know of no retailer that sells skinless duck breasts. And even though it sounds like a crime, pulling the skin off a bunch of Pekin ducks is worth it to make some of the recipes in this book. Just be sure to render the fat in the skin later so you do not waste anything.

Cooking a skinned duck breast is exactly like cooking a venison steak, and it's very similar to cooking beef flank steak: there is no fat in a duck breast at all, so you need to be careful not to overcook it or you will have a piece of shoe leather. Under no circumstances should you cook a piece of duck breast past medium. Unlike the medium heat you use for a skin-on duck breast, most skinless breasts are best cooked right from the fridge over medium-high to high heat. The exception is a very large breast, such as one from a Canada goose. This needs to be treated more like a London broil and roasted in the oven. All skinless waterfowl breasts will need a coating of melted duck fat or oil before it hits the fire, plus a generous sprinkling of salt.

STEP ONE. Get the pan good and hot before you pat the breasts dry with a paper towel and start cooking them. Lay the duck breast skinned side down in the pan and turn your hood fan on high, as the breast will spit. You want a serious sear. When you hear that, turn the heat down a notch to medium-high and let the duck breast cook.

STEP TWO. The breasts of most wild ducks and of the domesticated Pekin duck will need 3 to 4 minutes on each side. The breasts of small wild ducks will need only 1 to 2 minutes per side, and Moulard, Rouen, and Muscovy duck breasts will need 4 to 5 minutes. Turn and continue to cook until you have the doneness you want, using the finger test to check when it is ready (see page 61).

STEP THREE. Take the pan off the heat; transfer the duck breast, to a cutting board; and tent loosely with aluminum foil. Let rest for 5 minutes before cutting and/or serving.

GRILLING DUCK BREASTS

What makes duck breasts so wonderful—fat—is what makes them tricky to grill properly. All that fat seeps onto the fire, which then flares up, blackening and charring your duck. Ruined. Many recipes gloss over this fact, and it's a pity: a wrecked piece of duck is a far more expensive loss than a charred chicken breast.

Thankfully, this is not an insurmountable challenge, but you do need to think about what sort of duck breast to use before you slap one on the grill. The breast of a typical Pekin duck from the supermarket will be awfully fatty for the grill. A leaner Muscovy breast is a better choice. If you are a hunter and live in a migration state, chances are your birds will be very lean; I've shot mallard near Winnipeg that were as skinny as old rooster pheasants. Although this kind of bird is not my ideal duck for the table, its lack of fat does make it easier to grill, because you'll get fewer flare-ups.

PAN SAUCE JAZZ

This chapter has several recipes for simply seared duck breast with specific sauces. But they all follow the same principles, and once you know these principles, you can improvise a pan sauce with whatever you have around. Here are the keys to a perfect pan sauce for four people:

- Once you have finished cooking the duck breast, you will want to have about 2 tablespoons of fat in the pan. In many cases, you will need to drain off some fat to arrive at that amount.

- With the pan over medium-high heat, add about 2 tablespoons minced shallot or yellow or white onion to the fat and sauté for a minute or so.

- Add about 1 cup stock (any kind), or ¼ cup Duck Glace de Viande (page 226).

- Add a shot glass of hard liquor (brandy, whisky, ouzo, or the like) or a wineglass of wine, then add a heaping tablespoon of something sweet, such as jelly, jam, syrup, honey, or molasses.

- Mix well, bring to a boil, and boil furiously until the mixture reduces by half or more. Finish by removing the pan from the heat, seasoning the sauce with salt, and then swirling in 2 tablespoons unsalted butter.

Species matters. A perfectly grilled eider is still going to be fishy, and an overcooked pintail or mallard is still likely to taste okay. A general rule is that if you're cooking skin-on breasts, the more "off" they are, the stronger the sauce: even a fishy shoveler can be palatable smothered in barbecue sauce. Conversely, don't kill the wonderful taste of a pintail or canvasback with a lot of sauce. Go light and enjoy the true flavor of these special birds.

One way of dealing with the fat comes from chef Chrysa Robertson of Rancho Pinot in Scottsdale, Arizona. Robertson pan sears just the skin side of her duck breasts to render out the fat before she finishes them on her mesquite-fired grill. If you choose to do this, follow the pan-searing instructions on page 58 but don't flip the breasts.

If you've skinned your birds, you have basically made steaks of them. I grill skinless breasts of snow geese and Canada geese like a London broil: high heat, lots of salt, cooked medium-rare, and sliced very thinly against the grain.

STEP ONE. Assuming you are using skin-on breasts, take them out of the refrigerator, salt well, and set aside to come to room temperature. Fire up your grill and get it good and hot (light all burners on a gas grill). If you are using charcoal, make a hole in the center of your coals once they are hot. Scrape down the grill grate well and then oil the grate: use tongs to grab a piece of paper towel, dip the towel into some vegetable oil, and wipe the grate down.

STEP TWO. Coat the duck breasts with a little oil. Lay the duck breasts, skin side down, between the burners of a gas grill if using gas, or over the area where there are no coals if using charcoal. This helps limit flare-ups by sending the dripping fat to the bottom of the grill, not right to hot coals or a burner. Have a spray bottle of water handy for dousing any fires, too. Keep the grill cover open and grill your duck breasts undisturbed for 3 minutes. Douse any flare-ups with the spray bottle.

STEP THREE. Lift the duck breasts and check the skin: if it is brown and crispy, it's time to flip them. If not, lay the breasts down at a 45-degree angle to where they were to get that pretty crosshatching and grill for another 2 minutes, until the skin crisps. When the skin side is ready, flip the duck breasts and grill for 2 to 5 minutes, until done to your liking. Use the finger test (see page 61) to test for doneness.

STEP FOUR. Transfer the duck, skin side up, to a cutting board and tent loosely with aluminum foil. The breasts of small wild ducks like teal or wood ducks need only about 5 minutes to rest. A large duck breast will need about 10 minutes. A goose breast will need closer to 15 minutes.

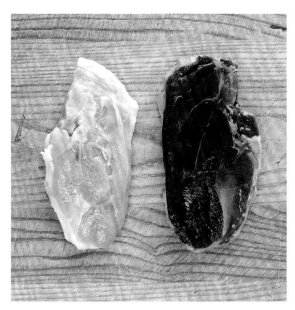

Duck breasts compared: on the left, supermarket pekin, on the right, wild mallard.

WHY IT IS SAFE TO EAT RARE DUCK

Duck breasts should be served rare to medium. This is a given in the cooking community, but many believe that they need to be cooked well-done, like a chicken. Indeed, the United States Department of Agriculture recommends an internal temperature of 165°F for duck meat. This is fine for a leg, but it absolutely ruins the breast meat.

But isn't rare meat unsafe? Studies on the causes of food-borne illness show that duck is one of the meats *least* likely to make you sick. A 2003 Danish survey of salmonella poisoning—a major source of food poisoning associated with poultry—found that less than 1 percent of all European cases were linked to eating duck. Most cases of salmonella poisoning come from eating chicken eggs (and even then, the incidence is relatively rare). Duck eggs also can carry salmonella, although not as often as chicken eggs do.

Also keep in mind that the interior of a solid piece of meat, such as a duck breast, is sterile. No pathogens will be lurking at its center. Any bacteria will be on the surface, and a good sear will kill them.

DUCK BIGARADE

This is a modern rendition of a nineteenth-century recipe that ultimately became the legendary *canard a l'orange,* though it bears little resemblance to the gloppy 1960s version of duck a l'orange served in this country. This is much lighter and just a little bitter. The sauce was originally made with sour Seville oranges (*bigarade* is the Provençal term for these sour citrus), and if you can find them, by all means use them. Citrus and waterfowl are a perfect pair, and they both happen to be in season at the same time. Any skin-on duck breasts will work with this recipe, but I prefer Muscovy or large wild duck breasts.

Serve this dish with roasted or mashed potatoes, polenta, or a wild rice pilaf. A soft white wine is a good choice here, such as a Viognier, a Roussanne, or an oaky Chardonnay.

DIFFICULTY: *

SERVES 4

PREP TIME: 30 MINUTES

COOK TIME: 20 MINUTES

1½ to 2 pounds duck breasts

Kosher salt

1 tablespoon all-purpose flour

1 cup Basic Duck Stock (page 222) or chicken stock

Juice of 1 orange, preferably Seville (½ cup)

1 shot glass Grand Marnier or other orange liqueur, optional

1 tablespoon cider vinegar or sherry vinegar

1 teaspoon sugar

Grated zest of 1 orange

½ sweet orange, quartered and thinly sliced

Remove the duck breasts from the refrigerator, salt them well, and set them aside at room temperature for 30 minutes.

Pan sear the duck breasts as directed on page 58. You may have to do this in batches. When the breasts are cooked, set them aside skin side up on a cutting board and let them rest, tented with aluminum foil, while you make the sauce.

To make the sauce, pour off all but about 2 tablespoons of the fat from the pan and place the pan over medium heat. Sprinkle the flour into the pan and stir to combine and make a roux. Let it cook, stirring occasionally, for 4 to 5 minutes, until it is the color of coffee with cream.

Add a pinch of salt and stir to combine, then slowly stir in the stock, orange juice, liqueur, and vinegar. Everything will spatter at first, but it will calm down. Add any accumulated juices from the duck to the sauce. Let this boil down until it is a little thinner than the consistency of Thanksgiving gravy. Add the sugar, then taste and adjust with salt. If you want a more refined sauce, pour it through a fine-mesh sieve into a bowl.

To serve, slice the breasts. Spoon some sauce on each plate and top with breast slices. Garnish with the orange zest and orange slices.

DUCK BREAST WITH BLACK CURRANT SAUCE

A venerable dish in both France and England, this preparation is almost as old as duck bigarade. Like that recipe and various others in this book, it is proof of the fundamental alliance between waterfowl and fruit. Black currants are a little musky, very tart, and not overly sweet. Cassis, if you've never heard of it, is black currant liqueur. You need at least one of these to do this recipe justice. I not only use black currant preserves and cassis, but also I will on occasion toss in a handful of fresh black currants at the end of the cooking just for good measure.

However, black currants can be difficult to find in any form, so you can hinge the dish on blackberries instead, using blackberry schnapps and blackberry preserves.

My rendition of this recipe is decidedly English, with a simple watercress salad and potato crisps. The watercress salad is supersimple: buy some watercress and dress it however you like; I recommend the Duck Fat Vinaigrette (recipe follows). If you cannot find watercress, use a mesclun mix or arugula. Pour a good red wine, such as a Côtes du Rhône, a Spanish Rioja, an Italian Aglianico, or a California Barbera.

DIFFICULTY: ✳ ✳

SERVES 4

PREP TIME: 30 MINUTES

COOK TIME: 30 MINUTES

1½ to 2 pounds duck breasts

Kosher salt

¼ cup minced shallot

⅓ cup cassis or port

1 tablespoon red wine vinegar

½ teaspoon dried thyme

½ teaspoon freshly ground black pepper

½ cup Basic Duck Stock (page 222) or beef stock

¼ cup black currant preserves or jelly

POTATO CRISPS

2 russet potatoes

⅔ cup duck fat or oil (such as peanut or olive)

Kosher salt

Remove the duck breasts from the refrigerator, salt well, and set aside at room temperature. Put a cooling rack on a baking sheet and put this baking sheet in the oven; this will be for your potato crisps. Preheat the oven to 200°F.

To prepare the potato crisps, have ready a large bowl of ice water. Using a mandoline or a sharp knife, cut the potatoes crosswise into ⅛-inch-thick slices and drop them into the ice water. In a wide sauté pan, heat the duck fat to 325°F. If you don't have a thermometer, put one of the potato end slices into the fat; if it sizzles nicely, you are ready to fry.

Remove the potatoes from the ice water and dry on cloth or paper towels. Working in batches, fry the potatoes in the hot fat, salting them as they cook and turning them once or twice. Remove them when they are golden brown. Each batch will take 5 to 8 minutes. Be sure to let the oil drain off the crisps before you put them on the cooling rack in the oven, and always let the oil temperature return to 325°F before adding the next batch.

When the final batch of potatoes goes into the hot oil, pat the duck breasts dry and pan sear according to the directions on page 58.

When the breasts are done, move them skin side up to a cutting board, tent with aluminum foil, and let rest while you make the sauce. Pour off all but about 2 tablespoons of the fat from the pan and place the pan over medium-high heat. Add the shallot and sauté for about 90 seconds, until the edges brown a bit. Take the pan off the heat and add the cassis. Return the pan to the stove top, turn up the heat to high, and scrape up any browned bits from the bottom of the pan with a wooden spoon.

Let the cassis boil down for 1 minute, then mix in the vinegar, thyme, pepper, stock, and preserves. Boil the mixture hard until it thickens: drag the wooden spoon through the sauce, and if it leaves a noticeable trail, you're ready. This should take 8 to 10 minutes. If you want a more refined sauce, pour it through a fine-mesh sieve into a bowl.

To serve, make a watercress salad as suggested in the headnote and put some on each plate. Divide the potato crisps among the plates. Slice the duck breasts and divide evenly among the plates. To finish, drizzle some of the sauce over each portion of duck and serve at once.

DUCK FAT VINAIGRETTE

DIFFICULTY: *

MAKES ABOUT 1 CUP

PREP TIME: 10 MINUTES

I can—and have—made this salad dressing in my sleep. It is my go-to for the annual Duck Hunter's Dinners we throw at our home; to get a seat at the table, you must be a duck hunter, or accompanied by one. At these dinners I unleash whatever crazy new duck recipes I've been working on during the season, and this dressing is the only constant: at some point in the multicourse meal, there will be a simple salad of bitter greens, dressed with this vinaigrette.

1 teaspoon Dijon mustard
1 shallot, chopped
½ teaspoon kosher salt
1 teaspoon sugar
¼ cup freshly squeezed Meyer lemon juice
　 or white wine vinegar
¾ cup duck fat, warmed

In a blender, combine the mustard, shallot, salt, sugar, and lemon juice, cover, and buzz on high speed to combine. Turn down the speed to low, remove the lid, and slowly pour in the duck fat. Re-cover, turn the speed to high, and blend for 30 seconds.

Use at once, or refrigerate for up to a week.

GRILLED DUCK WITH PANZANELLA

Duck is not normally associated with summertime eating in this country, but there is no reason it shouldn't be, especially if you can get your hands on Muscovy or wild ducks, which are lean enough to grill. Skinless Pekin duck breasts would also work well here.

Panzanella is an Italian summer salad made from day-old bread and fresh tomatoes, herbs, and garlic. I am always finding myself with aging bread, so when tomatoes from my garden are piling up, I wind up making this salad a lot. It is bright yet substantial and is a nice complement to the savory duck. Serve with a dry rosé or a light red such as a Grenache.

DIFFICULTY: *

SERVES 4

PREP TIME: 30 MINUTES

COOK TIME: 6 TO 10 MINUTES

1½ pounds lean duck breasts

Kosher salt

4 cups bite-size-cubed day-old bread from a baguette or other crusty loaf

4 cups coarsely chopped tomatoes (pieces about the size of the bread)

2 cups seeded and coarsely chopped cucumber (if the peel is bitter, peel it)

1 cup coarsely chopped red onion

1 to 2 tablespoons chopped fresh basil, oregano, or flat-leaf parsley

½ cup olive oil

1 tablespoon red wine vinegar

Take the duck breasts out of the refrigerator, salt well, and set aside.

While the duck breasts are coming to room temperature, make the *panzanella*. In a large bowl, combine the bread, tomatoes, cucumber, onion, basil, and olive oil and mix well. Set aside at room temperature to marinate; the salad is better after it sits a bit.

Set up the grill and grill the breasts as directed on page 62.

Transfer the duck breasts to a cutting board and tent loosely with aluminum foil. While the duck is resting, add the vinegar and any juices accumulated from the duck into the salad. Slice the breasts and arrange on dinner plates, with the salad alongside.

BRINING

I generally don't brine my duck breasts, but many cooks swear by the process, which removes some of the gamy flavor of wild birds and helps keep the meat moister. If you do brine, take this tip from chef Liam LaCivita of Lyon Hall in Arlington, Virginia. LaCivita brines his duck breasts only to the depth of the meat: he leaves the skin out of the brine. This keeps the skin dry, which helps it crisp later, and prevents any sugar in the brine from getting into the skin. Sugar will caramelize too fast when you're cooking the skin, causing it to burn.

DUCK BULGOGI

Bulgogi is one of the national dishes of Korea, though this is not an authentic version. It is an adaptation of an adaptation. Back in the 1960s, my mom and dad were invited to a barbecue at the home of a Korean War veteran and his Korean wife, who served their guests an authentic *bulgogi*. There is a reason this is a popular dish in Korea, and it was a hit that day, too. But all mom could get from the host was a list of ingredients, not the full recipe.

So mom did the best she could, and it eventually gelled into a dish that I remember longing for as a child: savory sweet, garlicky, and a little sticky. Mom made it with flank steak or London broil. I've since made it with venison, antelope, beef, and, yes, duck.

This is one of the easiest recipes in this book, and works with any skinless red meat. If you are serving a crowd, a domestic or Canada goose breast would be ideal.

DIFFICULTY: *

SERVES 4

PREP TIME: 10 MINUTES, PLUS 1 TO 24 HOURS MARINATING TIME

COOK TIME: 6 TO 8 MINUTES

¼ **cup rice vinegar**

⅓ **cup soy sauce**

2 **tablespoons toasted sesame oil**

4 **green onions, white and green parts, chopped**

2 **tablespoons peeled and chopped fresh ginger**

5 **cloves garlic, chopped**

2 **tablespoons sugar**

2 **pounds skinless duck breasts**

Kimchi and cooked white rice, for serving

Black sesame seeds, for garnish, optional

In a blender, combine the vinegar, soy sauce, sesame oil, onions, ginger, garlic, and sugar and puree until smooth. Put the duck breasts in a container just large enough to accommodate them, pour in the marinade, and turn to coat evenly. Marinate in the refrigerator for at least 1 hour or up to 24 hours.

When you are ready to cook, set up the grill as directed on page 62. Remove the duck breasts from the marinade, pat dry, and set aside. Pour the marinade into a small saucepan, bring to a boil over medium-high heat, and boil for 5 minutes. Remove from the heat and keep warm.

Coat the duck breasts with a little oil as directed in the grilling instructions, then grill as directed.

Transfer the duck breasts to a cutting board, tent loosely with aluminum foil, and let rest for 5 minutes. Slice the breasts thinly and arrange on dinner plates along with the kimchi and rice. Drizzle the hot marinade over the duck, then sprinkle the sesame seeds over everything. Serve with a cold lager or pilsner.

LAOTIAN DUCK SALAD

This is *larb*, one of the most famous dishes of Southeast Asia. It is a spectacular hot-weather salad, normally served with beef, chicken, or seafood. Duck *larb* does exist, however, in Laos, Cambodia, and Thailand. The list of ingredients is long, but the hardest part about making this recipe is chopping the herbs and vegetables. It's really that easy.

DIFFICULTY: *

SERVES 4

PREP TIME: 30 MINUTES

COOK TIME: 8 MINUTES

2 tablespoons short-grain white rice

1½ to 2 pounds skinless duck breasts

Kosher salt

2 tablespoons duck fat or vegetable oil

1 cup loosely packed chopped fresh cilantro

1 cup loosely packed chopped fresh mint

1 lemongrass stalk, white bulblike part only, trimmed, outer leaves discarded, and minced

2 large shallots, thinly sliced

3 green onions, white and green parts, thinly sliced

2 cloves garlic, minced

1 to 4 small fresh hot chiles, thinly sliced

2 teaspoons peeled and grated fresh ginger

Grated zest and juice of 1 lime

1 tablespoon fish sauce or soy sauce

1 teaspoon sugar

1 teaspoon toasted sesame oil

In a small, dry sauté pan over medium-high heat, toast the rice, shaking the pan often, for 4 to 5 minutes, until it browns. Pour onto a plate to cool, then grind coarsely in a spice grinder or with a mortar and pestle. Ready the remaining ingredients.

Pat the duck breasts dry with paper towels. In a large sauté pan, heat the duck fat over medium-high heat for 1 minute. Add the breasts skinned side down and sear for 3 minutes. Flip and finish cooking according to your liking, using the finger test for doneness (see page 61) and salting to taste. Transfer the duck to a cutting board and let rest for 15 minutes.

While the duck rests, in a bowl, combine the ground rice, cilantro, mint, lemongrass, shallots, green onions, garlic, chiles to taste, ginger, lime zest and juice, fish sauce, sugar, and sesame oil and mix well.

When the duck is ready, you can either slice or mince it; mincing is more traditional. Add the duck, plus any accumulated juices, to the bowl holding the rest of the salad and mix well. Serve with an ice-cold lager or pilsner.

DUCK JAGERSCHNITZEL

Jaegerschnitzel means "hunter's cutlet" in German, and the dish was originally made with thinly pounded venison backstrap. The Texas specialty chicken fried steak is believed to be an outgrowth of this dish, brought to the United States by German immigrants. But a pounded skinless duck breast works even better than beef or venison: duck has a denser grain, so it keeps its integrity better than coarser meats do.

At its core, *Jaegerschnitzel* is a thin cutlet of meat served with a mushroom gravy, traditionally made with chanterelles. Spaetzle or potatoes—boiled, mashed, or in a salad—are the traditional side dish. It is a manly meal, and the only green thing allowed is, reluctantly, parsley. Traditionally, the cutlet for *Jaegerschnitzel* is not coated with flour or bread crumbs, but I like a light coating of flour.

This is a superb recipe for "off" ducks that have been skinned. I love it with surf scoters and bluebills. If you are using a domesticated duck, stick to the smaller Pekin breasts. Larger breasts from Muscovy or Moulard ducks are just too big.

DIFFICULTY: ✱ ✱

SERVES 4

PREP TIME: 30 MINUTES, MOSTLY FOR CLEANING THE MUSHROOMS

COOK TIME: 20 MINUTES

1½ to 2 pounds skinless duck breasts

½ cup Basic Duck Stock (page 222) or beef stock

½ cup dry rosé or white wine

3 tablespoons duck fat, unsalted butter, or bacon fat

3 ounces smoky bacon, diced (about 4 slices)

Kosher salt and freshly ground pepper

All-purpose flour, for dusting

1 pound chanterelles or other mushrooms, coarsely chopped

½ cup minced shallots

¼ cup heavy cream

Chopped fresh flat-leaf parsley, for garnish

Place each duck breast between 2 sheets of plastic wrap and pound with a rubber mallet, meat mallet, or empty wine bottle until the meat is ⅛ to ¼ inch thick. Do this firmly but don't wail on the meat, or you will tear it. Trim the cutlets to an even shape, if you like.

Pour the stock and wine into a small saucepan and bring to a simmer; adjust the heat to maintain a bare simmer. Put a baking sheet in the oven and turn the oven on to the warm setting.

In a large sauté pan, heat the duck fat over medium heat. Spread the bacon out in the pan and fry until crispy. Using a slotted spoon, transfer to a plate and set aside.

Salt the cutlets well, then dust evenly with flour, tapping off the excess. Turn the heat to medium-high and add the cutlets to the fat remaining in the pan; ideally they should float a little in the fat. Fry them for 1 minute. Use a spatula to prevent them from curling up. Flip the cutlets and sear for another 1 to 2 minutes. Transfer the cutlets to the baking sheet in the oven. Pour all of the fat in the pan into a small heatproof bowl and reserve. Be sure to wipe the edge of the sauté pan or the fat will drip down to the burner and catch fire.

Add the mushrooms and shallots to the sauté pan and turn the heat to high. Shake them around so they don't stick too much and cook the mushrooms for 3 to 4 minutes, until they release their water.

Add 2 tablespoons of the reserved fat and sauté for about 4 minutes, until the shallots and mushrooms begin to brown. Add the stock-wine mixture and scrape up any browned bits from the bottom of the pan. Bring to a boil and boil for about 5 minutes, until the liquid has thickened. Turn off the heat, wait for the sauce to stop bubbling, and stir in the cream. Season with salt and pepper.

To serve, divide the cutlets among individual plates. Pour the sauce over the cutlets, and garnish with parsley—if you must. Serve at once with lots of beer.

DUCK BREAST WITH MORELS AND RAMPS

This is an ode to early spring. Ramps and morels are a natural combination, and spring peas complete the classic trio. The duck brings a thwack of savory punch to the dish. Any skin-on duck breasts will work with this recipe, but I prefer Muscovy or large wild duck breasts.

You really owe it to yourself to try to make this recipe with fresh morels and ramps, both of which are available in markets during April and May. The rest of the year you can make it with dried morels and those little pearl onions you can get in supermarkets. If you use pearl onions, boil them for 1 minute and then toss them in an ice-water bath to peel away those pesky skins.

If you don't know *farro*, it is an ancient variety of wheat that the Italians, especially the Tuscans and Umbrians, are particularly fond of. It adds heft to the dish, helps make it a complete meal, and gives it one more earthy note to go with those of the morels and the duck. *Farro* is sold in many supermarkets these days, but if you can't find it, use pearled barley, spelt, or wheat berries in its place. The barley will cook in about the same amount of time as the *farro*; the spelt and wheat berries will need at least an additional 30 minutes.

An acidic red wine, such as an Italian Sangiovese, or a dry rosé is a good choice here, as is an India pale ale or other hoppy beer.

DIFFICULTY: ✱ ✱

SERVES 4

PREP TIME: 30 MINUTES

COOK TIME: 30 MINUTES

1½ to 2 pounds duck breasts

Kosher salt and freshly ground black pepper

8 to 12 ounces fresh morel mushrooms, or 1 ounce dried morel mushrooms

2 cups hot water, if using dried morels

4 cups Basic Duck Stock (page 222) or chicken stock

1 cup farro

4 ounces ramp bulbs or pearl onions, halved lengthwise

½ cup Madeira, Marsala, or dry sherry

1 cup fresh or thawed shelled peas

Remove the duck breasts from the refrigerator, salt them well, and set aside at room temperature for 30 minutes.

If using dried morels, put them in a small bowl and pour in the hot water. Place a second bowl or small plate on the mushrooms to keep them submerged, and set the mushrooms aside.

In a saucepan, bring the stock to a boil over high heat. Add the *farro* and a pinch of salt, adjust the heat to a simmer, and cook uncovered for 25 to 30 minutes, until tender. Drain the *farro*, reserving ½ cup of the stock. Set the *farro* and stock aside separately.

Pat the duck breasts dry and pan sear them as directed on page 58. You may have to do this in batches. When the breasts are cooked, set them aside on a cutting board skin side up and let them rest, tented with aluminum foil, while you cook the morels and ramps.

If you are using dried morels, remove them from the water, squeeze them dry with your hands, and chop them coarsely. Pour off all but about 2 tablespoons of the fat from the pan in which you seared the breasts into a small heatproof bowl and reserve. Return the pan to medium-high heat and lay the ramps, cut side down, in the pan. As the edges of their layers caramelize, the ramps (or pearl onions) will start to lift up. Press them down a bit with a spatula as they cook. Once the cut side of the ramps has nicely browned, after about 90 seconds, mix in the morels and turn the heat to high. Fresh morels will begin to give up their water in a minute or

two. Let most of the liquid boil away. If you are using reconstituted dried morels, no liquid will be released. Add the Madeira and the reserved stock, bring to a boil, and boil furiously.

When the liquid has reduced by half, stir in the peas and cook for 2 minutes. Add the reserved *farro* and toss to combine. Add a little of the reserved duck fat to taste, and season with pepper.

To serve, slice the duck breasts and arrange on individual plates with the morels and ramps alongside. Serve at once.

DUCK BREAST WITH CHERRIES AND MARASCHINO LIQUEUR

Duck with cherries is the perfect combination for late spring or early summer. Sweet cherries, tart vinegar, and the zing of green peppercorns make this a sophisticated dish that also happens to be undemanding to prepare. Think of it as an easy dinner party dish. Maraschino liqueur is widely available in most large liquor stores, but regular brandy works fine here. This is a good dish for magret duck breasts, but any skin-on duck breast will work. Try to avoid really lean wild duck breasts.

Serve this dish with crusty bread or roasted potatoes (cooked in duck fat, of course!), a green salad, and a good red wine. A Chianti, a California Pinot Noir, or a French Burgundy would be a good choice.

DIFFICULTY: ✳ ✳

SERVES 4

PREP TIME: 30 MINUTES

COOK TIME: 15 MINUTES

1½ to 2 pounds skin-on duck breasts

Kosher salt

1 large shallot, minced

¼ cup maraschino liqueur or brandy

¼ cup Duck Glace de Viande (page 226), or
   1 cup Basic Duck Stock (page 222) or
   beef stock reduced to ½ cup

1 tablespoon green peppercorns

20 cherries, pitted and halved

1 tablespoon red wine vinegar

2 tablespoons unsalted butter, halved

Remove the duck breasts from the refrigerator, salt them well, and set aside at room temperature for 30 minutes.

Pat the duck breasts dry and pan sear them as directed on page 58. When the breasts are cooked, set them aside on a cutting board skin side up and let them rest, tented with aluminum foil, while you make the sauce.

Pour off all but about 2 tablespoons of the fat from the pan and return the pan to medium-high heat. Add the shallot and sauté for about 2 minutes, until it barely begins to brown.

Take the pan off of the heat and pour in the liqueur (this prevents the liqueur from igniting in your face). Set the pan back on the heat and use a wooden spoon to scrape up any browned bits on the bottom of the pan. Let the liqueur cook down by half, then add the *glace de viande* and peppercorns. Increase the heat to high and boil the mixture until reduced by half.

Add the cherries and vinegar and cook, stirring often to coat the cherries, for 2 minutes. Turn off the heat, and when the sauce stops bubbling, add the butter and swirl it around in the pan until it dissolves. Add salt to taste.

Slice the duck breasts and arrange on individual plates. Spoon the sauce over the duck and serve at once.

PAN-ROASTED GOOSE BREASTS WITH ORANGE AND OUZO

This is another combination of duck and citrus, only with a Greek twist: ouzo, an anise-flavored liqueur. Ouzo is available at most liquor stores, and you can substitute any similar liquor, such as Pernod, pastis, raki, *tsipouro*, *sambuca*, anisette, and so on. If you don't drink alcohol, double the amount of chopped fennel and add some fennel seeds or aniseeds.

I designed this recipe for specklebelly geese, which run five to seven pounds and are often pretty fatty. They are very similar to a Rouen or Moulard duck, the breasts of which can be used in place of the goose breasts here. Domesticated and Canada geese will work here, too. You can use smaller duck breasts to make this dish, too. Just follow the directions for pan-seared duck breasts on page 58.

I prefer to serve this dish with something simple that will sop up the sauce, such as mashed potatoes or celery root or a mound of polenta. Serve with a light red wine or a rich white, such as an oaky Chardonnay or a Viognier.

DIFFICULTY: ✳ ✳

SERVES 4 TO 6

PREP TIME: 45 MINUTES

COOK TIME: 20 MINUTES

2 pounds goose or duck breasts

Kosher salt and freshly ground pepper

1 teaspoon duck fat, unsalted butter, or olive oil

½ cup finely chopped fennel (bulb only)

1 shallot, minced (about 2 tablespoons)

1 small hot fresh chile (such as Thai or serrano), halved lengthwise

½ cup ouzo or other anise-flavored liqueur

1 cup goose or duck stock (page 222) or chicken stock

Juice of 1 orange (about ½ cup)

Mashed potatoes or celery root or cooked polenta, for serving

Small bunch of fennel fronds, for garnish

Remove the goose breasts from the refrigerator, salt well, and set aside at room temperature for 20 to 40 minutes. Preheat the oven to 425°F.

Pat the breasts dry with paper towels. If you are working with a domesticated goose or a very fat duck, use a sharp knife to score the skin (but not the meat) in a crosshatch pattern, making the slashes about 1 inch across. This helps the fat render and will give you a crispier skin. Do not score the skin of a wild goose unless it is very fatty.

Set the breasts, skin side down, in a cold ovenproof sauté pan with the duck fat and place on the stove top. Turn on the heat to high and let the sizzling rise to a comfortable level, the way it sounds when you cook bacon. Turn the heat down to medium-low, or even low, and let the breasts cook for 10 to 12 minutes at a gentle sizzle, until the skin has browned a bit.

Move the pan into the hot oven. Do not flip the meat. After 5 minutes, check for doneness using the finger test (see page 61). A very large domestic or Canada goose breast might take as long as 15 minutes to get warm at its center. If you prefer to use a thermometer, you will want it to read 125°F, which will yield rare meat after the breast rests a bit. Because the breast is larger, the carryover heat will increase the internal temperature more than for a typical duck breast.

When the meat is at the target temperature (remember, it will gain 5 to 10 degrees during the resting period), transfer the breasts, skin side up, to a cutting board and tent loosely with aluminum foil. Let rest a full 10 minutes before carving.

continued

continued from previous page

While the breasts are resting, start making the sauce. Remove an ice cube from the freezer and run it along the handle of your pan, which just came out of the oven. This should cool the handle enough for you to grasp it. I find that while I can remember to use an oven mitt to get the pan out of the oven, I always seem to slip up while I am making the sauce. I have the scars to prove it.

Pour off all but 2 to 3 tablespoons of the fat from the pan. Without turning on the burner, put the pan on the stove top, add the chopped fennel, shallot, and chile to the pan, and sauté for 2 to 3 minutes, stirring often. The vegetables should sizzle moderately. Do not let them burn.

Add the ouzo and use a wooden spoon to scrape up any browned bits on the bottom of the pan. Put the pan on the burner that heats the hottest and turn the heat to high. Let the ouzo boil down by half. Add the stock and orange juice and a little salt, bring to a boil, and boil furiously until a spoon passed through the sauce leaves a trail. Remove from the heat. If you want to a more refined sauce, pour it through a fine-mesh sieve into a bowl.

Slice the goose breasts on the diagonal. To serve, pour a little sauce on each plate and spoon the mashed potatoes on the sauce. The sauce will pool around the edges. Arrange the goose slices, skin side up, on the potatoes. Garnish with fennel fronds and pepper. Serve at once.

PENELOPE AND THE DUCKS

If you remember reading *The Odyssey* in high school, you might recall Penelope, the wife of the Greek hero Odysseus. She was the epitome of faithfulness, patience, and virtue. What you probably don't remember is that Penelope owed her life to ducks.

Penelope's parents were Prince Icarius of Sparta and the nymph Periboea. Being a typical Spartan, Icarius wanted sons, not a baby girl. Periboea hid the infant Penelope as soon as she was born, but Icarius found the baby girl and threw her into the sea to drown. But before she succumbed, a family of ducks rescued her. Icarius thought this was clearly an omen, so he relented and named the child Penelope after the Greek word for "duck" and raised her as his favorite child thereafter.

Those ducks were believed to be Eurasian wigeon, which are to this day known as *Anas penelope*. And yes, they do winter in Greece.

DUCK FRIED RICE, TWO WAYS

In China, duck fried rice is usually made with leftover duck, and while you can use leftovers here, I like it better with freshly cooked duck breast; shredded confit (page 144 or 146) is another good option. I have two versions here, one Chinese inspired and one Vietnamese inspired. I prefer to use skinless duck here, usually from wild birds, but a skinned Pekin duck breast works great, too.

If you've never made fried rice before, you need to start with cold cooked rice; otherwise, it gets all starchy and clumpy. You can use dried mushrooms in place of the fresh: soak ½ ounce dried shiitake mushrooms in 2 cups hot water until soft, then lift them out of the water, squeeze them dry, discard the stems, and slice the caps. This recipe goes together in a heartbeat, so have all of your ingredients ready to go before you start cooking.

DIFFICULTY: ✳

SERVES 4 TO 6

PREP TIME: 20 MINUTES

COOK TIME: 10 MINUTES

CHINESE

3 tablespoons duck fat, lard, or peanut oil

1 duck egg or 2 chicken eggs, lightly beaten

1 tablespoon peeled and minced fresh ginger

8 ounces baby bok choy, coarsely chopped

8 ounces skinless duck breasts, diced

4 ounces fresh shiitake mushrooms, stems discarded and caps sliced

½ cup chopped green onions, white and green parts

2 tablespoons soy sauce

1 tablespoon Shaoxing wine or dry sherry

4 cups cooked medium- or long-grain white rice

VIETNAMESE

3 tablespoons duck fat, lard, or peanut oil

1 duck egg or 2 chicken eggs, lightly beaten

1 tablespoon peeled and minced fresh ginger

1 tablespoon minced lemongrass (white bulblike part only), optional

1 bell pepper, seeded and diced

4 cloves garlic, thinly sliced

½ cup chopped green onions, white and green parts

2 to 4 fresh hot chiles, thinly sliced

8 ounces skinless duck breasts, diced

2 to 3 tablespoons fish sauce or soy sauce

1 tablespoon sugar

4 cups cooked medium- or long-grain white rice

¼ cup chopped fresh cilantro

¼ cup chopped fresh Thai basil, optional

Start by setting a wok or a large sauté pan over high heat for 1 to 2 minutes; you want it very hot. The Chinese and Vietnamese versions begin the same way: Add 1 tablespoon of the duck fat, swirl it around (it will probably start smoking), and immediately drop the beaten egg into the wok. Swirl that around, too, so it sets quickly. As soon as the egg sets, remove it from the wok and set it aside. If it is still in large pieces, chop it.

Set the wok back over high heat and add the remaining 2 tablespoons duck fat. When the fat is hot, add the ingredients in the following order, stir-frying as you go:

For Chinese rice, add the ginger and bok choy and stir-fry for 2 minutes. Add the duck and mushrooms and stir-fry for 1 minute. Add the green onions, soy sauce, wine, and rice and stir-fry for 2 to 3 minutes, until the rice is heated through and all the ingredients are will mixed. Return the egg to the wok, taste and adjust with more soy sauce, and serve.

For Vietnamese rice, add the ginger, lemongrass, and bell pepper and stir-fry for 1½ minutes. Add the garlic, green onions, and chiles and stir-fry for another 1 minute. Add the duck and stir-fry for 1 more minute. Add the fish sauce, sugar, and rice and stir-fry for 2 to 3 minutes, until the rice is heated through and all the ingredients are well mixed. Return the egg to the wok, add the cilantro and basil, taste and adjust with more fish sauce, and serve.

SICHUAN FRAGRANT DUCK

This dish is a mashup of several Chinese dishes I've eaten over the years, and it makes no claim to authenticity. It does claim awesomeness, however. It is a spicy umami bomb that, like most stir-fries, comes together quickly.

I prefer this with skinless duck breasts, sliced into shreds and then "velveted," a Chinese process in which you marinate the meat in a combination of egg white and cornstarch, then "pass it through" medium-hot oil to set the batter. It does require 2 cups of oil, but you can reuse the oil several times before discarding it. If this velveting process sounds too complicated, skip it. The meat will not be nearly as good, but the dish will still be fine. Look for the Chinese black vinegar and chile bean paste in an Asian market.

Be sure to do the stir-frying over your most powerful burner. Successful stir-frying requires serious heat. Serve this dish with steamed rice and a cold lager or pilsner.

DIFFICULTY: ✳ ✳

SERVES 4

PREP TIME: 1 HOUR, MOSTLY MARINATING TIME

COOK TIME: 5 MINUTES

1 pound skinless duck breasts

2 cups vegetable oil (such as peanut or canola)

2 tablespoons duck fat, lard, or peanut oil

2 tablespoons chile bean paste

1 tablespoon peeled and minced fresh ginger

2 cloves garlic, thinly sliced

2 to 5 small fresh hot chiles, thinly sliced

½ teaspoon ground Sichuan pepper, optional

1 (8-ounce) can bamboo shoots, drained and cut into matchsticks

4 green onions, white and green parts, thinly sliced

MARINADE

1 egg white

1 tablespoon Shaoxing wine or dry sherry

1 teaspoon toasted sesame oil

1 tablespoon cornstarch

1 teaspoon kosher salt

SAUCE

2 tablespoons Basic Duck Stock (page 222) or beef stock

1 tablespoon Shaoxing wine or dry sherry

1 tablespoon soy sauce

2 teaspoons Chinese black vinegar or malt vinegar

2 teaspoons toasted sesame oil

2 teaspoons sugar

1 heaping teaspoon cornstarch

Slice the duck breasts crosswise into thin slices, then cut the slices into thin slivers about ¼ inch wide. If you have ever eaten Chinese "shredded" dishes—usually pork, beef, or chicken—that's the size you are going for.

To make the marinade, in a bowl, whisk together all of the ingredients until the cornstarch and salt are dissolved. Add the duck to the bowl and mix until well coated. Cover and refrigerate for at least 1 hour. This step can be done up to 12 hours in advance.

To "velvet" the duck, pour the vegetable oil into a wok or a heavy saucepan and heat to about 275°F. Do not let the the oil exceed 300°F. Have ready a baking sheet. Add half of the duck to the hot oil and immediately swirl it around to separate the pieces; a chopstick is a good tool for this. Let cook for 45 seconds, then start fishing the meat out with a wire skimmer or slotted spoon and set it on the baking sheet to cool. Repeat with the remaining duck.

Let the oil cool for 15 minutes, then pour it into a container and set aside to strain later for another use. Wipe out the wok so that no browned bits remain in the bottom. You might need to wipe it down with a wet paper towel. Set the wok aside to use for cooking the dish.

continued

To make the sauce, in a small bowl, whisk together all of the ingredients until the sugar and cornstarch are dissolved. Set aside.

Put the duck fat into the wok and place over high heat. The moment the fat starts to smoke, take the wok off the heat and add the chile bean paste and ginger. Put the wok back on the heat and stir-fry for 30 seconds.

Add the garlic, chiles, Sichuan pepper, bamboo shoots, and green onions and stir-fry for 1 minute. Add the duck, pour in the sauce, bring to a boil, and boil furiously for 1 to 1½ minutes, until it has reduced slightly but has become glossy on the surface. Turn off the heat and serve.

"When I see a bird that walks like a duck and swims like a duck and quacks like a duck, I call that bird a duck."

—JAMES WHITCOMB RILEY,
AMERICAN POET AND WRITER
(1849—1916)

COOT OR DUCK RISOTTO

Believe it or not, this is a real dish: I did not just make it up to mess with coot-hating hunters. According to my colleague Kyle Phillips, an expert in Italian food, coot risotto is made around the marshes in Emilia-Romagna, where coots are known as *folaghe*.

Coots need to be stripped of all fat and skin to be tasty. Once you do that, they are perfectly good eating. The little breasts are the best part, and since they are small and cook quickly, I dice them and add the meat to the risotto at the end, where the residual heat cooks it. Skinless duck breasts also work well here. Another good option is to use 8 ounces duck confit (page 144 or 146), shredded. Serve with a Chianti, Nebbiolo, California Sangiovese, or other medium-bodied red wine.

DIFFICULTY: ✳ ✳

SERVES 4 TO 6

PREP TIME: 15 MINUTES

COOK TIME: 40 MINUTES

8 cups Basic Duck Stock (page 222) or chicken stock, plus more if needed to finish

3 tablespoons unsalted butter

1 large shallot, minced

2 cloves garlic, minced

2 cups Arboio or other risotto rice

½ cup white wine

1 heaping tablespoon tomato paste

1 tablespoon minced fresh sage

Kosher salt and freshly ground pepper

8 ounces skinless coot or duck breasts, diced

½ cup grated pecorino or Parmesan cheese

Pour the stock into a saucepan and heat until the stock is steaming.

In a saucier (a saucepan with rounded sides to facilitate stirring) or other saucepan, melt the butter over medium-high heat. When the butter browns, immediately add the shallot and sauté for 2 minutes. Add the garlic and cook for 1 minute longer. Add the rice and stir for 2 to 3 minutes, coating the grains well with the butter and heating them thoroughly.

Add the wine and tomato paste and stir to combine. When the liquid has nearly boiled away, add 2 ladles of the hot stock (about 1 cup). Stir vigorously and then stir gently and almost constantly as the stock is absorbed by the rice. When the liquid is almost gone—you do not want the bottom of the pot to sizzle—add another ladleful of stock and repeat the stirring. If you don't stir almost constantly, you will not get the creamy starch to come off the rice, which is what makes a risotto a risotto.

Continue to add the stock, a ladle at a time, stirring almost constantly and adding more stock only after the previous addition has been absorbed. After three ladles of stock have been added, stir in the sage. Taste for salt and add as needed; how much you need will depend on your stock. Continue cooking, adding a ladle of stock at a time and stirring for 25 to 30 minutes. Taste the rice after 20 minutes, and then monitor it. You may need more or less than the 8 cups stock. I like my risotto loose, so I add another splash of stock at the end. The grains should be tender but still slightly firm at the center.

Once the rice is done to your liking, stir in the duck and cheese and let it cook for another 1 to 2 minutes; you want the meat pink inside. Serve at once.

DUCK BREAST WITH KASHA AND MUSHROOMS

Russians and eastern Europeans eat a lot of duck and goose, mostly roasted whole and stuffed with kasha or other grain. I decided to modernize that idea and serve it as a duck breast dish, with the kasha on the side. This is winter food: brooding, hearty, bold.

Kasha (buckwheat groats) is readily available in the grains (though it is not a grain) or Jewish-foods section of supermarkets. As for the mushrooms, Russians are manic about them, so use lots here. I used two full ounces of dried mushrooms for this dish, but an ounce will do.

This can be a one-bowl dish if you mix the duck breast with the kasha, or you can serve the kasha alongside for a more elegant dish. In either case, it would not be complete without another Russian obsession, pickles. Pickles provide the acid this recipe needs. If you don't serve pickles on the side, add another tablespoon of vinegar to the kasha when you serve it. Pour a hearty, malty beer with this robust dish.

DIFFICULTY: ✱ ✱

SERVES 4

PREP TIME: 30 MINUTES

COOK TIME: 35 MINUTES

1 to 2 ounces mixed dried mushrooms
    (see headnote)

3 cups hot water

1½ to 2 pounds duck breasts

Kosher salt

1 cup kasha

1 egg, lightly beaten

2 tablespoons duck fat, unsalted butter, or oil

1 cup chopped white or yellow onion

1 teaspoon caraway seeds

¼ teaspoon ground cloves

1 tablespoon malt vinegar or cider vinegar

¼ cup chopped fresh chives, plus more for garnish

In a bowl, soak the mushrooms in the hot water to reconstitute them. Weight the mushrooms down with another bowl or a small plate to keep them submerged for 30 minutes.

Remove the duck breasts from the refrigerator, salt them well, and set aside at room temperature for 30 minutes.

In a bowl, mix together the kasha and egg until the kasha is evenly coated. In a large sauté pan, preferably nonstick, cook the kasha over medium heat, stirring, until the egg has completely hardened on the kasha. Set aside.

When the mushrooms are soft, lift them out of the water, squeeze them dry, and chop coarsely, discarding any tough stems. Line a fine-mesh sieve with a plain paper towel or cheesecloth, and pour the soaking water through the sieve into a measuring cup. Reserve the mushrooms and soaking water separately.

In a sauté pan, heat the duck fat over medium heat. Add the mushrooms and onion and sauté for 8 to 10 minutes, until the onion begins to brown. Remove from the heat and add to the kasha along with 2½ cups of the mushroom soaking water, the caraway seeds, the cloves, and a healthy pinch of salt. Stir to combine and bring to a simmer. Cover, turn the heat down to low, and cook for about 7 minutes, until the kasha has absorbed all of the liquid. Remove from the heat.

Once the kasha is cooking, wipe out the pan you cooked the mushrooms in and pan sear the duck breasts as directed on page 58. You may have to do this in batches. When the breasts are cooked, set them aside on a cutting board skin side up and let them rest, tented with aluminum foil.

To serve, add the vinegar and chives to the kasha and toss to mix. Slice the duck breasts and divide among individual plates. Garnish with more chives.

DUCK PHO

Pho is typically made with beef broth, and the broth made from duck's flavorful, dark meat is an excellent substitute. A bowl of this Vietnamese standard is a warm, flavorful, and filling meal. The key is in the broth, which is sweet smelling from ginger, star anise, and other spices. You cannot make good *pho* without good broth. Two key things about *pho* broth: First, you do not roast the bones. The broth should be light. Second, it needs body, which is why it is traditionally made with knuckle bones. My solution is to add duck feet, which have collagen in them to add body. Be sure to hack at them a few times with a cleaver or heavy knife to open them up to the broth. No duck feet? Use a pig's foot, which you can buy at a butcher shop or Asian market. Score the pig's foot all over before it goes into the pot. Or, skip the feet altogether.

Making *pho* is pretty time-consuming on the front end, but once you make the broth, the recipe goes together quickly. And once the broth is made, it can be frozen or pressure canned (see page 221) for months or refrigerated for a few days before using. Any skinless breasts will do in this recipe.

DIFFICULTY: ✳ ✳ ✳

SERVES 6 TO 8

PREP TIME: 40 MINUTES

COOK TIME: 3 HOURS

BROTH

3 to 5 pounds duck carcasses, necks, feet, and giblets (except the liver)

10 cardamom pods

5 star anise pods

1 tablespoon coriander seeds

6 whole cloves

1 tablespoon fennel seeds

2 white or yellow onions, sliced

6-inch piece fresh ginger, peeled and sliced

3 tablespoons sugar

2 tablespoons kosher salt

½ cup fish sauce

TO ASSEMBLE

2 white or yellow onions, thinly sliced

4-inch piece fresh ginger, peeled and sliced

8 ounces mung bean sprouts

1 large bunch cilantro and/or Thai basil

4 fresh hot chiles, thinly sliced

Fish sauce, hot-pepper sauce, and hoisin sauce, for serving

Kosher salt

2 pounds dried Vietnamese rice noodles or Japanese buckwheat noodles

1 pound skinless duck or goose breasts

To make the broth, put all of the duck bits into a large stockpot, add water to cover, and bring to a boil. Skim the scum that rises to the surface, then turn the heat down to a simmer. Do not let the broth boil from here on in.

While the water is coming to a boil, in a small, dry frying pan, toast the cardamom pods, star anise, coriander seeds, cloves, and fennel seeds over medium-high heat, stirring often to prevent scorching, until fragrant. Pour the spices onto a plate.

Once the water in the stockpot is pretty much free of scum, add the onions, ginger, toasted spices, sugar, salt, and fish sauce and stir well. Move the pot slightly off the center of the burner and simmer for 2 to 3 hours, until the broth tastes rich and lovely. By positioning the pot off center, you will concentrate the impurities and fat on one side of the pot, where you can easily skim them off frequently.

When the broth is ready, turn off the heat. Using a slotted spoon or wire skimmer, scoop out and discard all of the duck bits, onion, ginger, and the like. Then line a fine-mesh sieve with a paper towel or cheesecloth, place the sieve over a container, and strain the broth through the sieve, pouring slowly and discarding the last dregs of the broth, which will contain sediment. If you want to be fancy, cool the broth now, and once it has been refrigerated for a while, pick off the fat cap that forms on the surface.

To assemble the soup, pour the broth into a large saucepan, add the onions and ginger, and heat gently; do not allow the broth to boil. Cook for about 10 minutes, or until the onions are wilted.

Meanwhile, set out an array of condiments: bean sprouts, herbs, chiles, fish sauce, hot-pepper sauce, and hoisin sauce. These condiments are traditional, although you can improvise with what you have, if necessary. The one thing you must have is fresh herbs, however.

Bring a large pot filled with water to a boil and season with salt. Add the noodles and cook according to package directions. Traditional *pho* noodles (available at Asian stores), thin rice noodles about ¼ inch wide, are best, but I also like Japanese buckwheat noodles, which, although nontraditional, taste wonderful with duck. (In a pinch, you can use Italian vermicelli.) When the noodles are done, drain them and divide them evenly among individual serving bowls.

Slice the duck breasts as thinly as possible. (One way to get it super thin is to partially freeze the meat for 30 minutes or so before you're ready.) Dividing the slices evenly among the bowls, lay them on the noodles.

Pick out the ginger from the broth, then pour some hot broth over the noodles and duck. Be sure to give everyone some of the onions in the broth. Serve at once. Invite everyone to add condiments as they like.

TEA-SMOKED DUCK

Tea-smoked duck is a classic Sichuan dish, and it normally involves an entire duck, lots of time, and at least three different cooking preparations, much like Peking duck (page 54). It is daunting. So I've modified the process to make it slightly quicker and much easier, while retaining the same flavors.

You will need a wok to make this recipe, and if you want to be traditional, you will need to use Insta Cure No. 1, a curing salt. You can skip it if you must, but the flavor will be different. Note that for an especially large breast, that is, goose or Rouen or Moulard duck, adjust the recipe by dropping the amount of kosher salt from 2 tablespoons to 1 tablespoon plus 1 teaspoon, then increase the curing time to a full 24 hours.

Sichuan peppercorns are also a must here. Some large supermarkets carry them, or you can find them at Asian markets or buy them online. As for the tea, black tea is traditional, but I've seen jasmine tea used in some recipes. Go for the loose-leaf variety if at all possible, as it burns better than the finer tea you see in tea bags. Round out the menu with steamed rice and beer.

DIFFICULTY: ✳ ✳ ✳ ✳

SERVES W4

PREP TIME: 12 HOURS, MOSTLY CURING TIME

COOK TIME: 40 MINUTES

2 to 6 duck breasts, about 2 pounds

DRY RUB

2 tablespoons kosher salt

1 tablespoon Sichuan peppercorns

2 teaspoons black peppercorns

¼ teaspoon Insta Cure No. 1 (see page 196), optional

2 tablespoons Shaoxing wine or dry sherry

SMOKING INGREDIENTS

½ cup rice

½ cup loose-leaf tea

½ cup firmly packed brown sugar

1 star anise pod, optional

1 teaspoon dried orange peel, optional

TO FINISH

2 teaspoons peanut or other vegetable oil

8 ounces mushrooms, sliced

1 teaspoon toasted sesame oil

8 ounces bok choy, coarsely chopped

1 tablespoon peeled and minced fresh ginger

1 tablespoon sugar

1 tablespoon soy sauce

⅓ cup Basic Duck Stock (page 222) or chicken stock

2 to 4 fresh hot red chiles, thinly sliced

Remove the duck breasts from the refrigerator. To make the dry rub, combine the kosher salt, Sichuan peppercorns, black peppercorns, and curing salt in a spice grinder and grind to a powder, or grind together in a mortar with a pestle. Moisten the duck breasts evenly with the wine, then coat with the spice mixture. Wrap each breast individually in plastic wrap, place in the refrigerator, and let cure for at least 4 hours or preferably 12 hours. If using large breasts, leave them to cure for 24 hours (see headnote).

Once the breasts have cured sufficiently, rinse off the cure and pat them dry. Set them, skin side up, on a cooling rack and let dry for 2 to 3 hours. If you can, direct a fan on the duck so it dries thoroughly.

Line a wok with aluminum foil so that about 2 inches of foil extend beyond the rim around the perimeter. You will use this to seal the wok. Put all of the smoking ingredients in the bottom of the wok, followed by a rack (or use 4 cheap chopsticks or wooden skewers to improvise a rack). Place the duck, skin side down, on the rack. Seal the wok and set it on the stove top. If you are just using foil, drape it over the top of the wok and crimp the edges. If you have the lid, put the lid down and use the excess foil lining the wok to seal everything. Be sure to

continued

have your stove exhaust fan on high. (If your exhaust fan is not very powerful, you might want to consider doing this outside on the grill.)

Turn on the heat to high for 3 to 5 minutes, until the smoking ingredients just begin to start smoking. You will hear lots of snapping, crackling, and popping. Turn the heat to medium and smoke the duck for 20 to 30 minutes: normal-size duck breasts will need 20 minutes; really large ones such as Moulard or goose breasts will need the full 30 minutes.

Remove the lid and take the duck breasts out. You can let them cool and store them in the fridge for a day or two at this point. To finish them, in a sauté pan, heat the peanut oil over medium-high heat. Add the breasts, skin side down, and cook until the skin is crisp. Do not cook the meat side, which will be cooked already. Remove the breasts from the pan, slice them, and set them aside while you cook the vegetables.

To cook the vegetables, turn the heat to high under the same pan you used to crisp the skin of the duck. Add the mushrooms and toss to coat with the oil remaining in the pan. Let the mushrooms sit undisturbed for 2 to 4 minutes, until they begin to release their water. Add the sesame oil, the bok choy, and the ginger and stir-fry for 1 minute.

Add the sugar, soy sauce, and stock and toss to combine. Boil this furiously for 4 minutes, letting the liquid cook down and thicken. Turn off the heat, add the sliced duck and the chiles to taste, and toss to combine. Serve at once.

"The snow goose need not bathe to make itself white. Neither need you do anything but be yourself."

—LAO-TZU

DUCK SLIDERS

Sliders (little hamburgers) have become all the rage: you can even buy slider buns in supermarkets now. For a dinner party a few years back, I made a batch using ground duck meat, and instead of regular pork fat, I ground the meat with bacon. It was awesome, rich, and smoky. But these burgers cry out for something sharp and acidic. Pickled onions are ideal, as are mustard and ketchup. And no burger is complete without a little cheese; I suggest provolone or Monterey Jack. Make more sliders than you think you will need, because they will fly off the plate. (The recipe is easily doubled.) And, of course, you can also serve these as full-size burgers.

DIFFICULTY: ✳ ✳ ✳

MAKES 10 SLIDERS

PREP TIME: 45 MINUTES

COOK TIME: 10 MINUTES FOR GRILL, 20 MINUTES FOR STOVE TOP

1 pound skinless duck breasts, coarsely chopped

4 ounces bacon, chopped

1 teaspoon chipotle chile powder, optional

Duck fat or bacon fat, if cooking on the stove top

Slider buns (little potato dinner rolls work great), for serving

Cheese slices of choice, for serving

Pickled onions, for serving

Mustard and ketchup, for serving

Put the duck and bacon in a bowl and sprinkle with the chile powder. Put the bowl in the freezer for 30 minutes or so.

Fit your meat grinder with the fine die, and pass the duck mixture through the grinder. With your hands, shape the mixture into 10 small patties (look at the size of the buns and match the size).

Prepare a medium-hot fire in a charcoal or gas grill, or heat a little duck fat in a large frying pan over medium-high heat. Grill or fry the patties, turning once, for 3 to 5 minutes on each side, until they are at least medium-rare. The timing will depend on the thickness of the patties.

Toast the buns, if you like, then add your burgers and fixin's—cheese, pickled onions, mustard, ketchup—and serve at once. Needless to say, this is beer food.

POACHED DUCK BREAST WITH ROOT VEGETABLES

This is a beautiful holiday meal: perfectly cooked duck or goose breast, roasted mixed vegetables, and a zingy, rich German sauerbraten sauce that may change your mind about German food forever. You can make the sauerbraten sauce up to a week in advance and store it, tightly covered, in the refrigerator. It is especially nice with a simply seared duck breast, too, so it is a good recipe to get under your belt.

The key to cooking all of the vegetables properly is to stagger their addition to the roasting pan. Beets need longer cooking than carrots, for example, so you need to get the beets in the oven first, and then add the other vegetables as you finish making the sauce and cooking the meat. You can use any combination of vegetables you want, or you can use just one vegetable. Other good candidates are turnips, rutabagas, Jerusalem artichokes, and small onions.

Serve this hearty dish with a medium-bodied red wine or a dark beer.

DIFFICULTY: ✷ ✷ ✷

SERVES 4 TO 6

PREP TIME: 30 MINUTES

COOK TIME: 1 HOUR

2 pounds skinless duck or goose breasts

Kosher salt and freshly ground pepper

8 ounces beets

¼ cup duck fat or unsalted butter, melted, for roasting the vegetables, plus 2 tablespoons, melted

Smoked salt, for seasoning, optional

8 ounces Yukon Gold or other yellow-fleshed potatoes, peeled

6 cups Basic Duck Stock (page 222) or chicken stock

8 ounces large parsnips

8 ounces large carrots

1 teaspoon dried dill, or 1 tablespoon chopped fresh dill

1 teaspoon caraway seeds

2 tablespoons malt vinegar or cider vinegar

SAUERBRATEN SAUCE

1½ cups dry red wine

½ cup water

¼ cup red wine vinegar

1 teaspoon freshly ground pepper

1 teaspoon juniper berries, crushed

1 teaspoon mustard seeds

2 whole cloves

2 bay leaves

1 teaspoon dried thyme

1 celery stalk, cut into a few large pieces

1 small carrot, peeled and cut into a few large pieces

1 small yellow or white onion, thickly sliced

4 gingersnaps, crushed

Kosher salt and sugar, for seasoning

1 tablespoon unsalted butter, optional

Remove the breasts from the refrigerator and salt well with kosher salt.

Preheat the oven to 400°F. If you are using large beets, peel and cut them into 2-inch chunks. If you are using small beets, peel but leave them whole. Coat the beets with some of the melted duck fat, sprinkle smoked salt over them, and put in a roasting pan in the oven.

Do the same with the potatoes. If they are small, leave them whole. If large, cut into 2-inch chunks. Coat in duck fat, sprinkle with kosher salt, and put them in the roasting pan. By the time you have done this, the beets should have a good 10-minute head start.

Now bring the stock to a boil in a heavy saucepan with a lid. Once it boils, remove from the heat and when the stock stops simmering drop in the duck breasts, cover, and set aside. (Keep them in the stock until just before serving.)

To make the sauerbraten sauce, in another saucepan, combine the wine, water, vinegar, pepper, juniper berries, mustard seeds, cloves, bay leaves, thyme, celery, carrot, and onion and bring to a simmer over medium-high heat. Let the sauerbraten sauce simmer while finishing the vegetables.

Return to the root vegetables. Peel the parsnips, cut them into 2-inch pieces, coat them with some duck fat, season with kosher salt, and sprinkle with the dill. Add them to the roasting with the beets and potatoes. Peel the carrots, cut them like the parsnips, coat them with the remaining duck fat, and sprinkle them with kosher salt and the caraway seeds. Add them to the roasting pan.

Strain the sauerbraten sauce and pour it into a blender. Fish out the large pieces of carrot, celery, and onion and add them to the blender along with the gingersnaps. Puree the sauce, then season to taste with salt and sugar. The sauce should be as thick as Thanksgiving gravy and be tart, a little sweet, and warm in a pumpkin-pie spice sort of way. Return it to the saucepan and cover to keep warm. If it is too acidic, swirl in a tablespoon of butter.

After the beets have cooked for 1 hour, they should be done, and because you staggered the addition of the rest of the vegetables, they also should be nicely cooked.

To finish the dish, remove the duck breasts from the stock, slice them, and toss the slices with the vinegar and the remaining 2 tablespoons melted duck fat. Spoon some of the hot sauce onto a platter. Pour the rest into a gravy boat to serve at the table. Arrange the duck slices over the sauce, with the root vegetables alongside. Grind a little pepper over everything and serve.

POACHING DUCK

A skinless duck breast is a good candidate for poaching. The result is mild, tender, perfectly cooked meat all the way through to the center. It is a departure from the bold, crispy world that duck normally inhabits, but a slice of poached duck (or goose) breast, served with Duck Fat Hollandaise (page 206) or Duck Fat Saffron Aioli (page 205) is a beautiful thing. It's also wonderful served cold as sandwich meat.

A good ratio of stock to meat is 4 cups stock to 4 Pekin, mallard, or pintail breast halves; 2 Muscovy or Rouen breast halves; or 1 Moulard or goose breast half. Err on the side of more stock, not less.

The method works for skin-on breasts, too. You will want to finish the duck or goose breast by patting the breast dry with paper towels and then crisping the skin in a hot pan. Don't cook the meat side, as it will already be cooked.

DUCK CHILI

This is another hunter's special, a perfect dish for duck camp. If you're using store-bought ducks and geese, it can get expensive, however, so I would cut the duck with other ground meats. Some people prefer chili with minced instead of ground meat, so if you're one of them, go for it.

For the dried chiles, you want about sixteen of them of various varieties. The exact mixture can vary to your liking (and availability), but you are looking for large, relatively mild chiles to make up the bulk of the mixture. Go heavy on the ancho, guajillo, pasilla, and mulato chiles, as they are not as hot as cascabel or mirasol. Those last two are genuine hot chiles, and should be used with care.

DIFFICULTY: ✱ ✱ ✱

SERVES 8 TO 10

PREP TIME: 1 HOUR, PLUS SOAKING TIME FOR THE BEANS AND CHILES

COOK TIME: 2½ HOURS

1 rounded cup (8 ounces) dried pinto beans
   or kidney beans
About 16 assorted dried chiles (such as ancho,
   guajillo, pasilla, cascabel, mirasol, or mulato)
1 cup weak brewed coffee
8 ounces bacon, chopped
2 pounds ground duck or goose (see page 102)
1 pound sausages (such as duck, Italian, or chorizo),
   casings removed and meat broken up
1 large yellow or white onion, chopped
6 to 8 cloves garlic, chopped
2 tablespoons sweet paprika
2 tablespoons ground cumin
1 tablespoon ground coriander
2 tablespoons kosher salt
2 large tomatoes, peeled, seeded, and chopped, or
   1 (14-ounce) can crushed tomatoes (with their juices)
3 tablespoons molasses
2 to 4 cups Basic Duck Stock (page 222) or beef stock
1 habanero chile, optional
Cooked white rice, for serving
Chopped fresh cilantro, for garnish
Shredded cheese, for garnish
Sour cream, for garnish, optional

Pick over the beans, discarding any grit or misshapen beans, then rinse well. In a bowl, combine the beans with water to cover and let soak overnight. (If you are pressed for time, you can pour boiling water over the beans and let them soak for 4 hours, changing the water after 2 hours.)

Stem the dried chiles and break them up, discarding the seeds. Place in a heatproof bowl, pour in boiling water to cover, and let stand for 1 hour or so.

Drain the chiles, reserving about 1 cup of the soaking water. In a blender, combine the drained chiles, the coffee, and the reserved soaking water and puree until smooth. Set aside.

In a Dutch over or other large, heavy ovenproof pot with a lid, fry the bacon over medium heat until crispy. Using a slotted spoon, transfer the bacon to a plate and set aside. Reserve the fat in the pot.

Turn the heat to high, add the ground duck and sausage meat, and cook, stirring occasionally, until browned. You want the highest heat on your most powerful burner here or the meat will steam and stew rather than brown. If you don't have a powerful burner, brown the meat in batches.

When all of the meat is browned, add the onion and cook for 3 to 4 minutes, stirring often. Return half of the bacon to the pot. Add the garlic, stir, and cook for 1 minute. Drain the beans and add to the pot. Then add the paprika, cumin, coriander, and salt one at a time, stirring to combine after each addition. Mix in the chile puree, tomatoes, molasses, and enough stock to cover everything. You want it to be stewlike, rather than thin like a soup. I typically need a pint of stock, but sometimes I use a full quart.

Stir to combine, cover, and simmer gently for at least 2 hours. Check at 2 hours to see if you need more salt and stock, and to see how the beans are doing (they should be tender at this point, but old beans will need to cook longer). If you have the habanero, this is the time to add it. When the beans are tender, turn off the heat and let rest for 15 minutes.

Serve the chili with the rice. Top each serving with cilantro, cheese, sour cream, and the remaining half of the bacon.

ITALIAN DUCK MEATBALLS

Spaghetti with meat sauce is one of my most favorite things in the world. And I'm talking about those giant, juicy Italian American meatballs: plenty of fat, and a fine grind. Lean meatballs suck.

Perfect meatballs are not all meat, although that might seem counterintuitive. To achieve that pillowy, yet substantial texture in a perfect meatball, you must add bread to the mixture. You also want to work the ingredients together gently, and not completely. It is okay to have some uneven spots. It makes things more interesting. Think cake, not bread. Do not squeeze.

You need to fry the meatballs before finishing them in sauce. And when I say "fry," I mean fry, not sauté. This means you must use lots of oil. Meatballs require the buoyancy of hot fat. Don't worry, you can strain the oil and reuse it later, say, for the velveting step in Sichuan Fragrant Duck (page 85).

The fried meatballs can be used right away, or they can be cooled, packed into an airtight container, and refrigerated for a week or frozen for several months. Serve the meatballs in any tomato sauce. The Duck Arrabbiata Pasta Sauce (page 210) is ideal. Red wine is a must, preferably a Chianti or other Sangiovese, a Pinot Noir, a Merlot, or a Côtes du Rhône blend.

DIFFICULTY: ✱ ✱ ✱

MAKES 20 TO 25 LARGE MEAT-BALLS; SERVES 8 TO 10

PREP TIME: 1 HOUR

COOK TIME: 25 MINUTES

3 pounds skinless duck breasts, ground with 1 pound pork fat (see page 102)

⅔ cup milk

3 slices stale good-quality bread, crusts removed and torn into pieces

2 cups dried bread crumbs

1 tablespoon kosher salt

1 tablespoon freshly ground pepper

1 teaspoon fennel seeds

1 teaspoon dried thyme

2 cloves garlic, finely minced

¼ cup grated pecorino or Parmesan cheese

2 eggs

Vegetable oil (such as safflower or olive), for frying

If the ground meat is not already in the refrigerator, put it in the refrigerator to chill.

Pour the milk into a small saucepan and set it over low heat. Add the bread to the pan and it will begin to absorb the milk. When it absorbs all of the milk, remove the pan from the heat and mash the moistened bread into a paste. Let cool to room temperature.

Put the bread crumbs in a shallow bowl. Line a baking sheet with waxed or parchment paper. Take the meat out of the refrigerator, place it in a large bowl, and scatter the salt, pepper, fennel seeds, thyme, garlic, and cheese on top. Crack the eggs into the bowl, then pour in the bread-milk mixture. With clean hands, gently mix everything together. Do not knead the mixture like bread, and do not squeeze the ingredients together. Just gently work the mixture: think cake, not bread.

When it is mostly combined, grab a palmful and roll it into a ball between your palms, not with your fingers. You want a nice round ball about 2 to 3 inches in diameter that just barely holds together. Gently roll the meatball in the bread crumbs and place on the prepared baking sheet. (You may need to reshape the balls before you put them on the baking sheet.) Repeat with the remaining meat mixture. If you have time, refrigerate the meatballs for 1 hour to firm them up.

continued

Get a large pan ready; I use a cast-iron frying pan. Place it over medium-high heat and pour in oil to a depth of about ½ inch. I use a combination of safflower oil and olive oil. The oil is ready when a drop of flour splashed into it immediately sizzles away. Add the meatballs to the pan, being careful not to crowd them. You want the oil to come about halfway up the sides of the meatballs. Add a little more oil if necessary. (Don't worry, you can strain the oil and put it to other uses.) You want a strong sizzle, not an inferno, so you may need to lower the heat to medium. Fry the meatballs for 4 to 6 minutes. You are looking for the first side to be golden brown. Turn the meatballs only once, and fry the second side for 3 to 5 minutes, until golden brown.

When the meatballs are ready, set them on paper towels on a wire rack on a baking sheet to drain, then use or store as directed in the headnote.

GROUND DUCK

Ground duck is nearly impossible to find commercially, so you will have to grind your own. I only do this with wild birds, but there's no reason you can't do it with domesticated birds. The easiest duck (or goose) meat to grind on waterfowl is the breast, and it's important to use skinless meat and to add fat back in, specifically pork fat. For the most part, duck fat is simply too soft for ground meat recipes. Your ratio of meat to fat can change according to your taste, but the fat should not go below 15 percent. You can make a leaner grind with just 10 percent fat, but the resulting mixture will taste dry. I prefer a 20 percent grind, that is, 1 pound pork fat to 4 pounds duck meat.

Cut the meat and fat into 1-inch pieces (or pieces that will fit into your grinder), then freeze it for 1 hour before grinding: you want it to be at 28°F to 35°F when you grind it. If you are grinding the meat and fat for future use, divide the mixture into 1-pound batches, wrap them well, and freeze them. They will keep for up to a year. Once you have thawed a batch, do not refreeze it or the texture will suffer. If you have cooked the meat, it is okay to refreeze it, however.

GOOSE MEATBALLS, GERMAN STYLE

Königsberger Klopse is a classic German recipe that uses several ingredients Americans don't normally associate with German food: capers, anchovies, and lemon zest. My version is an adaptation of a recipe in Mimi Sheraton's classic, *The German Cookbook: A Complete Guide to Mastering Authentic German Cooking.* The dish originates in East Prussia, where Königsberg once stood. The Russians leveled the city during World War II and rebuilt it as Kaliningrad.

Historically, these meatballs (pronounced something like ker-nigs-burger klop-shuh) are made from veal or pork, but as both the Germans and the Russians eat a lot of goose, I made them with ground goose. Duck, of course, works as well.

Serve the meatballs with boiled or mashed potatoes or a good German bread and a dark, malty beer.

DIFFICULTY: ✱ ✱

SERVES 4 TO 6

PREP TIME: 30 MINUTES

COOK TIME: 35 MINUTES

MEATBALLS

2 tablespoons duck fat or unsalted butter

1 cup minced yellow or white onion

Kosher salt

1½ pounds ground goose or duck (see opposite)

⅔ cup dried bread crumbs

2 teaspoons anchovy paste, or 5 anchovies, mashed

Grated zest of 1 lemon

2 tablespoons chopped fresh flat-leaf parsley

½ teaspoon freshly ground white or black pepper

2 eggs

1 teaspoon Worcestershire sauce

4 cups Basic Duck Stock (page 222) or beef stock

SAUCE

3 tablespoons duck fat or unsalted butter

½ cup minced yellow or white onion

3 tablespoons all-purpose flour

2 tablespoons capers

2 tablespoons minced fresh flat-leaf parsley

2 to 4 tablespoons sour cream

Salt and freshly ground black pepper

To make the meatballs, in a small frying pan, heat the duck fat over medium heat. Add the onion and cook, stirring often, for about 5 minutes, until soft and translucent. Do not allow it to brown. Sprinkle a little salt over the onion as it cooks. When the onion is ready, remove from the pan and set aside to cool.

If you are not using meat that is already ground, you can make a better, smoother meatball by doing the following: cut the meat and fat into 1-inch pieces, and put them in a large bowl. Add the cooked onion, bread crumbs, anchovy paste, lemon zest, parsley, 1 teaspoon salt, and the pepper to the bowl. Fit your meat grinder with the fine die, and pass the meat mixture through the grinder. Then add the eggs and Worcestershire sauce and mix in by hand. If using already-ground meat, in a bowl, combine the meat with all of the other ingredients and mix together with your hands.

Line a baking sheet with waxed or parchment paper. Form the meat mixture into small meatballs with a teaspoon, placing them on the prepared baking sheet as they are shaped. You can make them bigger, but a heaping teaspoon makes a nice size.

Pour the stock into a pan large enough to accommodate all of the meatballs at the same time. A wide, deep sauté pan with a lid is a good choice. Place the stock over

continued

continued from previous page

medium-high heat and bring to a simmer. When the stock is simmering, carefully add the meatballs. When all of the meatballs are in the pan, turn down the heat as low as it will go. If all of the meatballs are not submerged in the stock, it will be okay. Cover the pan and let the meatballs cook gently for 25 minutes. Using a slotted spoon, carefully remove the meatballs and set them aside on a platter.

Pour the stock into a heatproof container and reserve it. To make the sauce, wipe the pan out with a paper towel, set it over medium-high heat, and add the duck fat. When the fat is hot, add the onion and cook, stirring often, for about 5 minutes, until translucent. Do not allow the onion to brown. Add the flour, mix well, lower the heat to medium, and cook, stirring often, for a few minutes, until the mixture is the color of coffee with cream.

Add the reserved hot stock, a little at a time, stirring constantly. Continue to add the stock until you have a sauce the consistency of thin gravy—not as thick as Thanksgiving gravy and not thin like soup. You probably will not need all 4 cups of the stock.

Return the meatballs to the sauce and add the capers. Turn down the heat to low and heat until the meatballs are heated through. Add the parsley and remove from the heat.

Serve the meatballs at once. Pass the sour cream and pepper at the table, and invite diners to add as much as they like. This ensures the sour cream won't curdle from overheating on the stove top and will allow diners to make their servings as creamy as they like.

LEGS AND WINGS

When it comes to birds, there are two kinds of people: those who reach first for the breast, and those who fight over the legs. I'm a leg man myself. Cooked slow and low, leg meat is just as tender as a seared breast but is far more interesting. Legs and wings work harder, and all that work builds up connective tissue and a texture in the meat that reminds me of eating good pulled pork barbecue.

But the key to delicious duck legs and wings is to cook them long and slow. Because the legs from domesticated ducks are wrapped in a thick, insulating layer of fat, they present a special challenge for the cook. That fat needs to be rendered away, and that cannot be done in a hurry. You can get away with quickly cooking the legs from a young wild duck, but the legs of older wild ducks have too much sinew and connective tissue for that to work. So if you have not successfully determined the age of your duck (see page 16), you could be in for a chewy time of it. As for the wings, they can be tough as nails, even on a domesticated duck that doesn't do much flying. And wild ducks and geese fly thousands of miles each year, so imagine how strong these muscles are. They need special handling.

For the most part, you will want to stick to a quintet of cooking techniques when working with duck and goose legs: braises and stews, barbecue and roasting, and confit.

BRAISES AND STEWS

Braising is an especially good method for duck legs because the slow, moist heat tenderizes the meat by gradually breaking down the connective tissues. Most duck legs and wings you will be working with have skin on them, however. That skin, when braised, gets flabby and gelatinous. The solution is to cook the legs skin side up, and never let the braising liquid cover the skin on the legs. Most of the cooking is done in a covered pot. Once the meat is tender, you uncover the pot and continue cooking until the skin dries out and eventually crisps: tender meat, crispy skin. Perfect. Always adjust the amount of braising liquid you use depending on the size of your pot: you want enough liquid to bathe the meat but leave the skin high and dry.

Stews are just braises with more liquid. The difference is no crispy skin, so I either remove the skin from the legs before I make a duck or goose stew, or I pull it off before I serve the stew. A second step I always take with stews is to remove all the meat from the bone. This makes the stew (or soup) easier to eat.

FLAVORED FAT

You skim off lots of delicious duck fat in the process of making, say, Red-Cooked Duck (see page 114), but don't chuck it! This stuff is golden. Because the fat came off of a slow-simmered dish, its structure has not broken down, which is what can happen when duck fat reaches extremely high temperatures. What's more, the fat is now infused with a complex Chinese flavor.

Here's what you do: put the fat in a container and set it in the fridge to solidify. When it is hard, spoon it out, leaving any liquid (which may have jelled) behind. This liquid is fantastic, too, but it will go bad in a week or so. The fat, once freed of impurities, will last months in the fridge. If you want to take an extra step, melt it again, line a fine-mesh sieve with a plain paper towel or cheesecloth, and pour the fat through the sieve into a glass container. This removes even more debris.

Now, the next time you make any Chinese dish, you already have a flavor bomb sitting in your refrigerator. It is a secret many chefs use to boost flavor what they cook. Now you know it, too.

BRAISED DUCK WITH RED CABBAGE AND JUNIPER

This is a classic dish of Alsace-Lorraine. It is traditionally made with goose, but duck legs are perfectly fine prepared this way; however, domestic duck legs work better than wild ones. Mashed potatoes are a good accompaniment, as they are a great way to sop up the braising juices.

Red currant jelly is available in most supermarkets, but if you can't find it, use lingonberry or cranberry jelly. And although it may seem weird to put jelly in a savory dish like this, the hit of sweetness really perks up the cabbage.

DIFFICULTY: ✳

SERVES 4 TO 6

PREP TIME: 15 MINUTES

COOK TIME: 2½ HOURS

3 pounds domesticated duck legs or wild or domesticated goose legs

Kosher salt

1 large yellow or white onion, sliced

1 head red cabbage, shredded

1 teaspoon caraway seeds

1 teaspoon crushed juniper berries, optional

½ teaspoon freshly ground pepper

½ cup red wine vinegar

2 cups dry red wine, or as needed

2 apples, peeled and diced

2 tablespoons red currant jelly

Mashed potatoes, for serving

Preheat the oven to 325°F.

Trim the legs of any excess fat. Pierce the skin of the duck legs all over with a clean needle or the tip of a sharp knife, positioning the tool at an angle so that you are piercing just the skin and not the meat. Salt the legs well, then place them skin side down in a Dutch oven or other large, heavy pot with a lid. Brown the duck legs slowly over medium to medium-low heat. Transfer them to a plate and set aside.

Pour off all but about 3 tablespoons of the fat from the pot and return the pot to medium-high heat. Add the onion and cook slowly until it begins to brown. Take your time with this step, and keep the heat at a steady medium-high. Once the onion begins to caramelize, mix in the cabbage. Sauté for 3 to 4 minutes, stirring often. Sprinkle salt over the cabbage as it cooks.

Add the caraway, juniper, pepper, and vinegar and stir and toss to mix. Return the duck legs, skin side up, to the pot. Add the red wine to come up to the level of the skin on the legs. Do not submerge the legs. Bring the liquid to a simmer, then cover the pot and put it in the oven. Cook gently for about 1 hour (or up to 3 hours if you decide to go with an old wild goose), until the meat yields easily when pierced with a knife.

Uncover the pot and cook for another 30 minutes, until the meat on the duck legs comes off the bone and the skin is crispy. Move the pot from the oven to the stove top and gently transfer the legs to individual plates. Turn the heat to medium-high, add the apples and jelly to the cabbage, and mix well. Cook for about 5 minutes, until the jelly melts and the apples soften.

Spoon the cabbage and mashed potatoes alongside the duck legs and serve at once.

BRAISED DUCK WITH LEEKS AND SAUERKRAUT

The combination of slow-cooked leeks and duck legs is ideal. The leeks caramelize much like onions do, but unlike onions, they don't fall apart, offering just enough bite to back up their silky sweetness. That texture flows naturally into the braised duck meat, which, moistened from the fat of the legs, melts into the leeks seamlessly.

You brown the duck or goose legs well in duck fat, sauté the leeks and some mushrooms in the same fat, and then make a nest with the leeks and mushrooms. The legs go on top of the nest, and you braise everything until the meat wants to fall off the bone.

This dish is best served with something mashed or soft, either garlicky mashed potatoes or polenta with a little grated pecorino mixed into it. I prefer a heavy white wine here, like a buttery Chardonnay, as the higher acidity of a white tempered by the soft edges of the Chardonnay complements the leeks and duck. An Italian red would also be a good choice.

DIFFICULTY: ✳ ✳

SERVES 4 TO 6

PREP TIME: 30 MINUTES

COOK TIME: 9½ HOURS

Small handful of dried mushrooms (such as porcini, morel, or black trumpet), broken into pieces

1 cup hot water

2 pounds duck or goose legs

Kosher salt

2 cups Basic Duck Stock (page 222) or chicken stock

4 leeks, white and light green parts only, thinly sliced

2 teaspoons dried thyme

2 teaspoons caraway seeds

2 bay leaves

1 to 2 shots Cognac, Armagnac, or other brandy

1 cup sauerkraut

Mashed potatoes or cooked polenta, for serving

1 tablespoon unsalted butter

Aged balsamic vinegar, for finishing

Preheat the oven to 325°F.

In a bowl, combine the mushrooms and hot water, cover, and let soak for 30 minutes. Remove the duck legs from the refrigerator, salt them well, and set aside at room temperature.

In a Dutch oven, a braiser, or a deep, ovenproof frying pan with a lid, brown the duck legs over medium-high heat. Take your time to get them well browned. Transfer them to a plate and set aside.

While the duck legs are browning, lift the mushrooms out of the soaking water, squeeze them dry, chop finely, and reserve. Line a fine-mesh sieve with a plain paper towel or cheesecloth and pour the soaking water through it into a small saucepan. Add the stock to the pan, place over medium-high heat, and bring to a simmer.

Add the leeks to the pot in which you browned the duck, which should now have lots of duck fat in it, and turn the heat to medium-high. Sauté the leeks, stirring often, for 2 minutes. Add the mushrooms and continue cooking over medium-high heat until you get a little color; you don't want to char anything. Add the thyme,

continued

continued from previous page

caraway, bay, and a little salt, and then add the brandy. You can flame it if you like, or just cook it down by half. Once it is reduced, mix in the sauerkraut.

Nestle the duck legs, skin side up, on the bed of leeks and sauerkraut. Add the hot stock to come up to the level of the skin on the legs. Do not submerge the legs. Bring the liquid to a simmer, then cover the pot and put it in the oven. Cook for at least 1 hour, until the meat yields when pierced with a sharp knife. This should take 1 hour for young Pekin duck, 1½ to 2 hours for most ducks or geese, or 3 hours or more for very old wild geese. Uncover the pot and cook for another 30 minutes, until the skin is crispy.

To serve, spoon mashed potatoes onto individual plates, spreading them fairly flat. Gently remove the duck legs, and stir the butter into the pot. Spoon the braised leeks and sauerkraut in the center of each portion, and top with the duck legs. Sprinkle the duck with a little vinegar and serve at once with the sauce passed at the table.

"No kind of domestic fowl has been seen here, with the exception of some ducks in the houses in Zuruquia; these ducks were larger than those of Spain, though smaller than geese—very pretty, with tufts on their heads, most of them white as snow, but some of them black."

—FIRST RECORDED REFERENCE TO A MUSCOVY DUCK, BY CHRISTOPHER COLUMBUS ON HIS SECOND VOYAGE IN 1494

DUCK GUMBO WITH SHRIMP

Louisiana gumbo is a dark, powerful stew with lots of meat and lots of vegetables. Spicy, warming, and complex, it is one of the world's great stews. Pretty much everything under the sun can and does find its way into the gumbo pot, and while this is listed as a duck gumbo, I designed it for the unloved coot.

Coots, known as *poulets d'eau*, or "water chickens" in Cajun parlance, are in fact more closely related to chickens than to ducks. Maybe you've seen them: black, with a white beak rimmed with a little red, bobbing their heads as they paddle around ponds.

If you actually do use coots, you must skin them and remove all of their fat, which tastes and smells fishy. Save the breasts, legs, hearts, and gizzards. You can certainly use duck or goose gizzards if you are making this gumbo with domestic or wild waterfowl. And if you don't have giblets lying around, chop or grind up some other duck meat.

You will also note that this gumbo has no okra. Okra tends to be used in Creole gumbos, not Cajun gumbo, which is traditionally thickened with a roux and *filé* (fee-lay) powder, the powdered leaves of the sassafras tree.

DIFFICULTY: ✱ ✱

SERVES 8 TO 10

PREP TIME: 30 MINUTES

COOK TIME: 2 TO 3 HOURS, DEPENDING ON HOW OLD AND TOUGH YOUR BIRDS ARE

1 cup all-purpose flour

1 cup duck fat or peanut oil

4 cups Basic Duck Stock (page 222) or chicken stock

4 cups water

1 tablespoon tomato paste

2 cups chopped yellow or white onion

1 pound gizzards, cleaned (see page 167) and chopped, optional

2 pounds duck legs

1 green bell pepper, seeded and chopped

1 cup chopped celery

4 cloves garlic, chopped

3 bay leaves

1 teaspoon dried thyme

2 tablespoons Cajun seasoning

Kosher salt

1 pound andouille sausage, sliced

1 pound peeled shrimp

Cooked white rice, for serving

Tabasco sauce, for serving

Filé powder, for serving, optional

In a Dutch oven or other large, heavy pot with a lid, combine the flour and duck fat over medium heat. Cook, stirring constantly, for about 15 minutes, until the roux is the color of dark chocolate. The closer it gets to that color, the closer you need to watch it, because if the roux burns, you must start over.

Meanwhile, pour the stock and water into a saucepan, bring to a simmer over medium heat, and whisk in the tomato paste until combined. Keep the mixture at a simmer.

When the roux is ready, mix in the onion and cook for 5 minutes, stirring occasionally. Add the gizzards and duck legs and coat evenly with the roux. Cook for another 5 minutes, stirring once in a while. Mix in the bell pepper and celery and cook for another 2 minutes. Add the garlic and cook for another minute.

Pour in the hot stock mixture, a little at a time, stirring constantly to mix well with the other ingredients. Add the bay leaves, thyme, and Cajun seasoning and season with salt. Simmer gently for 2 to 3 hours, until the gizzards are tender and the duck meat is falling off the bone.

Fish out the duck legs and strip the meat from the bones. Add it back to the pot. Add the sausage and shrimp and simmer for another 10 minutes, until heated through.

Serve the gumbo with the rice. Be sure to put Tabasco sauce and *filé* powder on the table, for diners to add as they like. *Filé* thickens the gumbo, so your guests can add as much as they want.

RED-COOKED DUCK

Red braising is a Chinese technique popular in Hunan and Sichuan provinces. The "red" comes from soy sauce and caramel. Although it is typically done with pork belly, I like it with duck or goose legs. The result is salty, sweet, spicy, and savory all at once. It is a powerfully flavored dish, so you need only one leg per person—plus a lot of rice to sop up the amazing sauce. I like something acidic on the side: Chinese pickled mustard greens or kimchi. Or, you can just sauté some greens yourself and douse them with vinegar at the end.

This recipe is ideal for the legs of Muscovy ducks or wild geese because they are less fatty. Regular duck legs work fine, but you will need to trim excess fat and spoon off some of the fat before you serve. If you use wild ducks, skip the boiling step, which is intended to render out a little fat before you braise the legs. You will also need to braise it longer, normally 2 to 3 hours.

DIFFICULTY: ✳

SERVES 4

PREP TIME: 20 MINUTES

COOK TIME: 1¾ HOURS

2 pounds duck legs

5 or 6 green onions, white and green parts, chopped

5 to 10 shiitake mushrooms, stems discarded and caps sliced, optional

2-inch piece fresh ginger, peeled and minced

⅓ cup soy sauce

¼ cup Shaoxing wine or dry sherry

¼ cup firmly packed brown sugar

2 small dried hot chiles (such as Thai or Chinese)

½ teaspoon five-spice powder

1 teaspoon ground Sichuan pepper, optional

2 cups Chinese Duck Stock (page 225), optional

Toasted sesame oil, for finishing

Chopped fresh cilantro, for garnish

Fresh red chile slices, for garnish

Cooked white rice, for serving

Preheat the oven to 325°F. Trim the legs of any excess fat. Select a pot large enough to hold all of the duck legs, fill with water, and bring to a boil over high heat. Add the duck legs and boil for 3 minutes, then remove the legs and set aside. Reserve the water. Using a cleaver or heavy kitchen shears, roughly cut each leg into 3 pieces.

Spread the green onions in a Dutch oven, a braiser, or a large, deep ovenproof frying pan with a lid. Arrange the leg pieces, skin side up, on the onions.

In a bowl, combine the mushrooms, ginger, soy sauce, wine, brown sugar, dried chiles, five-spice powder, and Sichuan pepper and mix well. Pour the mixture over the duck legs. Add enough stock or reserved water to come up to the level of the skin on the leg pieces. Do not submerge the duck. Bring the liquid to a simmer, then cover the pot and put it in the oven. Cook gently for about 1 hour (or up to 3 hours for legs of old wild geese), until the meat yields easily when pierced with a knife. Uncover the pot and cook for another 30 to 45 minutes, until the skin is crispy.

There will be a lot of fat. You can either roll with it, or you can carefully spoon the fat off and save it for using later (see page 107). Or, you can remove the duck legs, pour the sauce into a fat separator, and then pour the sauce from the separator when you serve.

Arrange the duck and sauce on individual plates. Drizzle the sesame oil over the duck, garnish with the cilantro and fresh chile, and accompany with rice.

GOOSE STEW WITH BARLEY AND CELERY ROOT

I originally designed this recipe for wild snow geese, and because many of California's snow geese spend their summers on Wrangel Island, near Siberia, it seemed fitting to give the stew a Russian feel. But of course the legs of any goose or duck, wild or domesticated, will work here.

It's important to remove the meat from the bones before you serve this stew, otherwise everyone will be picking through their bowls for small, sharp objects. It takes only a few minutes, and your family and friends will thank you for it.

This stew keeps well in the fridge for a week, though the grain in it will continue to swell over time, absorbing moisture and making this more like a French potage. It also freezes well.

DIFFICULTY: *

SERVES 4 TO 6

PREP TIME: 10 MINUTES

COOK TIME: 3 HOURS

8 goose legs (2 to 3 pounds)

3 tablespoons duck fat, lard, or unsalted butter

Kosher salt and freshly ground pepper

1 large yellow or white onion, sliced

1 pound small mushrooms (such as yellow foot chanterelle or beech), halved or left whole

2 teaspoons dried marjoram

7 cups Basic Duck Stock (page 222) or beef stock

1 cup pearled barley

1 cup peeled and sliced carrots

1 celery root, peeled and cut into 1-inch cubes

2 tablespoons chopped fresh dill

4 to 6 tablespoons sour cream

Trim the legs of any excess fat. In a Dutch oven or other large, heavy pot with a lid, heat the duck fat over medium-high heat. Add the legs and brown them, salting them as they cook. Take your time to get them well browned. Transfer them to a plate and set aside.

Add the onion and mushrooms to the pot, turn the heat to high, and stir to combine. Sauté for 6 to 8 minutes, until the onion begins to brown. Add the marjoram, return the legs to the pot, and then pour in the stock. Bring to a simmer, cover, and cook for 2 to 3 hours, until the meat is tender. If a lot of fat begins to accumulate on the surface of the stew, skim it off.

When the goose legs are tender, remove them, let them cool a bit, and then pull all of the meat off the bones. Return the meat to the pot. Add the barley, carrots, and celery root, stir well, and cook for about 30 minutes, until the barley and celery root are tender. Season with salt.

Serve garnished with the dill and a sprinkle of black pepper, and top each bowl with a dollop of sour cream at the table.

FRENCH DUCK WING SOUP

This is a traditional soup from the French region of Languedoc, where an awful lot of ducks and geese are eaten. It takes a lot of wings to make this recipe, but I include it for two reasons: first, to give hunters something to do with all those wings from the birds they bring home, and second, for nonhunters to get in on some cheap meat. If you can find them, bags of duck wings at Asian markets are very inexpensive.

I prefer to strip the meat from the bones in this recipe, because I don't like to pick bones out of my soup, and there will be a lot of bones in the pot if you don't strip the meat. But the French don't bother with this step, so you don't have to, either. Serve the soup with boiled potatoes or crusty bread.

DIFFICULTY: ✷ ✷

SERVES 4 TO 6

PREP TIME: 20 MINUTES

COOK TIME: 2½ TO 4 HOURS, DEPENDING ON THE AGE OF THE BIRDS

1 head garlic

2 teaspoons olive oil

4 tablespoons duck fat or unsalted butter

2 to 3 pounds duck or goose wings

1 tablespoon minced fresh sage

1 teaspoon dried thyme

2 teaspoons dried oregano

1 bay leaf

1½ cups dry white wine or rosé

3 cups Basic Duck Stock (page 222), chicken stock, or water

Kosher salt and freshly ground pepper

1 large yellow or white onion, thinly sliced stem
    to root end (about 2 cups)

2 carrots, peeled and sliced

2 celery stalks, coarsely chopped

¼ cup chopped fresh flat-leaf parsley

Preheat the oven to 400°F. Slice off the top of the garlic head, removing the top one-fourth of the cloves. Nest the garlic in aluminum foil, and drizzle the oil onto the cloves. Close up the foil and put the garlic in the oven. Bake for 35 minutes, until the cloves are browned and soft. Set aside.

Get out a large sauté pan and a Dutch oven or other large, heavy pot. Divide the duck fat evenly between them and turn on the heat to medium-high. Divide the wings between the pans and brown them well. Take your time with this to get the wings good and browned.

When all of the wings are browned, put them all in the Dutch oven and add the sage, thyme, oregano, and bay

and pour in the wine and stock. Mix well and bring to a simmer. Season with salt, cover the pot, and simmer gently for 2 hours.

Squeeze the roasted garlic into the simmering soup and stir well.

While the wings are simmering, turn on the heat under the sauté pan to medium, add the onion, and cook, stirring occasionally. After the onion slices begin to brown around the edges, turn the heat to medium-low, and continue cooking for about 30 minutes, until the onion is soft and has mostly turned a caramel color. If the pan begins to dry during this time, cover it and the steam will keep the onion moist. Turn off the heat and let the onion sit in the pan for now.

The meat on wings of domesticated ducks should be falling off the bone after 2 hours, but the meat on wild ones may not be. Wild ducks and geese will all be different ages, so I've found that cooking an extra hour ensures that even the wings from really old birds in your pot are cooked enough.

When the wings are tender, fish them all out and lay them out on a baking sheet to cool. Stir in the caramelized onion along with the carrots and celery and continue cooking the soup while you pull the meat from the bones. This step takes me 10 to 15 minutes. Return the meat to the pot, cover, and simmer for 20 to 30 minutes, until the carrots and celery are tender.

When everything is tender, stir in the parsley, season with salt and pepper, and serve.

SPANISH DUCK WITH GREEN OLIVES AND SHERRY

Andalusia is the home of this recipe, specifically the city of Jerez. Jerez is also the home of sherry, which is a dominant flavor in this dish. Combining sherry, orange, *serrano* (dry-cured) ham, and green olives is just about the most Spanish thing you can do, and there is a long history of duck hunting in the marshes around Jerez, so this has become a classic dish of Spain for good reason.

Traditionally, this recipe is made with a dry fino sherry and a little honey, but the sweeter amontillado or even oloroso sherry will work, too. Just cut the honey by half. Be sure to buy a sherry for this recipe that you also want to drink, because that's what you should be drinking when you eat it. Serve this dish with roasted potatoes or rice.

DIFFICULTY: ✷ ✷

SERVES 4

PREP TIME: 15 MINUTES

COOK TIME: 2½ HOURS

2 to 3 pounds duck or goose legs

Kosher salt

Olive oil, for cooking

1 large yellow or white onion, thinly sliced stem to root end (about 2 cups)

⅓ pound serrano ham, diced

5 cloves garlic, coarsely chopped

1 cup Spanish sherry

Zest of 1 orange, cut into wide strips

1 teaspoon dried thyme

2 bay leaves

1 tablespoon honey

1 cup Basic Duck Stock (page 222)

Juice of 1 orange (about ½ cup)

12 green olives, pitted and halved

Minced fresh flat-leaf parsley, for garnish

Preheat the oven to 325°F. If using domesticated duck or goose legs, trim off any excess fat, then pierce the skin of the legs all over with a clean needle or the tip of a sharp knife, positioning the tool at an angle so that you are piercing just the skin and not the meat. Skip this step if using wild ducks or geese. Separate the drumsticks and thighs with a cleaver or heavy kitchen shears, and salt them well.

Set the pieces, skin side down, in a *cazuela* (earthenware cooking pot), Dutch oven, or other wide, heavy pot and turn on the heat to medium. If you are using wild ducks or geese, pour about 3 tablespoons oil into the pot. If using domesticated birds, pour in only 1 tablespoon oil. Brown the skin side of the pieces well, and set them aside on a plate.

Turn the heat to medium-high and add the onion and ham. Sauté, stirring often, until the onion and ham begin to brown. Mix in the garlic and cook for another 1½ minutes. If you find you have a lot of fat in the pot, move the onion, ham, and garlic to one side of the pot, tip the pot a little, and spoon some of the fat out.

Add the sherry and bring to a boil. Mix in the orange zest, thyme, bay leaves, and honey. Nestle the thighs and drumsticks, skin side up, in the pot, and add enough stock and orange juice to come up to the level of the skin. Do not submerge the pieces.

Bring to a simmer, cover, and put the pot in the oven. Cook gently for about 1 hour if using legs from domesticated ducks or about 3 hours if using legs from old wild geese, until the meat yields easily when pierced with a knife.

Uncover the pot and add the olives. Cook, uncovered, for another 30 minutes, until the skin is crispy. To serve, transfer the drumsticks and thighs to individual plates and spoon the sauce around them. Garnish with parsley and serve at once.

ARROZ DEL CAZADOR (SPANISH HUNTER'S RICE)

If you like paella, you will love this dish. It is a cousin of that famous Spanish rice dish, and what makes it so special is that it relies on whatever a hunter brings back that day: the meats in the rice change with every hunt. Obviously, duck (or goose) is vital to this recipe, but feel free to include any other meat you'd like. I've included chicken thighs here because they are easy to get, but rabbit would be my first choice with the duck.

DIFFICULTY: ✳ ✳ ✳

SERVES 4 TO 6

PREP TIME: 30 MINUTES

COOK TIME: 2 HOURS

SOFRITO

¼ cup olive oil

2 cups minced yellow onion

1 green bell pepper, seeded and minced

4 cloves garlic, minced

1 bay leaf

½ teaspoon cayenne pepper

1 teaspoon dried thyme

1 teaspoon dried rosemary

¼ cup chopped fresh flat-leaf parsley

Kosher salt

¼ to ½ teaspoon saffron threads

¼ cup hot water

1 teaspoon sweet paprika (preferably smoked)

1 cup crushed canned tomatoes

MEATS

2 to 3 pounds duck legs

1 teaspoon olive oil

1 pound chicken thighs

Kosher salt

1 cup fino or other dry sherry

RICE

2 tablespoons olive oil

2 cups short-grain rice
   (such as Bomba, Arborio, or Carnaroli)

GARNISHES

2 to 4 cloves garlic, minced

½ cup chopped fresh flat-leaf parsley

3 roasted piquillo or other red peppers,
   seeded and coarsely chopped

To make the *sofrito*, in a large sauté pan, heat the oil over medium heat. Add the onion, bell pepper, and garlic and cook gently, stirring often, for 10 minutes. Mix in the bay, cayenne, thyme, rosemary, and parsley, season with salt, and cook slowly for 30 more minutes, stirring occasionally. Do not let it burn. While the onion and pepper are cooking, in a small glass, crumble the saffron into the hot water, stir briefly, and let the saffron bloom. When the vegetables have cooked for the full 40 minutes, mix in the saffron, paprika, and tomatoes and simmer gently for 20 minutes. Turn off the heat and set aside.

While the *sofrito* is cooking, prepare the meats. Preheat the oven to 400°F. If using domesticated duck legs, trim off any excess fat. In a Dutch oven or other large, heavy pot with a lid, heat the oil over medium-high heat. Add the duck legs, skin side down, and cook until they give up some of their fat. Add the chicken thighs, again skin side down. Brown the duck legs and chicken thighs well on both sides. Sprinkle salt over the meats as they cook.

When the meats are well browned, check to see how much fat is in the pan, and pour off all but about 3 tablespoons. Turn the duck legs and chicken thighs skin side up, add the sherry, and then add enough water to come up to the level of the skin. Do not submerge the meats. Bring to a simmer, cover, and put the pot in the oven. Braise for about 1 hour, until the meats are tender.

Remove the pot from the oven, fish out the meats, and put them on a baking sheet to cool. Turn the heat to high and boil down the braising liquid until it is reduced to about 4 cups. This should take about 8 to 10 minutes.

Pour in the *sofrito*, bring to a boil, then turn off the heat and set aside.

Strip all of the meat from the bones, discard the bones, and put the meat in a bowl. Save the skin as a cook's treat—or toss it, if you must.

To cook the rice, put the oil in a large, wide sauté pan—if you have a *cazuela* (earthenware cooking pot) or paella pan, this would be the time to use it—and set it over medium heat. Add the rice and sauté for 2 minutes.

Add 4 cups of the *sofrito* mixture and the meats, bring to a simmer, and cook for 10 minutes. Put the pot in the oven and cook for another 10 minutes, until the rice is tender.

To serve, you can either sprinkle the garlic, parsley, and red peppers over each person's dish, which is traditional, or you can move everything to a large bowl and mix in the garlic, parsley, and red peppers. Pour a Spanish red, a Côtes du Rhône, a Chianti, or a California Pinot Noir at the table.

"To give counsel to a fool is like throwing water on a goose."

—DANISH PROVERB

DUCK TAGINE
WITH CHESTNUTS

A Moroccan lamb *tagine* is the inspiration for this simple braised dish. Moroccans don't eat a lot of duck, but this dish works well with the other earthy flavors, and the result is a smooth, "brown" effect that's comforting on chilly days. Sometimes I add a little lemon juice at the end; other times I just eat it with lots of pickles on the side. Use any chestnuts that are available; I prefer the ones in jars, but fresh, canned, or vacuum sealed is just fine. If you cannot find chestnuts, walnuts are a good alternative. Serve the *tagine* with bread, couscous, or rice.

DIFFICULTY: *

SERVES 4

PREP TIME: 20 MINUTES

COOK TIME: 3 HOURS FOR DUCK LEGS, 4 HOURS FOR GOOSE LEGS

2 tablespoons duck fat or olive oil

2 to 3 pounds duck or goose legs

Kosher salt

1 large yellow or white onion, sliced from stem to root end

5 cloves garlic, chopped

1 tablespoon tomato paste

1 teaspoon ground ginger

1 teaspoon ground cinnamon

½ teaspoon ground cloves

1 cup Basic Duck Stock (page 222) or chicken stock, or as needed

1 pound chestnuts, cooked, peeled, and quartered (see headnote)

10 dates, pitted and coarsely chopped

Dash of rose water, optional

Preheat the oven to 325°F.

In a Dutch oven or large, heavy pot with a lid, heat the duck fat over medium-high heat. Add the legs and brown them, taking your time to get them well browned. Transfer them to a plate and season with salt. Check to see how much fat is in the pot, and pour off all but about ¼ cup.

Turn the heat to medium-high and add the onion, and cook, stirring occasionally, for 8 to 10 minutes, until browned. When the onion is almost done, add the garlic and season with salt. Mix in the tomato paste, ginger, cinnamon, cloves, and ½ cup of the stock. Nestle the duck legs, skin side up, on top of the onion mixture. Add enough of the remaining ½ cup stock, or more as needed, to come up to the level of the skin. Do not submerge the legs. Bring to a simmer, cover, and put the pot in the oven. Cook gently for about 1 hour if using legs from domesticated ducks or up to 3 hours for legs from old wild geese, until the meat yields easily when pierced with a knife.

At the hour mark, add the chestnuts by tucking them in among the legs. Cover and cook for another 15 minutes. When everything is tender, uncover the pot, add the chopped dates, and cook uncovered for 30 minutes more.

Sprinkle the rose water over everything and serve.

DUCK WITH WALNUTS AND POMEGRANATE

Called *fesenjan*, this is one of the hallmarks of Persian cooking, and although it is most often made with chicken these days, it is originally a duck dish. According to Gil Marks in his *Encyclopedia of Jewish Food*, *fesenjan* originated on the shores of the Caspian Sea, "where wild ducks were in abundance," and it became a favorite dish for Rosh Hashanah. Flavorwise, it is a knockout: the walnuts make it rich and luxurious, and the pomegranate adds a sweet-and-sour tang. The Spice Road flavors underlie everything, making it a wonderful main course for a cool night.

Pomegranate molasses is sold in Middle Eastern markets and in some specialty supermarkets. You can also substitute pomegranate jelly, but be sure to omit the honey. Or, you can boil down pomegranate juice until reduced by half and use that.

DIFFICULTY: ✳ ✳

SERVES 4 TO 6

PREP TIME: 20 MINUTES

COOK TIME: 3½ HOURS

3 pounds duck legs

Kosher salt

1 tablespoon duck fat or clarified butter

1 large yellow or white onion, chopped

2 cups Basic Duck Stock (page 222), or as needed

2 cups (about 8 ounces) walnut halves, toasted and finely ground

5 tablespoons pomegranate molasses (see headnote)

2 tablespoons honey

1 teaspoon freshly ground pepper

½ teaspoon ground nutmeg

¼ teaspoon ground cinnamon

¼ teaspoon saffron threads, dissolved in 2 tablespoons hot water

Pomegranate seeds, for garnish

Chopped fresh flat-leaf parsley, for garnish

Cooked white rice, for serving

Preheat the oven to 350°F. Pierce the skin of the duck legs all over with a clean needle or the tip of a sharp knife, positioning the tool at an angle so you pierce just the skin, not the meat. Salt well and set aside.

In a large sauté pan, heat the duck fat over medium-low heat. Add the duck legs, skin side down, and brown slowly, rendering their fat. Remove the legs as they brown and set aside.

Add the onion to the pan and sauté over medium heat for 6 to 8 minutes, until translucent. Return the duck legs, skin side up, to the pan. Add enough stock to come up to the level of the skin on the legs. Do not submerge the legs. Bring to a simmer, cover, and put the pan in the oven. Cook gently for about 1 hour if using legs from domesticated ducks or up to 2½ hours for old wild ducks, until the meat yields easily when pierced with a knife.

Remove from the oven, fish out the duck legs, and put them on a baking sheet to cool a bit. Strip off the skin and set aside. Strip off the meat in large pieces and return the meat to the pan. Stir in the nuts, pomegranate molasses, honey, pepper, nutmeg, cinnamon, and saffron and its soaking water.

Re-cover the pan, return it to the oven, and cook for 1 hour longer, stirring every 20 minutes or so to keep the walnuts from sticking to the bottom of the pan.

If you like, while the dish is in the oven for the last hour, slice the duck skin into narrow ribbons and fry them until crispy.

When the dish is ready, remove from the oven, taste, and adjust with more honey and salt. Sprinkle with the crispy skin, if using, and garnish with pomegranate seeds and parsley. Serve spooned over rice.

MEXICAN DUCK
WITH GREEN MOLE

Duck is one of the few animals domesticated in the Western Hemisphere, and the indigenous Muscovy duck has an ancient history in the cuisines of Mexico and South and Central America. Mole is an equally ancient style of sauces, believed to have been invented by the Mayans and perfected in the centuries since Spanish contact. This particular mole is an adaptation of one in Diana Kennedy's *The Cuisines of Mexico*.

Note that this is a recipe for legs from domesticated ducks. If you are using legs from wild ducks or geese, you will want to make the sauce first, then braise the legs in the sauce for the whole time; this will keep the legs moist.

DIFFICULTY: ✱ ✱ ✱

SERVES 4

PREP TIME: 15 MINUTES

COOK TIME: 2¼ HOURS

2 to 3 pounds duck legs

Kosher salt

1 cup pepitas (hulled pumpkin seeds)

1 teaspoon black peppercorns

2 teaspoons cumin seeds

2 cups Basic Duck Stock (page 222) or beef stock

1 cup chopped tomatillos

4 serrano chiles, seeded and chopped

1 yellow or white onion, chopped

2 cloves garlic, chopped

1 tablespoon dried epazote, optional

¼ cup loosely packed chopped fresh cilantro, plus more for garnish

Leaves from 1 bunch radishes (about ½ cup loosely packed)

Cooked white rice, for serving

Lime wedges, for garnish

Preheat the oven to 325°F.

Trim off any excess fat from the duck legs. Separate the drumsticks and thighs with a cleaver or heavy kitchen shears, then salt the pieces well and put them, skin side up, in a single layer in a baking dish. Put the dish in the oven and bake, uncovered, for 1½ hours.

While the duck cooks, reserve 3 tablespoons of the *pepitas* for later. Put the remaining *pepitas*, the peppercorns, and the cumin seeds in a spice grinder or mortar and grind

to a paste. Transfer to a bowl, add about ½ cup of the stock, and stir to form a thick sauce. Set aside.

In a blender, combine 1 cup of the stock, the tomatillos, chiles, onion, garlic, epazote, cilantro, and radish leaves and puree until smooth. Pour into a bowl and set aside.

After an hour, check your duck legs. They should have given off some fat by now. Spoon out 2 tablespoons and put them in a sauté pan. Put the duck legs back in the oven to keep cooking. Add the pureed vegetables to the sauté pan and bring to a simmer. Simmer gently for 10 minutes, stirring occasionally. Season with salt.

Turn off the heat under the sauté pan and whisk in the *pepita* mixture. Add enough of the remaining ½ cup stock to create a sauce with the consistency of thick gravy. Coarsely chop the reserved *pepitas* and stir them into the sauce.

When the duck has cooked for 1½ hours, remove the dish from the oven and turn the heat down to 300°F. Pour off all of the fat in the baking dish and reserve for another use. Dredge the duck legs in the sauce and return them, skin side up, to the baking dish. Pour enough of the sauce into the baking dish to come up to the level of the skin; you want most of the duck skin out of the sauce. Return the baking dish to the oven and allow the duck to cook for 30 minutes more, until it is almost falling off the bone. Be sure to monitor the duck as it cooks to make sure the sauce does not boil.

Serve with the rice and garnish with cilantro and lime.

THAI DUCK CURRY

Ducks are believed to have been domesticated in Southeast Asia some twenty-five hundred years ago, so duck has a long tradition in Thai cooking. In most versions of this dish, the duck legs are not crisped up before you make the curry, but I prefer to slowly crisp the skin to render the fat. The result is leaner and has a better mouthfeel at the end.

If you are using the legs from wild ducks (or geese), which have far less fat, you will not need to brown them quite as long. And if you are dealing with skinless legs, skip that step altogether.

DIFFICULTY: ✱ ✱

SERVES 6 TO 8

PREP TIME: 20 MINUTES

COOK TIME: 1¾ HOURS

2 pounds duck legs

1-inch piece fresh ginger, peeled and minced

2 tablespoons minced lemongrass
   (white bulblike part only), optional

1 tablespoon minced galangal root, optional

¼ to ⅓ cup store-bought Thai green curry paste

3 cups coconut milk

1 yellow or white onion, sliced

5 lemon or lime leaves, optional

2 tablespoons fish sauce

1 cup Basic Duck Stock (page 222) or chicken stock

5 small Thai green eggplants, quartered, or 1 cup
   seeded and chopped green bell pepper

3 to 5 fresh green chiles (such as Thai, cayenne,
   or serrano), thinly sliced

¼ cup fresh Thai basil or mint leaves,
   torn into small pieces

¼ cup fresh cilantro leaves, chopped

Freshly squeezed lime juice, for seasoning

Cooked white rice, for serving

If using domesticated duck legs, trim away any excess fat. Separate the drumsticks and thighs with a cleaver or heavy kitchen shears. Pierce the skin of the duck pieces all over with a clean needle or the tip of a sharp knife, positioning the tool at an angle so that you are piercing just the skin and not the meat. If cooking legs from wild ducks, pierce the skin only if the legs are very fatty.

Arrange the duck pieces, skin side down, in a large sauté pan and turn on the heat to medium. Let them render out some of their fat and brown, about 15 minutes. Do not cook the meat side.

Spoon out about 2 tablespoons of the accumulated fat from the sauté pan and put it into a Dutch oven, a large wok, or other large, heavy pot. Place over high heat and heat just until the fat begins to smoke, then add the ginger, lemongrass, galangal, and curry paste and stir-fry for 1½ minutes. Add 1 cup of the coconut milk, mix well, and bring to a boil. Cook, stirring often, for 5 minutes.

Mix in the duck pieces, onion, citrus leaves, fish sauce, the remaining 2 cups coconut milk, and the stock. Cover the pot, adjust the heat to maintain a gentle simmer, and cook for 1 hour. Add the eggplants and simmer for about 20 minutes more, until the meat is almost falling from the bones.

I don't like to mess around with bones in my curry, so I pull out all of the duck pieces, strip all the meat from the bones, and then return the meat to the curry for the final few minutes of cooking. You can choose to do this or not.

Add the chiles, basil, and cilantro and simmer for 2 minutes. Taste and adjust with fish sauce if needed, then season to taste with lime juice. Serve at once with the rice.

CASSOULET

Cassoulet is a thick, meaty, beany dish that is somewhere between a stew and baked beans. It is a triumph of French cookery, something to center a dinner party on. It takes time to come together, however, so give yourself a nice window to do it right.

You will need confit and good sausages for this recipe. You can buy confit in some specialty stores, and while I prefer duck sausages for this dish, they are hard to find, so if you don't make them, good sweet Italian sausages or even bratwurst can be substituted.

Believe it or not, this is something of a stripped-down cassoulet. Most "authentic" versions have a lot more meat in them. A splash of sherry or red wine vinegar cuts the dense richness of the cassoulet nicely. Keep a bottle of high-quality vinegar at the table when you serve, and a nice salad of bitter greens alongside is also a good idea. Serve with a burly red wine.

DIFFICULTY: ✳ ✳ ✳

SERVES 6 TO 8

PREP TIME: 15 MINUTES, PLUS SOAKING TIME FOR THE BEANS

COOK TIME: 3½ HOURS

1 pound dried white beans (such as cannellini or Great Northern)

2 heads garlic

4 teaspoons olive oil

2 pounds confit duck legs (about 5 legs), page 144 or 146

3 tablespoons duck fat

4 ounces pancetta or salt pork, cut into bite-size pieces

1 pound pork shoulder, cut into 2-inch chunks

Kosher salt

1 large yellow or white onion, chopped

2 carrots, peeled and sliced

2 tablespoons tomato paste

2 bay leaves

2 teaspoons dried thyme

6 cups Basic Duck Stock (page 222)

1 pound duck sausages, homemade hunter's style (page 185), or store-bought sweet Italian, thickly sliced

2 tablespoons dried bread crumbs

¼ cup chopped fresh flat-leaf parsley

2 tablespoons walnut oil

Pick over the beans, discarding any grit or misshapen beans, then rinse well. In a bowl, combine the beans with water to cover and let soak overnight. (If you are pressed for time, you can pour boiling water over the beans and let them soak for 4 hours, changing the water after 2 hours.)

Preheat the oven to 400°F. Slice off the top of each garlic head, removing the top one-fourth of the cloves. Nest the garlic heads in aluminum foil, and drizzle the oil onto the cloves. Close up the foil and put the garlic in the oven. Bake for 35 minutes, until the cloves are browned and soft. Set aside. Turn off the oven.

Put the confit duck legs in an ovenproof pan and set in the still-warm oven to melt the fat.

In a large Dutch oven or other large, heavy pot with a lid, heat the duck fat over medium heat. Add the pancetta and fry until crispy, turning to cook on all sides. Using a slotted spoon, transfer the pancetta to a plate and set aside.

Turn the oven back on to 325°F. Increase the heat to medium-high under the Dutch oven. Working in batches if necessary to avoid crowding, add the pork shoulder and brown well on all sides, salting the meat as it cooks. As the pieces are browned, transfer them to a plate and set aside.

When all of the meat has been browned, increase the heat to high, add the onion and carrots and cook, stirring often, until the onion begins to brown on the edges. Mix in the tomato paste and cook for another 2 to 4 minutes, until the tomato paste turns brick red. Squeeze in the roasted garlic and mix well.

Return the pancetta and pork shoulder to the pot. Then drain the beans and add them to the pot along with the bay and thyme. Pour in the stock. As the stock is heating, take the duck legs out of the oven and strip off all of the meat in large pieces from the bones. Add the duck pieces along with the sliced sausages to the pot and mix well.

Bring to a gentle simmer, cover, and put the pot in the oven. Cook for about 2 hours, until the beans are tender but still hold their shape. You want this stew to be very

thick, so let the beans absorb more of the stock than you might think proper in another stew. Add water only if the pot dries out.

When the beans are tender, remove the pot from the oven and raise the oven temperature to 375°F. Uncover the pot, sprinkle the bread crumbs evenly over the top of the cassoulet, return it to the oven, and bake, uncovered, for about 30 minutes, until the bread crumbs are nicely browned.

To serve, spoon into shallow bowls and sprinkle with the parsley. Drizzle a little walnut oil over each serving. Serve with a burly red wine.

MARTHA WASHINGTON'S "FRENCH" STEWED DUCK

I do not recommend that you try this recipe; it sounds nasty. But this is what a recipe looked like in the eighteenth century. We've come a long way.

"First halfe roste her, then cut her up & lay her in a stew pan with a little salt & water, as much as will cover it. Take a little time, margerum, winter savory, rosemary, & an ounion cut in 2, a blade of mace & 2 or 3 pepper cornes, some claret wine, & soe let her stew together. When it is allmoste enough, put in a piece of butter and beat the youlks of 6 eggs with a spoonfull or 2 of clarret, & mix with beaten butter and put it in with the ducks after they have had a walme or 2 together. Shake & serve them up."

—from Martha Washington's *Booke of Cookery* (1799)

BAKED BEANS WITH GOOSE "HAM HOCKS"

Here is a good way to use your so-called goose wing ham hocks. It is an Italian-inspired recipe for baked beans that has at its core the idea of Boston baked beans. The dish is good enough to warrant making even if you have no goose ham hocks around. Buy a smoked turkey leg and use that instead. Serve the beans with a salad of bitter greens and a good malty beer.

DIFFICULTY: *

SERVES 4 TO 6

PREP TIME: 25 MINUTES, NOT INCLUDING BEAN SOAKING TIME

COOK TIME: 2 TO 6 HOURS

1 pound dried borlotti or cranberry beans

2 tablespoons duck fat or olive oil

1 cup chopped red or yellow onion

1 cup chopped fennel

1 or 2 Goose Wing "Ham Hocks" (page 134)

4 cups Basic Duck Stock (page 222) or chicken or vegetable stock

1 cup tomato puree

¼ cup molasses

¼ cup red wine

1 tablespoon hot paprika, or 1 teaspoon red pepper flakes

2 teaspoons kosher salt

Pick over the beans, discarding any grit or misshapen beans, then rinse well. In a bowl, combine the beans with water to cover and let soak overnight. (If you are pressed for time, you can pour boiling water over the beans and let them soak for 4 hours, changing the water after 2 hours.)

Preheat the oven to 250°F.

In a Dutch oven or other large, heavy pot with a lid, heat the duck fat over medium heat. Add the onion and fennel and cook, stirring occasionally, for several minutes, until soft and translucent. Do not allow them to color.

Drain the beans, add them to the onion and fennel, and mix well. Add the goose wings, stock, tomato puree, molasses, wine, paprika, and salt and mix well. Increase the heat to high and bring to a boil. Cover the pot, put it in the oven, and cook until the beans are tender. Check after 2 hours. It might take as long as 6 hours, depending on how old the beans are.

Ladle into bowls to serve.

GOOSE WING "HAM HOCK"

Let's face it: goose wings, although large and seemingly meaty, are just about the toughest meat in the animal kingdom. It makes sense, if you think about it. A typical wild goose lives well beyond seven years, and geese over the age of twelve are not uncommon. Each year a goose flies thousands of miles in migration, and then flies all over the place wherever it is wintering. Even a domesticated goose, which will be far more tender than its wild cousin, lives a lot longer than a chicken, or even a domestic duck, which makes its wings pretty tough, too. And although you can braise goose wings or use them to make French Duck Wing Soup (page 118) or German *Ganseklein* soup (page 159), I often use them as a flavoring agent rather than for their meat.

The idea here is to smoke the hell out of those goose wings and then use them like a ham hock for flavoring beans, broth, or soup. If you have one of these smoked wings around, you can make superior baked beans (page 132). And yes, you can do this with duck wings, too.

I smoke my geese with hickory, oak, maple, or apple wood. Walnut would be another good choice.

DIFFICULTY: ✱ ✱

MAKES 4 GOOSE HAM HOCKS

PREP TIME: 24 TO 72 HOURS FOR CURING, PLUS 2 HOURS FOR DRYING

COOK TIME: 5 TO 8 HOURS

3 tablespoons kosher salt

2 tablespoons brown sugar

1 teaspoon garlic powder

1 teaspoon dried thyme

1 teaspoon crushed juniper berries, optional

½ teaspoon (2 grams) Insta Cure No. 1 (see page 196)

4 goose wings, separated into drumettes and tips

In a small bowl, stir together the kosher salt, sugar, garlic powder, thyme, juniper, and curing salt to make the dry cure. Massage the dry cure evenly into the goose wings, then place the wings in a container just large enough to hold them. Cover and refrigerate for at least 24 hours or up to 3 days.

Remove the wings from the refrigerator and rinse off the cure. Dry well with paper towels and arrange on a cooling rack. Place the rack in a cool, breezy place (or in front of a fan) and let the wings dry further for an hour or two.

If you have a smoker, just follow the directions that came with it to set it up and smoke the wings. If you have only a kettle grill, you can turn it into a smoker with a handful of relatively simple steps (see page 43). Smoke the goose wings at 250°F for at least 5 hours, until they are well cooked. They may take up to 8 hours. You want them firm, smoky, and a little dry.

Let the wings cool, then seal them in butcher paper or a vacuum-sealed bag. They will keep in the fridge for 10 days or in the freezer for up to 1 year.

BARBECUE AND ROASTING

Once the weather warms, it's time to turn off the oven and fire up the barbecue. While grilling ducks hot and fast can be fraught with challenges, waterfowl are practically made for the 'cue: all that fat and their relatively thick skin make them perfect for the slow and low caresses of smoke and time.

Domesticated ducks and geese are best for barbecue, but skin-on wild birds will work almost as well, though they will need lower heat and more time. I often brine my wild duck and goose legs to keep them moist during the long cooking time. I prefer a brine of ¼ cup kosher salt to 4 cups water. Mix well to dissolve the salt, then brine the legs and wings for at least 2 to 3 hours or up to overnight. Any more time than that will make them too salty.

Marinades are optional. Keep in mind that a marinade will not penetrate deeper than ¼ inch into the meat per day, which is not a problem with duck and goose legs. My typical marinade is the barbecue sauce I plan to baste the meat with later, and I often marinate the legs overnight. I don't normally both marinate and brine the same duck leg—doing so would take a couple of days—but you can if you like.

When it comes time to cook, low indirect heat is the key, somewhere between 225°F and 300°F. You will need some sort of drip pan underneath the duck legs, as they will render out a lot of fat as they cook, and you don't want flare-ups. I use sheets of heavy-duty aluminum foil. Also, keep the grill cover down throughout the cooking. Be prepared to spend some time with your duck legs as they cook; it can take several hours.

Hold off on applying barbecue sauce until the duck is at least half-cooked. Paint on the barbecue sauce and cook for 10 minutes. Flip, paint, and cook for another 10 minutes. Barbecue is forgiving, so you can repeat this process a couple of times before the meat begins to dry out
too much.

CHINESE CHAR SIU BARBECUED DUCK

This is classic Chinese barbecue, and it is damn good. This *char siu* sauce was meant for pork, but it also works well with duck or goose—or any fatty meat. The spices, the heat, and the sweetness cry out for a rich meat to partner with, so duck legs—and I'm talking domesticated duck legs here—are ideal. My advice? Make a double batch of the sauce and store it in the fridge for up to a month. You will want to put it on everything.

With the exception of the Shaoxing wine, black vinegar, and chile bean paste, all of these ingredients are readily available in most supermarkets. Dry sherry and malt vinegar are good substitutes for the wine and vinegar, respectively. Serve the duck with steamed white rice, some pickled or sautéed mustard greens, and cold beer.

DIFFICULTY: ✻ ✻

SERVES 4 TO 6

PREP TIME: 30 MINUTES

COOK TIME: 2½ HOURS

SAUCE

¼ cup Shaoxing wine or dry sherry

2 tablespoons honey

2 tablespoons soy sauce (preferably dark soy)

2 tablespoons hoisin sauce

1 tablespoon chile bean paste

3 cloves garlic, minced

2 tablespoons peeled and grated fresh ginger

½ teaspoon five-spice powder

2 to 3 pounds duck legs

1 to 2 fresh green or red chiles, sliced, optional

1 to 2 tablespoons Chinese black vinegar or
   malt vinegar, optional

Cooked white rice, for serving

To make the sauce, in a blender, combine all of the ingredients and puree for 1 minute. Pour into a bowl. Put the duck legs in a plastic container just large enough to hold them snugly and coat them with a little of the sauce. Reserve at least half of the sauce for basting later. Cover the duck and marinate for at least 30 minutes at room temperature or up to overnight in the refrigerator. If the legs have been refrigerated, bring them to room temperature before you put them on the grill.

When it comes time to cook, set up your grill with an open space to one side so the duck legs cook away from direct heat. In a gas grill, this means leaving two of the three burners off. With a charcoal- or wood-fired grill, put the fuel on one-half of the grill floor and leave the other half open. Make a drip pan out of aluminum foil or buy a disposable foil pan at the supermarket and put it below the grate where the duck legs will be to catch the drips. If using a gas grill, place the drip pan on an unused burner. You are looking for slow, steady heat here, about 300°F. Alternatively, you can cook the duck in the oven at this temperature.

Set the duck legs on the grill grate or rack over the drip pan, cover the grill, and cook until the legs are tender. This will take between 2 and 3 hours; the meat should pierce easily with a knife. Baste the legs with some of the remaining sauce every 45 minutes or so, and turn the legs once every hour.

Remove from the grill, garnish with the chiles and a splash of the vinegar, and serve with the rice.

SOUTH CAROLINA–STYLE BARBECUED DUCK

For a taste of South Carolina rather south China, use this mustardy sweet-and-sour sauce instead of the *char siu* sauce. I recommend serving this with potato salad and corn on the cob.

DIFFICULTY: ✳ ✳

SERVES 4 TO 6

PREP TIME: 30 MINUTES

COOK TIME: 2½ HOURS

SAUCE

4 tablespoons unsalted butter

½ cup grated yellow onion

½ cup prepared yellow mustard (the ballpark kind)

½ cup firmly packed brown sugar

½ cup cider vinegar

1 tablespoon dry mustard

1 bay leaf

Cayenne pepper, for seasoning

Kosher salt

2 to 3 pounds duck legs

To make the sauce, in a saucepan, melt the butter over medium-high heat. Add the onion and sauté for about 3 minutes, until translucent. Do not let it brown. Stir in the prepared mustard, sugar, vinegar, dry mustard, bay leaf, and cayenne pepper and season with salt to taste. Turn down the heat to low and simmer gently for 30 minutes to blend the flavors.

Turn off the heat and remove the bay leaf. Pour the sauce into a blender and puree.

Put the duck legs in a plastic container just large enough to hold them snugly and coat them with a little of the sauce. Reserve at least half of the sauce for basting later. Cover the duck and marinate for at least 30 minutes at room temperature or up to overnight in the refrigerator. If the legs have been refrigerated, bring them to room temperature before you put them on the grill.

When it comes time to cook, set up your grill with an open space to one side so the duck legs cook away from direct heat. In a gas grill, this means leaving two of the three burners off. With a charcoal- or wood-fired grill, put the fuel on one-half of the grill floor and leave the other half open. Make a drip pan out of aluminum foil or buy a disposable foil pan at the supermarket and put it below the grate where the duck legs will be to catch the drips. If using a gas grill, place the drip pan on an unused burner. You are looking for slow, steady heat here, about 300°F. Alternatively, you can cook the duck in the oven at this temperature.

Set the duck legs on the grill grate or rack over the drip pan, cover the grill, and cook until the legs are tender. This will take between 2 and 3 hours; the meat should pierce easily with a knife. Baste the legs with some of the remaining sauce every 45 minutes or so, and turn the legs once every hour.

Remove from the grill and serve.

BUFFALO DUCK WINGS

Football is one of the only sports I get worked up about, and Buffalo wings are my go-to snack for game day. Named for the city in upstate New York, not the bison—which, as you may know, lacks wings—Buffalo wings are essentially a way to eat the least desirable part of the chicken: marinate the wings in a hot sauce, roast or fry them, toss them in some more sauce, and serve them with blue cheese dressing and a few celery sticks.

What's not to love? Actually, quite a lot. I have eaten scores of crappy wings, where the skin is flabby or the meat isn't done enough. I've worked hard to perfect my wing recipe, and for duck wings the trick is to simmer the wings in stock for a couple of hours and then roast them in the oven.

If you are a hunter who has saved the wings of many ducks, you're in business. If you are not a hunter, you can buy duck wings at Asian markets ridiculously cheap: big bags go for something like five bucks. That's a lot of yummy protein for a low price—and we can all use a good deal these days.

DIFFICULTY: ✳ ✳

SERVES 4

PREP TIME: 10 MINUTES, PLUS
1 HOUR FOR MARINATING

COOK TIME: 3 HOURS

2 pounds duck wings, separated into drumettes and tips

4 cups Basic Duck Stock (page 222) or chicken stock

2 bay leaves

⅓ cup hot-pepper sauce (such as Frank's or Tabasco's Buffalo style)

1 tablespoon sweet paprika

3 tablespoons unsalted butter or duck fat, melted, or vegetable oil

½ teaspoon kosher salt

SAUCE

½ cup crumbled blue cheese

½ cup sour cream or plain Greek-style yogurt

¼ cup mayonnaise

Celery sticks, for serving

In a large Dutch oven or large, heavy pot with a lid, combine the wings and stock. If the wings are not fully submerged, add water as needed to cover by about ½ inch. Toss in the bay, cover, place over medium heat, and bring to a simmer. Adjust the heat to maintain a gentle simmer and cook for at least 1½ hours or up to 3 hours. You want the meat on the wings to be thinking about falling off the bone. The wings from domesticated ducks will be on the short end of this spectrum; the wings from wild ducks will be on the other end of the time spectrum.

Remove the pot from the heat and drain the wings. In a container large enough to hold all of the wings, mix together the hot-pepper sauce, paprika, butter, and salt. Add the wings and toss to coat them evenly. Let the wings marinate for at least 1 hour at room temperature or up to overnight in the refrigerator. The longer you marinate the wings, the hotter they will be.

Preheat the oven to 400°F. Oil 1 or 2 baking sheets. Remove the wings from the marinade and arrange them in a single layer on the pan(s). Pour the marinade into a small saucepan and set aside.

Roast the wings for 30 to 45 minutes, until crispy. Turn them after the first 15 minutes, and then start watching them after 30 minutes to make sure you get the crispiness you want.

While the wings are roasting, make the sauce. In a small bowl, stir together the cheese, sour cream, and mayonnaise, mixing well.

Just before the wings are ready, bring the marinade to a boil over medium heat and simmer for 5 minutes. Remove from the heat and keep warm.

When the wings are done, remove them from the oven, transfer to a shallow bowl, add the hot marinade, and toss to coat evenly. Serve at once with the sauce and celery. Oh yeah, and with beer—lots of beer.

CONFIT

Indoors or out, no method of cooking duck legs is more revered than confit, whose combination of curing, braising, and crisping makes what is quite possibly the perfect duck leg. Simply put, confit is the cooking and preservation of something in fat or sugar syrup. In my case, duck legs in duck fat.

In the past, duck legs were heavily salted and packed with herbs, then slowly cooked in duck fat, and finally stored in earthenware crocks, completely submerged in the fat in which they were cooked. Stored in a cool, dark place, the meat would keep for six months or more. Even modern confit, which is not so heavily salted, is far tastier "ripened" for a week or so than it is when served fresh.

My advice is to cure and confit large batches of legs at once. Stored in the refrigerator, there is nothing better for a midweek meal than to pull out a few legs, sear them in a hot pan on the stove top or in a hot oven until the skin gets crispy, pull the meat off, and eat it with, well, pretty much anything: in a salad, with a pasta or cooked grain, in a taco, or over polenta—it's incredibly versatile.

There are many ways to go about making confit. The traditional method requires several cups of duck fat, and although wonderful, it gets a little costly if you don't have a ready supply of fat on hand. A more modern way is to vacuum seal the duck with a smaller amount of fat, then submerge the sealed bag in warm water to cook in a *sous vide* water oven, in a stockpot on the stove top, or even in a cooler filled with hot water. A slow cooker also works well (see page 149).

Long-Aged Confit

If you want to age your confit longer than a week or two, you will need to shift it to a clean container, preferably glass or ceramic. Pour melted duck fat to a depth of ¼ inch into the bottom of the container. Put the container in the fridge and let the fat set. Take the container out again and pack the confit into it. Pour more melted fat around the confit to submerge it fully. If you are using the fat you cooked the confit in, be careful to avoid any liquid that has come off the duck during cooking. This stuff is a flavor grenade (use it in place of *glace de viande* in sauces), but it can spoil your confit if left in contact with the meat and fat longer than a couple of weeks. See Reusing the Fat (page 146) for how to separate the liquid from the fat.

Cover the container and store it in a cool place for up to 1 month for normally cured confit (cured overnight) and for up to 5 months for long-cured confit (cured 48 hours). Serve the confit as directed in Confit of Duck (page 144).

DUCK AND SOUS VIDE

Duck is particularly suited to the gentle cooking that a *sous vide* water oven provides. If you've never heard of it, *sous vide* is incredibly precise "boil in the bag" cooking. You have a tub of water, you can heat it to an exact temperature of, say, 137°F for duck breast. You seal your duck in a vacuum bag with seasonings, drop it into the tub, and let the hot water cook it gently—and perfectly. It does not heat up your house, and given enough time, it will render even the toughest meats tender.

Using *sous vide*, confit is made easier (page 146), a duck breast is cooked with precision, and typically dense gizzards are transmogrified into meltingly tender tidbits. You can even make something magical from duck tongues using this technique (page 158).

I use a Sous Vide Supreme water oven at my house, and while it is not cheap at $330, it is incredibly useful for the serious home cook—especially one who cooks wild game with any frequency. To use one, you also need a vacuum sealer; mine is a heavy-duty one made by FoodSaver.

Here is a list of cuts, times, and temperatures for *sous vide* cooking of ducks and geese:

Legs, tender and pink: 150°F for 8 to 10 hours*

Duck breasts: 137°F for 45 minutes

Goose breasts: 139°F for 1 hour

Duck or goose livers: 135°F for 45 minutes

Duck gizzards: 160°F for 12 to 24 hours**

Duck tongues: 190°F for 5 hours

Duck eggs, flowing yolk: 145°F for 30 minutes

Duck eggs, pretty soft-boiled yolk: 149°F for 30 minutes

CONFIT

Pekin duck legs: 180°F for 3 to 6 hours

Mallard or other large wild duck legs: 180°F for 3 to 7 hours

Moulard duck legs: 180°F for 4 to 7 hours

Muscovy duck or domestic goose legs: 180°F for 4 to 7 hours

Wild goose legs: 180°F for 6 to 12 hours

Wings: Add 1 hour to the legs cooking time

* For geese or the wings of duck or geese, use the higher end of this range.
** Some people like their gizzards firm, almost crunchy. The short end of this range reflects that.

You will note that the cooking times are long here, even in the case of tender cuts such as duck liver or breast. The reason for this is because when you are cooking at such low temperatures, you need to hold that temperature for a long time to kill any potentially harmful bacteria. (Note that these are my temperature preferences; some chefs cook *sous vide* at lower temperatures.) The long cooking time essentially pasteurizes the meat. And don't worry, the meat will not overcook. That's one of the beauties of *sous vide*.

CONFIT OF DUCK

Confit is a technique that you will want to master. Like pan searing duck breasts, this is one of the bedrock skills of a good waterfowl cook. But unlike pan searing, confit has all sorts of room for individuality and experimentation. What follows will get you started on that journey.

Confit begins by coating the duck legs or wings in salt, herbs, and spices and curing them in the fridge for hours or even days. In some cases, curing salt (sodium nitrite) is also used, which gives the confit a rosy color and a slightly hamlike flavor. I've done it both ways, and each is good. It can be challenging to get the salt in your confit exactly how you like it. Everyone's salt tolerance is different, so when you're just starting out, err on the side of less salt rather than more, less curing time rather than more. A general rule I learned from cookbook author and food anthropologist Paula Wolfert is to use 22 grams (¾ ounce) salt per pound of duck or goose. Weight, incidentally, is the best way to gauge salt in cured meats.

I prefer to stick to a few seasonings with my confit, especially if I am making confit to store for a long period outside the freezer. That's because some fresh herbs and other seasonings can compromise the keeping qualities of the meat. Plus, the more you dress up your confit, the less versatile it will be in the kitchen. Confit is a beginning, not an end.

You can cook confit in the oven, sealed in a vacuum bag in hot water, or in a slow cooker. But no matter which cooking method you choose, you must be patient. You must cook the meat gently so it is close to falling off the bone, without actually doing it, and so as much fat as possible has been rendered out. This takes hours. You can overcook confit, however. When this happens, the skin completely gelatinizes and is impossible to crisp later and the meat becomes mushy, like stringy baby food. Even if you plan on stripping the skin off the confit, don't cook it longer than seven hours. Gizzards are an exception to this, as are the wings and legs of very old wild geese.

You finish confit by crisping the skin, either in a hot oven or in a pan on the stove top. Once the skin is crispy, you have achieved something magical: silky, melting, ever-so-salty meat wrapped in crackling crisp skin. Its uses are limitless.

DIFFICULTY: ✳ ✳

MAKES ABOUT 3 POUNDS
CONFIT DUCK LEGS OR WINGS

PREP TIME: 12 HOURS

COOK TIME: 3 TO 5 HOURS

3 pounds duck or goose legs or wings
   (about 8 domesticated duck legs)

4 tablespoons plus 1 teaspoon (2¼ ounces or 66 grams)
   kosher salt

1 tablespoon sugar

1 tablespoon dried thyme

1 tablespoon freshly ground pepper

1 teaspoon garlic powder, or 1 large clove garlic, minced

1 cup duck fat, for nontraditional method, or
   5 to 6 cups duck fat, for traditional method

3 or 4 bay leaves

Put the duck legs in a storage container just large enough to hold them comfortably. In a small bowl, stir together the salt, sugar, thyme, pepper, and garlic. Pack the legs with the salt mixture, pressing it into the skin and exposed meat and making sure every part has some cure on it. Cover and refrigerate overnight for normal confit and for no more than 48 hours for confit you plan to store unfrozen for long periods.

When the meat is cured to your liking, rinse off the cure and dry the legs well. Put them on a cooling rack to dry further while you prepare to cook them. My preferred method is to use a vacuum sealer to seal the legs in bags and then cook them in a pot of hot water. This saves a lot of fat over the traditional oven method, which requires up to 6 cups, more than most people have lying around. So if you are using a vacuum sealer, make vacuum bags large enough to hold 2 legs from domesticated ducks or geese, or 6 to 8 legs from wild ducks. It is very important for the meat to be in a single layer. Divvy up the 1 cup fat into the bottom of each vacuum bag, and then divide the bay leaves evenly among the bags. Vacuum seal the bags.

Fill the largest pot you have with water and heat it to around 180°F, which is a bare simmer. Submerge the bags in the water, topping them with a plate or other weight if necessary, and cook for at least 3 hours, monitoring the temperature every 30 minutes or so to prevent the water from boiling. The legs are cooked when you see the meat beginning to separate from the bone.

Just before the legs are cooked, ready a large bowl of ice water. When the legs are cooked, retrieve the bags from the pot of water and plunge them into the ice water; leave to cool for 20 minutes. Then transfer the cooled bags to cooling racks and let dry.

If you don't have a vacuum sealer, cure the legs as directed, then rinse off the cure and pat dry thoroughly. In a small pot, totally submerge the legs in the 5 to 6 cups fat, then put the pot, uncovered, in the oven set to 200°F. Alternatively, put the pot on the stove top over a burner turned on very low or on a burner turned low with a heat diffuser (flame tamer). Watch that the fat never

sizzles. Cooking time will be a little less, so check the legs after only 2 hours. Again, you should see the meat beginning to separate from the bone. Transfer the meat to a storage container, cover with the fat, and let cool.

You can eat your confit as soon as it is cooked, but you can also age it, which improves the flavor. To age it, store it fully submerged in fat in the refrigerator for up to a week or two before serving.

When it comes time to serve the confit, you will need to extract it from its fatty bed. Remove the bags or container from the refrigerator. If you have cooked your confit submerged in fat, bring it to room temperature. The fat will soften, so you can reach in and grab a leg or two. If you have cooked your confit in a vacuum bag, immerse the bag in warm water to melt the fat. Pull out the legs and scrape off any excess fat. If you don't plan on eating the skin, just pull it off and discard it. Do not discard the fat, however. See page 146 for directions on reusing it.

The easiest way to finish your confit is in the oven. Preheat the oven to 400°F. Set a cooling rack inside a baking sheet and place the confit, skin side up, on the rack. Roast for 20 to 40 minutes, until the skin crisps. The fattier the bird, the longer it will take.

You can also crisp the skin in a sauté pan. Lay the legs or wings skin side down in a cool pan and turn the heat to medium-high. Turn the fan on, as the fat will spit and sputter. Sear until the skin is crispy, about 5 minutes. Use tongs to move the legs around so you get as much of the skin crisped as possible.

EASY CONFIT

This is not a real confit, but the end result is similar, though not nearly as complex in flavor. Its advantage is that it takes just a little more than two hours and is supereasy. Just be sure to do this only with domesticated bird legs. Wild birds are too old and tough for this method to work well.

DIFFICULTY: *

SERVES 4

PREP TIME: 10 MINUTES

COOK TIME: 2 HOURS

4 to 6 domesticated duck or goose legs
Kosher salt
Melted duck fat or olive oil, for greasing

Pat the duck legs dry with paper towels. To ensure crispy skin, pierce the skin of the duck legs all over with a clean needle or the tip of a sharp knife, positioning the tool at an angle so that you are piercing just the skin and not the meat.

Salt the duck legs well. Coat the bottom of a baking dish—one just big enough to hold the legs—with a thin layer of melted duck fat. Place the duck legs, skin side up, in the baking dish close together but not overlapping. Put the baking dish in the oven and turn on the oven to 275°F (do not preheat the oven).

After 1½ hours, check the duck. It should be partly submerged in melted fat and the skin should be getting crispy. Turn up the heat to 375°F. Check after 15 minutes. You are looking for a light golden brown. The whole process should take about 2 hours.

Remove the confit from the oven and let cool for 10 to 15 minutes before eating. Save the accumulated fat and use for cooking vegetables or other meats. If you want to save the fat for at least a few weeks, strain it through a fine-mesh sieve lined with a plain paper towel or cheesecloth into a glass container, cover tightly, and refrigerate. It will keep for up to 6 months. To store the confit, wrap well and refrigerate for up to 2 weeks.

REUSING THE FAT

All confit fat can be reused. It will be salty, but it will also be infused with ducky flavor and with whatever herbs you used. But you must separate the fat from any juices that came off of the duck during cooking. Pour the whole shebang into a plastic or glass container, cover it, and set it in the fridge. The fat will float on top of the liquid. Keep this overnight before messing with it.

The next day, spoon or pick off the fat and put it into a pot. When you get close to the level of the liquid—which will probably have set into a gel—leave a little fat. Save this liquid and use it in place of *glace de viande* for pan sauces.

Put the pot of fat on the stove top over medium heat. As the fat melts, watch for little bubbles. This is stray water in the fat. As the fat heats, the bubbles will spatter and pop a little—and it will be just "a little," if you've done it right, which is why you leave some fat with the confit liquid. In 5 to 15 minutes, the fat should be free of bubbles and look placid. Turn off the heat, let cool a bit, and pour into glass storage containers. Cover and store in the refrigerator for up to 6 months.

CONFIT SALAD WITH FRISÉE

This is a traditional French way to eat confit. Many cooks simply plunk a crispy confit leg on each plate and call it a day, but I prefer to shred the meat, crisp it, and toss it in with the salad. Add a little Duck Fat Vinaigrette and something tart and fruity and you have a perfect summertime lunch or light supper. Pour a white wine or a dry rosé at the table.

DIFFICULTY: *

SERVES 4

PREP TIME: 15 MINUTES

COOK TIME: 5 MINUTES

1 pound confit duck or goose legs,
  (page 144 or page 146)
Duck Fat Vinaigrette (page 67)
4 to 6 cups loosely packed chopped frisée or
  other bitter green
Tangerine sections or pomegranate seeds, for garnish

Pick all of the meat and skin off the duck legs and shred it coarsely. Toss with a little of the vinaigrette. In a large bowl, combine half of the duck and the all of the frisée and toss to combine. Taste and adjust with more vinaigrette, toss well, then top with the remaining confit. (The remaining vinaigrette will keep in a tightly covered container in the refrigerator for up to a week.) Garnish with the tangerine sections and serve.

CONFIT OF DUCK
WITH PASTA AND LEMON

This is one of my favorite things to do with duck confit (though you can also use the slow-roasted duck on page 31). It is a sumptuous pasta dish that has its origins in old Venice, where it is traditionally served with tagliatelle, a long, flat pasta. If you can't find tagliatelle, shoot for linguine, spaghetti, or *pappardelle*.

Make sure you have all of the ingredients prepped before you start cooking, as this dish comes together quickly. Have the water boiling, and give it plenty of salt; you want it to taste of the sea.

DIFFICULTY: *

SERVES 4

PREP TIME: 10 MINUTES

COOK TIME: 10 MINUTES

2 confit duck legs (page 144 or page 146)
1 tablespoon unsalted butter
1 tablespoon duck fat, or as needed
Kosher salt and freshly ground pepper
1 pound fresh tagliatelle
4 cloves garlic, finely chopped
2 tablespoons freshly squeezed lemon juice
Grated lemon zest, for garnish

Bring a large pot of water to a rolling boil.

Meanwhile, pick all of the meat off the duck legs and reserve the skin. Tear the meat and skin into small pieces. Heat a large sauté pan over medium-high heat for 2 minutes. Add the butter, 1 tablespoon duck fat, and the duck meat and skin. Turn the heat down to medium.

Generously salt the boiling water, then add the pasta and stir well.

Add the garlic to the sauté pan and mix well. Watch the garlic: the moment it begins to brown, turn off the heat.

When the pasta is al dente, drain it into a colander, then add it to the sauté pan. Alternatively, use tongs to transfer it from the boiling water to the sauté pan. Turn on the heat to medium and toss the pasta to coat well with all of the ingredients, adding more duck fat if the mixture seems too dry. Season with pepper, add 1 tablespoon of the lemon juice, and toss again. Taste and add the remaining 1 tablespoon lemon juice if you want. Serve immediately, garnished with the lemon zest.

SLOW-COOKER CONFIT

You can use your slow cooker to make confit, too. You will need several cups of duck fat, but if you run short, you can supplement with olive oil. And yes, you can strain and reuse the fat later. Slow cookers generally run hotter than the oven and stove-top methods, so the confit will cook in less time. But the result is still great.

Cure the legs as directed, then submerge them in fat in the slow cooker. Turn the heat to low, or if your cooker has a temperature gauge, turn it to 185°F. Once the fat hits at least 175°F, start timing the confit. Leave the legs to cook for 2 hours before checking them. As with other methods, the larger the leg and the older the bird, the longer it will need to cook. You want the meat almost ready to fall off the bone.

When the legs are done, carefully remove them from the cooker and put them in a storage container. Pour in the fat to cover completely, let cool, cover, and refrigerate. Store and serve the confit as directed in Confit of Duck (page 144).

EXTRAS

GIBLETS

Giblets—such a homey name. Makes you think of a warm fire, cider, a Thanksgiving turkey, and gravy, doesn't it? Most of us associate good things with the word *giblet*. Most of us are not so accepting when we call those same giblets innards, offal, or the ever-cryptic variety meats.

Properly defined, giblets are the heart, liver, and gizzard of a bird. In Asian cooking, you would add the tongue and feet. Some people include the neck in the giblet category, but I prefer to consider it part of the catchall carcass, suitable primarily for stock making.

Poultry giblets are probably North America's most widely eaten wobbly bits. Fried gizzards are a regular menu item in places as far-flung as Tennessee and Montana. Duck Liver Pâté (page 179) is an acceptable hors d'oeuvre in most households in America, and chopped chicken liver is an iconic dish of Jewish cuisine. Only the heart seems lost, which is ironic considering it is just muscle meat, like the breasts, legs, and thighs of the rest of the bird.

It is interesting to note that poultry giblets are the only innards commonly packaged with the animal from which they come. Buy a whole chicken without that little packet of giblets inside and you feel cheated, even if your only plan for them was to toss them all into the stockpot.

While I am happy that so many people do use their giblets for stocks, my hope is that you'll do more than that. I am a firm believer in the nose-to-tail ethic of meat eating: if an animal died for your dinner plate, you ought to use as much of it as you can. Sermon over. Even if you don't buy into this belief, two good reasons exist for learning how to cook what is sometimes called the fifth quarter of the animal: thrift and flavor.

Admittedly, I was not an offal evangelist before I began hunting. Sure, I loved to order sweetbreads in restaurants. And I became a committed heart eater after I had them grilled and served with mole sauce while on vacation in La Paz, Mexico. But I've never enjoyed the texture of liver, and I ate kidneys once on a dare.

Hunting changed everything. When I began hunting, I was not very good at it. My first year of duck hunting, I came home with fewer than a dozen birds. Each bird represented a step in my evolution as a duck hunter, and I wanted to get as much out of these precious birds as I could. The giblets of a duck or goose can weigh as much as a pound, and it seemed terrible to waste that much good meat. So I learned how to cook the giblets.

At first I put them into the stockpot. Then I learned to grind the hearts and gizzards with some pork fat to make duck burgers or ground duck for sausages (page 102). If I could convince every duck hunter to do at least this, I would be a happy man. But over time, thanks to chefs like Chris Cosentino in San Francisco and Fergus Henderson in London, I learned that there is far more to giblet cookery than this. Gizzards are best when slowly cooked for hours. Hearts are wonderful seared hard on the outside but still pink inside. Livers make a surpassing ravioli filling. As my hunting skills improved, I began to look forward to gathering enough giblets to make some of recipes included here. They have become some of my favorite dishes in the book and are worth every bit of trouble it might take to collect or seek out a source for duck giblets. And if you can't get your hands on any, chicken giblets are an almost seamless substitute.

DUCK AND GOOSE GIBLETS BY THE NUMBERS

Duck giblets are not that different from their chicken cousins, although in general, a duck gizzard will be larger—a goose gizzard is downright huge—as will the heart. A wild duck or goose heart will be even larger that their domesticated counterparts, which is not surprising considering how much these birds fly every year. The liver from a normal domesticated duck will be about the same color and slightly larger than a chicken liver; the liver of a wild duck will be smaller and often as dark as a glass of Bordeaux.

Duck livers are incredibly high in vitamins A and B_{12}, as well as copper and iron. A single ounce of duck liver will give you 252 percent of your daily recommended dose of vitamin B_{12}, 223 percent of your vitamin A, 83 percent of your copper, and 47 percent of your iron. Chicken livers don't even come close to those numbers. Duck livers are, however, high in cholesterol: that single ounce is nearly half your daily allowance.

Most whole ducks in the supermarket come with the giblets inside, and it is not impossible to find duck gizzards sold separately, although you may have to head to your nearest Asian market. My advice is to collect them from the birds you buy and store them in the freezer until you have enough to make these recipes.

Hunters, who typically shoot dozens of ducks in a season, are actually in a better position to make duck and goose giblet recipes. On a banner day, Holly and I can come home from the marsh with fourteen ducks and a goose or two. We remove and clean the giblets (see page 22) and package each kind separately. Then, when the mood strikes, we can make a meal solely of slow-cooked gizzards, grilled duck hearts, or even crispy fried duck tongues.

A SHORT HISTORY OF FOIE GRAS

The most famous of all duck or goose giblets by far is foie gras, the fattened livers of ducks and sometimes geese. Foie gras is an ethereal food: creamy, ducky, almost sweet. But it is also extremely expensive, and controversial.

Most foie gras is produced by force-feeding ducks (and occasionally geese). The process, known as gavage, a French word, can involve everything from hand feeding with a funnel to a more mechanized system. The process works because waterfowl naturally store up fat for their long migration flights. These flights are so grueling that more birds sometimes die from exhaustion on the flight than fall to hunters' guns, disease, or other animal predation. Building up fat is a defense against death.

Humans have known about this since antiquity: an Egyptian tomb painting shows people force-feeding geese. The Romans were especially fond of fattened goose livers, and the practice became associated with Italy's Jewish community as early as the days of writer Bartolomeo Scappi in 1570. Criticism over force-feeding is nearly as old as Scappi's observations about it, especially in the English-speaking world. Gavage looks horrible, and if it were done on a human, it would constitute torture. But waterfowl are different: they have no gag reflex, and their trachea is a bony tube under their tongue, so the birds can breathe normally during feeding.

There is, however, ample evidence that shoving a tube down a duck's throat causes some harm. How much harm remains unclear. I take no position in the foie gras debate, and I am not including any traditional foie gras recipes in this book for two reasons: most foie gras in this country is eaten in restaurants, not at home, and because the stuff is so bloody expensive.

High-quality foie gras costs around seventy dollars a pound, if you can find it. It is nearly impossible to obtain fresh in all but the largest cities, though the canned product is often available in specialty stores in smaller markets. Foie gras can also be bought online through purveyors such as D'Artagnan. A Spanish producer, La Patería de Sousa, makes an exquisite foie gras without gavage by laying out lots and lots of figs, acorns, lupini beans, and olives for the geese to eat in fall. The Spanish liver is not as large as the French force-fed liver, but it did win a blind tasting in France in 2006. Since then, La Patería de Sousa has become the darling of the food world.

Hunters take note: wild foie gras exists. Under certain circumstances, wild ducks and geese will gorge themselves far beyond their normal nutritional needs, to the point where they develop livers that closely resemble the foie gras of domesticated waterfowl. Not all ducks seem to do this. You will rarely see a diver duck or a snow goose this fat. Most often, it is seed-loving ducks: mallard, gadwall, wigeon, green-winged teal, and most prominently, the northern pintail *(Anas acuta)*. Holly and I will bring home maybe a dozen of these birds with fattened livers a year, so it's not that rare for a bird to have a fatty liver, if you hunt in a wintering ground where the birds can fatten up after the migration.

Our wild foie gras in California is largely a product of two things: waterfowl recovering from their migrations—California is a wintering ground for ducks and geese—and the rice industry. Ducks eat what's around them. One study of pintail feeding behavior done in Kern County, about two hundred miles south of the rice fields, shows that during the hunting season pintail there eat mostly swamp timothy and barnyardgrass, supplemented by midge larvae. Pintail that far south do not put on the fat our ducks do. Another study conducted where we hunt in rice country north of Sacramento found that pintail were getting 97 percent of their food from plants, as opposed to 72 percent in Kern, and that close to 99 percent of the plant diet of the northern pintail was rice.

Rice is so high in energy and full of nutrients that the birds, like many omnivores (humans included), engage their "thrifty gene." This gene tells the body to store as much energy as possible because the animal is programmed to live in a feast-or-famine world. Incidentally, teal, wigeon, and gadwalls do the same thing in the rice fields. So, too, do specklebelly geese, the cousins of those Spanish geese with the naturally fattened livers. They become flying butterballs.

If you get one of these big livers, cook it simply with salt and something acidic, such as balsamic vinegar. And enjoy one of the great tastes in nature.

DUCK HEART TARTARE PUTTANESCA

The thing about hearts (of anything) is that they taste intensely of whatever they came out of, and duck hearts are no exception. They are one of the easier giblets to love, as they are just meat—muscle, not organ. Heart has a dense, slightly chewy texture that lends itself to being finely diced.

Tartare puttanesca hinges on the pantry staples of capers, olives, a little chile, and tomatoes. The result is surprisingly nonthreatening, tastewise, and makes a very good little starter. If you are not into duck hearts, or can't get them, use skinless duck breast instead.

I typically make this dish with Roma or San Marzano tomatoes, but in winter, when they are not in season, I substitute jarred roasted red peppers. Better a pickled pepper than a poor phantom of a real tomato.

DIFFICULTY: ✳ ✳

SERVES 4 AS AN APPETIZER

PREP TIME: 30 MINUTES

36 to 48 duck or goose hearts (about 12 ounces)

1½ tablespoons tiny (nonpareil) capers

3 tablespoons finely cut Roma tomato or roasted red pepper (pieces the size of the capers)

1 small fresh hot chile, seeded and minced

1 heaping tablespoon minced shallot

1 tablespoon minced, pitted green or black olives

1 teaspoon grated lemon zest

3 tablespoons olive oil

1 tablespoon freshly squeezed lemon juice

1 tablespoon minced fresh flat-leaf parsley

1 tablespoon minced fresh mint

Kosher salt

GARLIC CHIPS, OPTIONAL

2 or 3 large cloves garlic, thinly sliced lengthwise

2 cups milk

3 to 4 tablespoons olive oil

Trim off the top of each heart (the top end above the fat ring). Mince the hearts into pieces about the size of the capers and put in a bowl. Add the capers, tomato, chile, shallot, olives, and lemon zest and mix gently to combine. You can now hold this in the refrigerator for a couple of hours if you like.

To make the garlic chips, in a small saucepan, combine the garlic and 1 cup of the milk and bring to a boil. Remove from the heat and drain the garlic. Repeat with the garlic slices and the remaining 1 cup milk, then pat the garlic slices dry. This blanching is necessary to take any bitterness out of the garlic. If you skip this blanching step, the garlic will be quite bitter and ruin your pretty tartare. In a small frying pan, heat the oil over medium-high heat. Add the garlic slices and fry for 2 to 3 minutes, until they just begin to brown. Transfer to paper towels to drain.

When you are ready to serve, add the oil, lemon juice, parsley, mint, and salt to taste to the hearts mixture and mix gently. Put a large spoonful of the tartare on each plate, then select the 4 nicest garlic chips and top each tartare spoonful with one chip.

GRILLED DUCK HEARTS WITH CHIMICHURRI

If you've never eaten poultry hearts before, this recipe would be a good place to start. It's simple, quick, and flavorful. The hearts are brined for a while to season them and to keep them tender over the hot fire, then skewered, grilled, and finally doused with *chimichurri*, an Argentine staple that goes on everything. It is an herby, garlicky sauce that relies on parsley and usually some other herb. I like to use mountain pennyroyal, which is a sort of wild oregano that grows in the Sierra Nevada range not far from where I live. Regular oregano works just fine.

You can make this dish as fancy or as humble as you want. I have a rosemary bush in my front yard, so I like to take some long, woody sprigs, soak them in water, and use them as skewers. It adds a huge amount of flavor, but if you don't have your own rosemary bush, use regular metal or bamboo skewers instead.

If you can grill over hardwood—apple, oak, hickory, maple—you will notice a huge difference in flavor. Even some wood chips thrown in a charcoal fire, or on top of the burners in a gas grill, will make a difference. Serve the hearts with lots of crusty bread and a good rosé or a light red, like a Grenache.

DIFFICULTY: *

SERVES 4 AS AN APPETIZER

PREP TIME: 2 HOURS

COOK TIME: 3 TO 4 MINUTES

¼ cup kosher salt

4 cups water

8 to 12 ounces duck or goose hearts

2 tablespoons olive oil

CHIMICHURRI

1 to 2 cloves garlic, minced

1 cup loosely packed chopped fresh flat-leaf parsley

1 cup loosely packed chopped fresh oregano

1 small fresh hot chile (such as serrano, Thai, árbol, or mirasol), minced

2 to 3 tablespoons freshly squeezed lime juice

Kosher salt and freshly ground pepper

½ cup olive oil

To make the brine, mix together the salt and water until the salt dissolves. Pour the brine into a plastic container with a lid and add the duck hearts. Cover and set aside for 2 hours. If using bamboo skewers, put them in water to soak.

Meanwhile, make the *chimichurri*. In a food processor, combine the garlic, parsley, oregano, chile, lime juice, and a little salt and buzz just to combine. Do not puree.

With the motor running, slowly drizzle in the olive oil. Taste and adjust the seasoning with salt and pepper. Let stand at room temperature to blend the flavors.

Set up the grill and get the fire raging hot. Make sure the grill grate is clean.

Drain the duck hearts and pat them dry with paper towels. Toss the hearts with the olive oil, then push them onto skewers, leaving a little space between the hearts.

Right before you lay the skewers on the grill, oil the grate: use tongs to pick up a paper towel, dip it into vegetable oil, and wipe down the grate. Lay the duck skewers over the hot fire and cook, turning once, for no more than 2 minutes on each side.

To serve, either pour the *chimichurri* over the skewers or remove the hearts from the skewers and toss them with the sauce. You can slice the hearts in half if you think they might be too big for one bite.

CRISPY DUCK TONGUES

Admittedly, this is a sporty recipe, not only because you'll be eating duck tongues but also because it is technically difficult and time-consuming. That said, the results are nothing short of addictive. Make more of these than you think you will need, as they will be gobbled up like potato chips, which is essentially what they are. In Kansas City, chef Michael Smith of Extra Virgin serves these in tacos, and they are one of his best-selling appetizers.

This recipe is best when done with a *sous vide* water oven (see note), but you can still make it without one. If you have a vacuum sealer, you can use a stockpot of hot water and monitor the temperature, which is how I do it here. Or, you can cook the duck tongues in stock in the oven (see note). In every case, you will need to dry the tongues well before you fry them, or they will pop violently when they hit the hot oil and sometimes even fly across the room. Trust me, you don't want to skip the drying step. It is best done with a dehydrator, but you can get by drying them in your oven set to the lowest temperature.

Look for duck tongues in Asian markets, or if you are a hunter, save them up for this treat.

DIFFICULTY: ★ ★ ★ ★ ★

SERVES 4

PREP TIME: 5 MINUTES

COOK TIME: 6½ HOURS

1 pound duck or goose tongues

½ cup Duck Glace de Viande (page 226)
   or beef demi-glace or stock

2 tablespoons duck fat or unsalted butter

1 teaspoon kosher salt

1 cup vegetable oil (such as safflower or peanut)

Fine sea salt, for finishing

Mustard or Duck Fat Saffron Aioli (page 205), for serving

Put the duck tongues, *glace de viande,* duck fat, and salt in a vacuum bag and seal. You don't need to get all out of the air out, but get out as much as you can. Fill a large stockpot with water and heat to 190°F, which is a gentle simmer. Drop in the vacuum bag and turn the heat to low. Cover the pot and cook the tongues for 4 hours, until they are tender, monitoring the temperature every 30 minutes or so. Under no circumstances should the water boil. It is better for it to be a little too cool than too hot.

When the tongues are done, retrieve the bag, open it, and pour out everything into a bowl. Now you need to work fast. While the tongues are still warm, grab the end of the bone at the base of the tongue and gently pull it out. If the tongues are tender enough, this should be easy. Discard the bones—or use as earrings.

Now, arrange the tongues in a single layer on a dehydrator and dry on low heat (100°F) for 2 hours. If you don't have a dehydrator, arrange the tongues on a nonstick baking sheet, put the pan in the oven, turn on the oven to its lowest setting, and leave them for 2 hours. If you have a convection oven, use it. With either setup, turn the tongues over after the first hour.

You can prepare the tongues up to this point up to 2 days in advance. Pack them into an airtight container and store in the fridge.

To finish the dish, pour the oil into a deep sauté pan and heat to 350°F to 360°F. When the oil is ready, working in batches, add the tongues and fry for 2 to 3 minutes, until they puff up and brown. Using a slotted spoon, transfer to paper towels to drain. Always let the oil temperature return to 350°F to 360°F before adding the next batch. Sprinkle with fine sea salt.

Serve the tongues hot with mustard for dipping.

Note: If you have a *sous vide* water oven, seal the tongues in a bag and cook at 190°F for 4 hours. If you don't have a vacuum sealer, submerge the tongues in duck or beef stock, bring to the steaming point—don't let the liquid bubble—then cover the pot and cook in a 200°F oven for 4 to 5 hours, until the tongues are tender.

GANSEKLEIN, A GERMAN GIBLET SOUP

I've been fascinated by this venerable German soup ever since I first heard of it years ago. The Germans eat more goose than nearly any other country in Europe, and they make use of all parts of the bird. This sweet-and-sour giblet soup is traditionally served during the holidays, and it really does taste like Christmas, with hints of clove and nutmeg, the flavor of the giblets (giblet gravy, anyone?), and all those dried fruits. A similar dish in Poland is called *czarnina*.

Some versions of this recipe are thickened with goose blood, but as that's pretty much impossible to obtain—and would probably scare off too many people—this is a northern German version that omits the blood. If you don't want to use the giblets, you can also make the dish with the legs and wings of a goose or duck. The dish is typically served with little potato dumplings called *Kartoffelklosse*, which I have included here, or with small fingerling potatoes. Either is fine. Serve with white wine or a dark, malty beer.

DIFFICULTY: ✳ ✳

SERVES 6 TO 8

PREP TIME: 20 MINUTES

COOK TIME: 3½ HOURS

2 pounds goose or duck giblets (gizzard and heart but not liver), necks, and wings

6 cups water

3 or 4 whole cloves

1 teaspoon dried marjoram

2 bay leaves

Kosher salt and freshly ground pepper

2 tablespoons duck fat or unsalted butter

1 large yellow or white onion, sliced stem to root end

1 celery stalk, chopped

1 carrot, peeled and chopped

¼ cup raisins

¼ cup dried cranberries

10 prunes, pitted and halved

3 tablespoons malt vinegar or cider vinegar

2 teaspoons sugar

DUMPLINGS

2 pounds floury potatoes, such as russet

2 tablespoons duck fat or unsalted butter, melted

1 duck or chicken egg, lightly beaten

¼ cup dried bread crumbs

1 tablespoon kosher salt

½ teaspoon ground nutmeg

About ½ cup all-purpose flour

In a Dutch oven or large, heavy pot, combine the giblets and/or necks and wings and water and bring to a simmer over medium-high heat, skimming off any scum that floats to the surface. Add the cloves, marjoram, and bay leaves and a healthy pinch of salt. You want the broth to be a little undersalted now, as it will cook down over time. Cover, adjust the heat to maintain a gentle simmer, and cook for at least 2 hours or up to 3 hours, until the meat starts to fall off the neck and wings.

Meanwhile, in a large sauté pan, heat the duck fat over medium heat. Add the onion and cook slowly, stirring occasionally, to caramelize it. This will take about 20 minutes or so, and you may need to lower the heat or cover the pan to prevent the onion from burning. Once it is nicely browned, turn off the heat and set aside.

Make the dumpling dough while the soup is cooking. Preheat the oven to 400°F. Stab each potato all over with the tines of a fork, then rub with the duck fat (this helps them cook). Put the potatoes on a rack in the oven and bake for 1 hour, until tender when pierced with a knife. Remove them from the oven, break them open to release the steam, and let cool for 15 to 30 minutes.

continued

continued from previous page

Put the cooked potatoes through a ricer or food mill held over a bowl, or just peel them and mash the potatoes with a fork in the bowl. Add the egg, bread crumbs, salt, nutmeg, and flour and mix with a wooden spoon or your hands just until combined. The dough should be slightly tacky but should still hold together when compressed into a ball. Do not knead the dough like bread dough or the dumplings will be very heavy. Set the dough aside for now.

Once the meats are tender, turn off the heat and fish out the gizzards, hearts, necks, and wings. Roughly chop the gizzards and hearts, and pull off all of the meat from the necks and wings. Return all of the meats to the soup. Add the celery, carrot, caramelized onion, raisins, cranberries, and prunes. Turn on the heat again and bring the soup back to a simmer.

Meanwhile, bring a large pot of salted water to a boil for cooking the dumplings. Shape the dough into little balls, using about 1 tablespoon dough for each ball. When all of the dumplings have been formed, gently submerge them in the boiling water, which should drop in temperature to a simmer. Do not let it return to a boil; you want a gentle simmer for cooking the dumplings.

When the dumplings start bobbing on the surface, which should take 4 to 5 minutes, it is your signal to remove them with a slotted spoon or wire skimmer.

Add the vinegar and sugar to the soup, then season with salt and pepper. Taste and adjust the seasoning with more of any of these ingredients.

To serve, arrange some dumplings in each bowl and ladle the hot soup over the top. Serve at once.

SEARED DUCK LIVER

This is an excellent, über simple method for cooking any poultry liver that I picked up from chef Brad Farmerie of Public restaurant in New York City. He does it with domestic duck and chicken livers, which will almost always be fattier than a wild duck liver. I would not recommend doing this with a wild liver, unless you are blessed with wild foie gras. If you do not have a good aged balsamic vinegar on hand, boil down cheaper balsamic to reduce by half, until syrupy. This is an ecstatic bite, not a meal.

DIFFICULTY: *

SERVES 2

PREP TIME: 5 MINUTES

COOK TIME: 2 MINUTES

1 tablespoon vegetable oil with high smoke point
   (such as grapeseed, safflower, or rice bran)
2 duck or goose livers, or more
Fleur de sel or other fine sea salt
Aged balsamic vinegar, for drizzling

Get a small frying pan screaming hot. Add the oil and heat it until it smokes. Take the pan off the heat and gently lay the livers in the pan. As soon as they hit the hot oil, shake the pan a little so they do not stick. Set the pan back on the heat and sear the livers for 1½ minutes, all the while basting the other side with the fat in the pan. Remove from the heat.

Sprinkle the livers with salt, drizzle with vinegar, and serve immediately by themselves or with a simple green salad.

"What's sauce for the goose is sauce for the gander."

—GERMAN PROVERB

DUCK LIVER RAVIOLI

This is inspired by one of the signature dishes at Mario Batali's Babbo in Manhattan. That version calls for foie gras, but I use butter and it works fine. If you can afford it, use foie gras instead. All you need is a small tin of the stuff, available online. If you want to try this recipe and cannot find duck or goose livers, use chicken livers.

I often make the pasta dough with chestnut flour, available at specialty shops or online. If you can't find it—and it's really worth looking for—use spelt flour or barley flour. The key is to get an earthy flavor going.

How to serve? With the simple sauce here or in the Duck Consommé on page 228. Either way is wonderful.

DIFFICULTY: ✳ ✳ ✳ ✳

SERVES 6 TO 8

PREP TIME: 2 HOURS

COOK TIME: 35 MINUTES

DOUGH

3 cups all-purpose flour, plus more for rolling

1 cup chestnut flour

Pinch of kosher salt

4 duck eggs or 5 chicken eggs, lightly beaten

1 tablespoon olive oil, plus more for coating

Semolina flour or cornmeal, for dusting

FILLING

4 tablespoons duck fat or unsalted butter

½ cup chopped yellow onion

1½ pounds duck or goose livers

1 teaspoon red pepper flakes

1 cup red wine

2 teaspoons dried oregano

Kosher salt and freshly ground black pepper

4 tablespoons unsalted butter or 2 to 3 ounces foie gras, chilled and diced

SAUCE

3 tablespoons duck fat

¼ cup balsamic vinegar (use a decent one)

Minced fresh flat-leaf parsley, for garnish

Grated pecorino or Parmesan cheese, for garnish

Chopped scallion, for garnish

To make the dough, in a large bowl, whisk together the all-purpose and chestnut flours and the salt until combined. Make a well in the center, and pour the eggs and the 1 tablespoon oil into the well. Starting at the rim of the well, and using a fork, gradually draw the flour into the liquid ingredients. Continue to incorporate the flour until you get big clumps, then switch to kneading the ingredients together. Once the mixture has come together in a big ball, knead vigorously with the dough in the bowl for 5 to 8 minutes, until smooth. Coat the dough with a little olive oil, then wrap in plastic wrap and let rest at room temperature for 1 hour.

To make the filling, in a frying pan, heat the duck fat over medium heat. Add the onion and sauté for about 8 minutes, until it is translucent and soft. Turn up the heat to medium-high, add the livers and red pepper flakes, and sauté, turning once, for 1½ minutes on each side.

Add the wine, bring to a boil, and cook for 8 to 10 minutes, until reduced to about ¼ cup. Add the oregano, then remove from the heat and let the mixture cool a bit. Transfer the contents of the pan to a food processor and process until well chopped but not a smooth puree. Season with salt and black pepper and let cool to room temperature. When the mixture is cool, add the butter and mix until evenly distributed.

To shape the ravioli, divide the dough into 4 equal portions. Keep the portions covered when you are not working with them to prevent them from drying out. You can roll out the dough with a rolling pin on a floured work surface, or with a pasta machine, following the directions that came with the machine. You want the dough

continued

sheets to be very thin. If using a pasta machine, do not roll the dough on the thinnest setting, however, or it will be too delicate to hold the filling. I roll out my dough to no. 7 on my Atlas pasta machine, where no. 9 is the thinnest setting.

Dust a baking sheet with semolina flour or cornmeal. Lay a pasta sheet on the work surface and use a 3-inch biscuit cutter or a wineglass to cut out circles of dough. Using a teaspoon, place mounds of the filling in the center of each circle. Dip your finger in a little cool water, then wet the top half of the dough circle. Fold it over into a half-moon and press to seal, working carefully to create an even seal with no air bubbles. Repeat until you have used up all of the filling and dough.

When all of the ravioli have been shaped, you can refrigerate them for no more than a few hours, or you can freeze them individually on a baking sheet and then transfer them to zipper-top bags and store them in the freezer for up to 2 months.

To finish the dish, bring a large pot of generously salted water to a boil (it should taste like the ocean). Add the ravioli and boil until they float, and then for 1 minute longer.

Meanwhile, to make the sauce, combine the duck fat and vinegar in a large sauté pan and bring to a boil over high heat. Using a wire skimmer or slotted spoon, lift the ravioli from the water, draining well, and add to the sauté pan. Turn the heat down to medium and shake the pan to coat the ravioli with the sauce. Serve at once, garnished with the parsley and cheese.

HOW TO CLEAN A GIZZARD

Almost no cleaning is needed for giblets other than the gizzard. Once you have cleaned gizzards, they are pure, dense, red meat that is wonderful slow cooked (see page 168), ground up, or even just tossed into the stock-pot. But you need to clean them first. You will need a work surface, a small, sharp knife, and a large bowl of cool water.

Start by peeling away any excess fat on the outside of the gizzard. Discard. A gizzard is made up of two muscles separated by grinding plates. Slice in between these plates to open the gizzard. Rinse the gizzard in the bowl of water; don't do this in the sink because the gizzard will be full of stones that can damage your pipes.

Cut the two halves apart. Slice off the grinding plates and any soft tissue to reveal the dense, burgundy meat. To finish, slip the point of your knife under the silver skin that's on each side of each half of the gizzard and slice it off.

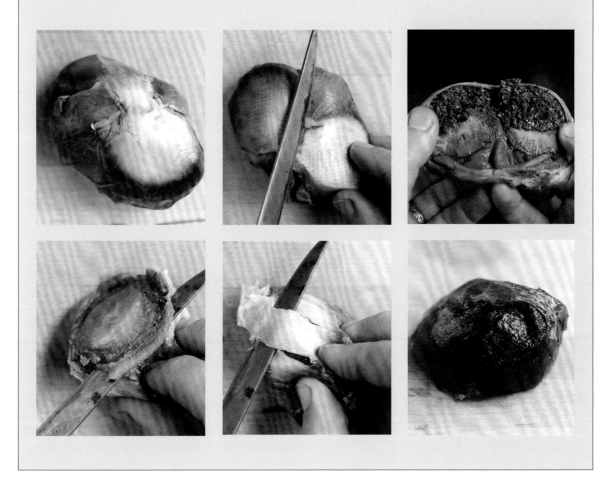

CORNED GIZZARDS AND "CABBAGE"

Duck gizzards, cured like corned beef, cooked slowly in duck fat for the better part of a day, glazed with a malt vinegar dressing, and served with cabbage buds or broccoli rabe, all dusted with toasted caraway—it's as wonderful to eat as it is time-consuming to make. Cooking gizzards this long makes them meaty, salty, slick with duck fat, ever-so-slightly herby from thyme, and so tender you can squash them with a fork. If you serve this even to confirmed gizzard haters, you will change them forever.

What is important when you decide to make this recipe is the corning process and the slow cooking of the gizzard, not the fancy garnishes or plating. Corning is a curing process that is followed by slow simmering. Time is the key here. The longer and slower you cook these gizzards, the more magical they will become. Eight hours is not enough for me. Twelve is about minimum, and twenty-four is not too much.

Cabbage buds can be hard to find unless you are a gardener, so use florets from broccolini or broccoli rabe. Be sure to toast the caraway seeds. It makes a difference. If you cannot find Insta Cure No. 1 (curing salt), skip it. You will not get that pretty pink color of real corned beef, and the flavor will be a little different, but the dish will still be fine.

DIFFICULTY: ✶ ✶ ✶ ✶

SERVES 4

PREP TIME: 6 HOURS

COOK TIME: 24 HOURS

---

1 tablespoon plus 1 teaspoon (22 grams) kosher salt

1 tablespoon dried thyme

Heaping ½ teaspoon (4 grams) Insta Cure No. 1 (see page 196)

1 pound gizzards, cleaned (see page 167)

½ cup duck fat, unsalted butter, or lard

About 4 cups Basic Duck Stock (page 222) or beef stock

1 cup small broccolini, broccoli florets, or cabbage flower buds

1 heaping tablespoon caraway seeds, toasted

Broccolini, broccoli, or cabbage flowers, for garnish, optional

DRESSING

¼ cup malt vinegar

2 teaspoons dry mustard

1 teaspoon kosher salt

½ teaspoon sugar

¾ cup neutral vegetable oil (such as safflower, grapeseed, or canola)

To prepare the gizzards, in a bowl, stir together the kosher salt, thyme, and curing salt. Add the gizzards and mix well to coat evenly. Put the gizzards in a nonreactive container, cover, and refrigerate for 4 to 8 hours. The longer you go, the saltier the gizzards will be, and the better chance you have that the cure will reach the center of each gizzard. I keep mine in for 6 hours.

Rinse the gizzards well and pat dry with paper towels. At this point, you can hold the gizzards for up to a day in the fridge before you cook them.

When you are ready to cook, in a Dutch oven or other large, heavy pot with a lid, heat the duck fat. Add the gizzards and enough stock just to cover them. Cover the pot, put it in the oven, and turn on the oven to 200°F (no need to preheat). Cook for at least 10 hours. If you have a slow cooker, turn it on low and cook for the same amount of time. After 10 hours, check to see if the gizzards are tender. If not, cook them for another 2 to 6 hours. (When the gizzards are tender, you can store them in the cooking liquid in the fridge for up to 1 week before continuing.)

When ready to serve, bring a pot filled with water to a boil. Fill a large bowl with ice water and place it near the stove. When the water is boiling, salt it generously, add the florets, and boil for 1 minute. Drain the florets and submerge them in the ice water to halt the cooking. Drain well, pat dry, and set aside.

To make the dressing, in a blender, combine the vinegar, mustard, salt, and sugar, cover, and buzz on high speed just until mixed. Turn down the speed to low, remove the lid, and slowly pour in the oil. Re-cover, turn the speed to high, and blend for 30 seconds. Taste and adjust the seasoning with salt.

To serve, toss the gizzards with a little of the dressing and arrange on a platter. Toss the florets with some of the dressing and add to the platter. You may have some dressing remaining, which you can save for another use. Sprinkle the caraway and flowers over the top and serve.

Note: If you have a sous vide water oven, put the dried-off gizzards and duck fat in a bag and vacuum seal. Set your water oven to 160°F, place the bag of gizzards in the water, and cook for 12 to 24 hours, depending on how tender you want the gizzards.

DUCKY DIRTY RICE

Dirty rice is a traditional Cajun preparation, and it happens to be quite possibly the greatest use of giblets ever—especially for those who think that they hate eating offal. What makes the rice dirty is ground gizzards and minced liver. And when I say "minced," I mean chopped almost to a puree.

This rice is roll-your-eyes-back-in-your-head-good: spicy, meaty, and richly flavored—a perfect side dish or a simple meal.

If you don't have enough duck or goose giblets to make this recipe, supplement them with giblets from chickens or turkeys. It is important that you use long-grain white rice, and that you let the cooked rice cool before you assemble the dish. You can cook the rice a day ahead, too.

DIFFICULTY: ✳ ✳

SERVES 4

PREP TIME: 20 MINUTES, PLUS AT LEAST 30 MINUTES FOR COOLING THE RICE

COOK TIME: 35 MINUTES

1½ cups long-grain rice

1 cup Basic Duck Stock (page 222) or chicken stock

1½ cups water

Kosher salt

½ to 1 pound duck, goose, or chicken gizzards and/or hearts

3 tablespoons duck fat, unsalted butter, or lard

1 or 2 jalapeño chiles, seeded and chopped

1 green bell pepper, seeded and chopped

1 cup chopped yellow or white onion

2 celery stalks, chopped

½ to 1 cup duck, goose, or chicken livers

1 to 2 tablespoons Cajun seasoning

2 green onions, white and green parts, chopped

To cook the rice, rinse it, put it in a saucepan, and add the stock, water, and a little salt. Place over high heat and bring to a boil. Cover, turn down the heat to low, and cook for about 20 minutes, until the liquid is absorbed and the rice is tender. Spread the cooked rice on a baking sheet and set aside to cool.

While the rice is cooking, if using gizzards, clean them as directed on page 167, then either chop finely or grind in a meat grinder fitted with the fine die. Do the same with the hearts, if using.

In a large sauté pan, heat the duck fat over medium-high heat. When the fat is hot, add the gizzards and/or hearts, chiles, bell pepper, yellow onion, and celery and cook, stirring occasionally, until well browned. Take your time with this step. You want the mixture nicely browned.

Meanwhile, chop the livers very finely. They should be almost a puree. When the gizzards and vegetables are nicely browned, add the livers and mix well. Let this mixture cook for a minute or two. Sprinkle some salt over everything. If the pan gets dry, add a little water or stock to loosen.

Add the cooled rice and a little water to the pan, stir to combine, and turn up the heat to high. Sprinkle in the Cajun seasoning to taste and stir and toss for 2 minutes, until the rice is well coated and beginning to brown. Add the green onions, toss to combine, and serve hot.

CHARCUTERIE

If you're looking for the place where the phrase "duck is the new pig" applies most, it is in the realm of charcuterie. Ducks, and especially geese, have a long history as cured meats. *Prosciutto d'oca* is a classic Italian preparation, said to be invented by that country's Jewish community, for whom regular pork charcuterie is forbidden. Smoked goose is a standard in the German and eastern European world, and duck liver pâté is common all over France. In China, smoked duck and duck liver sausage are sold in markets all over the country.

What follows is a primer on working with waterfowl as cured meats and fresh sausages and pâtés. If you have some familiarity with pork charcuterie, there are only a few key differences between waterfowl and swine. If you've never made a sausage or pâté, this section will get you started.

Be warned: charcuterie is an addiction. Once you learn how to manipulate meat with salt and time and smoke, you will want to do it often. Feel free to play with the seasonings in these recipes once you have made them as they are written a few times. For the most part, only the salt content must remain the same: although you can tinker a bit with the salt, it is the primary preservation agent here, so too little can result in spoiled meat. Other than that, your imagination is your guide.

GOOD MOLDS, BAD MOLDS

Sometimes as you cure the meat, mold will develop. White, powdery mold is okay; white fuzzy mold is not harmful but should be wiped off; green fuzzy mold needs to be wiped off the moment you spot it; and black mold is bad. I toss the meat if I get the black stuff. When green mold does appear, I wipe it off every other day with a paper towel soaked in red wine vinegar.

GOOSE PROSCIUTTO

Some recipes for this classic Italian prosciutto, especially those from the Veneto and Friuli regions, cure the leg and thigh of large geese; others stick to the breast meat. Either way, the result, when done correctly, creates a dark, rich, cured meat that stands out on any charcuterie plate. Serve it with melon, figs, good cheese, on top of a fried egg, with bruschetta—you get the point.

One of the best things about this recipe, which can also be made with a Moulard duck breast, is that it is probably the easiest curing project you can undertake. It is where you should start if you are a beginner.

DIFFICULTY: ✳ ✳

MAKES 2 SLABS PROSCIUTTO

PREP TIME: 30 DAYS OR MORE

1 whole goose breast or whole Moulard duck breast
   (both halves)
½ cup (3¾ ounces or about 100 grams) kosher salt
2 tablespoons sugar
2 tablespoons garlic powder
1 tablespoon sweet paprika
1 tablespoon red pepper flakes
1 tablespoon dried oregano
1 tablespoon freshly ground black pepper

Leave as much skin and fat on each breast half as possible; you get "tails" of skin on both the tail and the neck end of the bird, which you will use to hang the meat from later. Peel off the "tender" on the meat side of the breast. The tender makes a great snack: coat it in batter and deep-fry it.

In a large bowl, stir together the salt, sugar, garlic powder, paprika, red pepper flakes, oregano, and black pepper, mixing well. Coat the breast halves evenly with the mixture, massaging it into the meat and making sure that every bit of flesh has cure on it. Place the breasts in a nonreactive container just large enough to hold them, pour any remaining cure over the breasts, and cover the container.

Cure the breasts in the refrigerator for 1 to 3 days. The longer you cure, the saltier the prosciutto will be. The saltier it will be, the longer it will keep—but the thinner you will need to shave it when you eat it. Flip the breasts once a day to ensure even contact with the extra cure.

When the breasts are ready, rinse off most of the cure—a few bits here and there are a good thing—and dry the breasts thoroughly. Place the breasts, skin side down, on a cooling rack and leave to dry for an hour or two.

Now it's time to hang your prosciutto in a curing chamber. You will need a place with 60 to 85 percent humidity and a temperature of between 40°F and 65°F (see Aging Your Charcuterie, page 197). Poke a hole in one of the skin "tails" on each breast half and either run an S hook or some string through it. Hang the breasts on a rack so they are not touching each other or anything else.

How long to hang your prosciutto? From 2 weeks to 3 months, depending on the size of the breasts, the amount of fat, and the temperature and humidity. If you are a beginner, hang the breasts in the refrigerator for 2 weeks before eating them; this also absolves you of the need to create a proper curing chamber. The prosciutto will be tasty, and it should whet your appetite

continued

for a longer cure later. I cure my prosciutto for 2 months in a curing chamber (which is an old refrigerator I've modified) by starting the drying in 85 to 90 percent humidity, then ratcheting it down 5 percent a week each week until I get down to 60 percent, then I hold it there. The longer meat hangs, the more complex it gets: think about the difference between a nice young rosé and a Barolo that's been aging for a generation.

When the prosciutto is ready, you can eat it straightaway or wrap it and store it in the fridge for a few months. It will continue to dry out in the fridge, however. It also freezes well for a year or more. To serve, slice it on the diagonal as thinly as you can.

Note: What happens if while making prosciutto, you end up with something more like jerky? All is not lost. If you really can't slice it paper-thin because it has hardened too much, finely dice it and add it to a long-simmering stew. The prosciutto will soften and you'll appreciate its chewy texture in the stew. Or, you can do what my friend and fellow charcutier Bob del Grosso does. He wraps the meat in wet cheesecloth, vacuum seals it or sticks it in a zipper-top bag, and puts it in the fridge until it softens. The dark jerkylike color won't change, but the meat will be just as pliable as if you did it right the first time.

SPICKGANS, GERMAN SMOKED GOOSE BREAST

If you have a smoker, you can make a German variation on goose prosciutto called *spickgans*. This specialty of Pomerania, on Germany's Baltic coast, is cured goose breast smoked over a combination of juniper boughs, beech, alder or oak, and peat moss.

It is crazy good, and clearly always has been. A November, 1900 menu from New York City's Metropole Hotel and Golden Rod Rathskeller shows Pomeranian smoked goose selling for more than three times the price of regular smoked goose. An order would set you back a hefty $18.62 in today's dollars.

A domesticated goose is best for this recipe, but you could use a plump specklebelly or Canada goose breast, too.

DIFFICULTY: ✳ ✳ ✳

MAKES 2 GOOSE BREASTS

PREP TIME: 3 DAYS, TO CURE

COOK TIME: 7 HOURS, TO SMOKE

Skin-on breasts from 1 large goose (about 2 pounds)
½ cup peaty Scotch whisky, optional
3 tablespoons (1½ ounces or 44 grams) kosher salt
Heaping ½ teaspoon (4 grams) Insta Cure No. 1
  (see page 196)
2 tablespoons sugar
1 tablespoon crushed juniper
1 tablespoon freshly ground black pepper

If you are using the Scotch, put the goose breasts in a bowl and coat them with the whisky. Put the breasts into a sealable container just large enough to hold them and refrigerate overnight.

The next day, mix all the remaining ingredients in a bowl. Drain the goose breasts, or just pat them dry if you have not done the Scotch soak.

Massage the spice mixture into the meat, making sure every bit of the breasts is covered. Put the breasts into a container that just barely fits the meat. Pour in any excess spice mixture, cover tightly, and refrigerate for 3 to 4 days. Every day during the curing process, turn the goose breasts over so they are evenly coated.

When the meat has cured, it will be dark red and slightly firm to the touch throughout. Rinse it briefly under cold running water and pat it dry. Let the meat sit out in a cool place for 2 to 4 hours, preferably with some sort of breeze or fan on it. Alternately, you can leave it to dry in the refrigerator uncovered overnight.

Truss the meat as you would a roast or stuff it into sausage netting. If you use netting, wear an apron, as you will need to manhandle the goose breast into the netting. Take your time and do it little by little. Tie off the ends of the string or netting, leaving enough of the breast end with the most fat sticking out—this should be the thick end of the breast—to hang. You want the fattiest part of the goose breast at the top, so the fat can drip down and keep the meat moist.

Hang the breasts in a cold smoker and smoke over beech, alder, oak, cherry, or apple wood. Start the smoke cold and gradually bring the temperature up. Your goal is to have the internal temperature of the thickest part of the goose breast reach 140°F to 150°F by the end of cooking. Move the goose breasts out of the smoker and allow them to return to room temperature before refrigerating.

The smoked goose will last 10 days in the refrigerator, or a year if well sealed and frozen.

DUCK JERKY

Who doesn't love jerky? It is a staple in the duck blind and on a road trip, and it is the perfect use for "off" birds like spoonies, fishy divers, or snow geese. Once the fat is removed, there's no fishy flavor. If you're not a hunter, duck jerky makes a cool addition to a charcuterie plate.

This recipe makes a jerky that is dry enough to store at room temperature—although the fridge is best for really long storage—but pliable enough to keep it meaty.

I designed this recipe for a dehydrator, but if you don't have one, you can dehydrate it in your oven set to warm. Another option is to use the inside of your car in summer. I've done this when the temperatures get beyond 100°F, which is often in Sacramento. Works like a charm.

The porcini powder is made by grinding dried porcini (available in most supermarkets) in a spice grinder or coffee grinder.

DIFFICULTY: ✳ ✳

MAKES ABOUT 1½ POUNDS

PREP TIME: 24 TO 48 HOURS

COOK TIME: 6 TO 8 HOURS

3 pounds defatted skinless duck or goose breasts

2 cups water

½ cup Worcestershire sauce or soy sauce

2 tablespoons plus 2 teaspoons (1½ ounces or 40 grams) kosher salt

Heaping ½ teaspoon (4 grams) Insta Cure No. 1 (page 196), optional

3 tablespoons brown sugar

1 tablespoon cayenne pepper or hot paprika

1 teaspoon garlic powder

1 teaspoon dried thyme

1 teaspoon porcini powder

Slice the breasts into strips about ¼ inch wide. In a large bowl, combine the water, Worcestershire sauce, kosher salt, curing salt, sugar, cayenne, garlic powder, thyme, and porcini powder and mix well. Put the meat strips into the marinade and massage them well to to coat evenly. Pour everything into a zipper-top bag or nonreactive container, close tightly, and put in the fridge.

Let the meat cure for at least 24 and up to 48 hours. The longer the meat is in the mix, the saltier it will be, and the longer it will keep at room temperature. During the marinating process, massage the meat with the marinade every now and again to keep all the pieces in contact with the liquid.

Remove the meat from the bag and pat dry with paper towels. If you have a dehydrator, follow the instructions that came with it for making jerky (I dehydrate mine at 130°F). If you do not have a dehydrator, lay the strips on a wire rack set over a rimmed baking sheet to catch the drippings, and put the baking sheet in the oven. Turn the oven on to the warm setting and leave the meat in the oven for 6 to 8 hours, until it is dried out but still pliable. I leave the oven door ajar for air circulation.

Store the jerky in the fridge indefinitely, or at room temperature for up to 1 month.

PÂTÉS AND RILLETTES

These are the gateways to more involved charcuterie. Pâtés and rillettes are easy to make, require no special equipment, and will last for a couple of weeks in the fridge and for months in the freezer if vacuum sealed. Both use parts of the duck many cooks don't normally bother with: wings, meat from the carcass, and giblets.

Generally, a pâté is a relatively smooth meat spread meant to be eaten on bread. Rillettes are also best on bread, but they are much coarser. Both scream out for pickles as an accompaniment. Tradition would have you use those little French cornichons, which are nice, but any good pickle will do, from a Polish sour dill to Korean kimchi. It's the acidic tang you need to balance the richness of a pâté or rillettes.

DUCK LIVER PÂTÉ

This is probably the easiest charcuterie recipe you can make: it's basically sautéed duck livers and shallots, mixed with herbs, brandy, and duck fat, then buzzed in a food processor or blender. Easy peasy. This is my master recipe, which I play with depending on what herbs look good in the garden and how boozy I want to make it. Goose livers can be treated the same way. Serve the pâté with good bread—toasted is even better—and some pickles.

DIFFICULTY: ✴ ✴

SERVES 6 TO 8 AS AN
APPETIZER

PREP TIME: 25 MINUTES,
MOSTLY COOLING TIME FOR
THE LIVERS

COOK TIME: 10 MINUTES

3 tablespoons duck fat or unsalted butter

⅓ cup minced shallot or yellow onion

8 ounces duck livers

2 teaspoons minced fresh sage

1 tablespoon capers

Kosher salt and freshly ground pepper

2 shots of brandy

¼ cup unsalted butter, plus 1 tablespoon more, if needed

½ cup heavy cream

In a sauté pan, heat the duck fat over medium heat. Add the shallot and sauté for about 3 minutes, until soft but not browned. Add the livers, toss to coat with the fat, and turn up the heat to medium-high. Sear the duck livers for 2 minutes. Turn the livers over and add the sage, capers, and some salt and pepper. Let this cook for 1 minute.

Remove the pan from the heat and add the brandy. Return the pan to the stove top, turn up the heat to high, and scrape up any browned bits from the bottom of the pan with a wooden spoon. Let the brandy boil down for about 3 minutes, until syrupy. Turn off the heat and move the liver mixture to a plate or small baking sheet to cool. Let cool for 15 minutes.

While the liver is cooling, cut the ¼ cup butter into small pieces and set out at room temperature; you want the butter cool but not rock hard. Move the liver mixture to the bowl of a food processor or blender and add the butter and cream. Start by pulsing a few times. Scrape down the sides of the bowl with a rubber spatula. Repeat this twice, then run the food processor continuously until you have a thick puree. If you want a perfectly smooth puree, push it through a fine-mesh sieve to filter out any stray bits.

Taste the mixture and add salt, pepper, or even a little more brandy, if you like. If you think the pâté is too loose, add another 1 tablespoon cool butter. Remember, the pâté will tighten up in the fridge a bit.

Scrape the pâté out of the bowl with the spatula into a plastic container or ramekins. Cover with plastic wrap and chill for at least 1 hour before serving. Store any leftover pâté in a container with plastic wrap pressed directly onto its surface, or pour melted butter, lard, or duck fat over the surface to form a cap. The pâté will keep in the fridge for 2 weeks or in the freezer for 6 months.

DUCK OR GOOSE RILLETTES

Rillettes are basically a preserved, fatty meat product pulverized enough to be spread on bread. Some versions are smooth, but most are coarse. It is a great way to prepare meats that are very tough, yet very flavorful—like wild ducks and geese. Domestic birds work well, too, of course, and cook more quickly.

   If you are a hunter, rillettes are a fine use for the meat from legs and wings, and whether you hunt or not, rillettes are a fantastic appetizer or snack, spread over crusty bread and served with pickles. What's more, rillettes keep forever. Since the meat is presalted, and helped by the preserving nature of the alcohol and herbs, you can keep rillettes for months in the refrigerator.

   I normally make my rillettes with snow goose legs, Armagnac, and rue, an extremely bitter herb with a beguiling aroma. You can use parsley in place of the rue.

DIFFICULTY: ✶ ✶ ✶

MAKES A LITTLE MORE
THAN 1 PINT

PREP TIME: 13 HOURS

COOK TIME: 5 HOURS

2 pounds duck or goose legs and wings

3 tablespoons (1½ ounces or 44 grams) kosher salt

3 tablespoons dried thyme

8 cups duck or goose stock (page 222) or vegetable stock

3 bay leaves

About 1¼ cups duck fat or goose fat

2 to 3 tablespoons Armagnac or other brandy

**1½ teaspoons to 1 tablespoon minced rue leaves,
   or 1 to 2 tablespoons minced fresh flat-leaf parsley**

Freshly ground pepper

If you are using domesticated duck or goose legs, start by trimming them of excess fat. Use these trimmings to render your own duck fat (page 203) for use later (for mixing with the rillettes). In a large bowl, stir together the salt and thyme leaves. Add the legs and wings and massage the salt mixture into the meat, making sure everything is well coated.

Put the legs and wings in a nonreactive container and pour any salt-thyme mixture over the top. Cover and refrigerate for 8 to 12 hours. The longer you go, the saltier your rillettes will be, and the longer they will keep in the fridge. I like to salt them the night before and cook them around midmorning the following day.

When you are ready, rinse off the cure well. Arrange the legs in a large pot and cover with the stock; add water or white wine if the level of the liquid does not cover the legs. Add the bay leaves. Cover, then either cook on the stove top over low heat or in a 225°F oven for 4 to 8 hours; old, wild birds will need the full 8 hours. You want the meat to be falling off the bone. Check after about 2 hours to see if you have enough liquid and add more if needed.

When the legs and wings are cooked, turn off the heat and let them cool. Ideally, you refrigerate everything to solidify any fat (you can use the fat later for mixing with the meat). When the meat is cool, pull off the skin and discard it, or run it through the fine die of a meat grinder. Shred the meat and place in a large bowl with the ground skin, if using.

Taste the remaining stock to see how salty it is. You will need a little for the rillettes, but you want to know how much to add—without oversalting everything. Add a little of the stock to the rillettes and beat together with a stout wooden spoon or potato masher until the liquid is incorporated.

Add 2 tablespoons of the duck fat and beat it in. Keep adding duck fat until the mixture becomes creamy. Do this little by little. When a spoonful of the rillettes tastes creamy, not dryish, add 2 tablespoons Armagnac, half of the rue, and some pepper. Beat it in well. Taste it: you should be able to taste both the Armagnac and the rue; neither should be overpowering. Add more of both ingredients if needed.

Press the rillettes into ramekins or other nonmetal containers. Melt some duck fat and pour fat to a depth of ¼ inch on the rillettes to seal the top. Cover with a lid or foil and store in the fridge. It is best to let your rillettes ripen for a week before serving, but it is perfectly fine to eat them straightaway.

To eat the rillettes, pop off the cold fat cap and set it in a warm place; it will melt. Eat as much as you'd like, then flatten out the remaining rillettes, pour the melted duck fat over the top again, and return to the fridge. The rillettes will keep like this for at least 2 months.

"The key thing for me is embracing the fact that there's fat on a duck, and we use all that fat to the best of our ability."

—CHEF TONY MAWS, CRAIGIE ON MAIN

SAUSAGES

Sausages are a mainstay of the charcutier's art. Once you know how to control the seasoning, the fat content, the grind, the size, and the level of smoke in your links, you'll never look back.

The recipe for Duck Sausages, Hunter's Style on page 185 is a master recipe for a basic duck or goose sausage. Use it for all the detailed instructions on grinding, mixing, and forming links. Beyond that will be recipes that will increase in difficulty, until you get to salami: salami, or dry-cured sausages, are the pinnacle of the sausage maker's craft.

Equipment and Casings

You will need a few special pieces of equipment to make sausages. First, you must have a meat grinder. I use a dedicated grinder, but the grinding attachment on a KitchenAid or other stand mixer works fine. You also need a dedicated stuffer. I use an LEM brand stainless-steel vertical stuffer, which costs about a hundred dollars. Avoid both the KitchenAid stuffer attachment and any cornucopia-shaped stuffer; neither works well. Finally, you need a wooden rack on which to hang sausages to dry; a clothes rack will do.

If you are a beginner, you can skip stuffing the sausage meat into casings and make sausage patties instead. You can also wrap your sausage meat in blanched cabbage or chard leaves, roll it in bulgur to make Lebanese kibbeh, wrap it in caul fat (available at good butcher shops, though you may need to order it in advance), or enclose it in grape leaves.

If you plan on stuffing your sausages, you will need hog, sheep, or beef casings. Hog casings are the easiest to buy; they come in two diameters, narrow and large. Nearly every good butcher has them, and they are inexpensive. Most come heavily salted in plastic tubs and must be soaked in warm water for a half hour or more to reconstitute them. Because they are cheap, always soak more than you think you will need to be sure you have enough. You also can use narrow sheep casings or very wide beef casings, but you may need to special order them from your butcher, or buy them online from a dealer such as Butcher & Packer or The Sausage Maker. You can buy artificial casings made from edible collagen, but I never use them. They make me feel like I am eating cellophane.

Sausage Making 101

Temperature is vital. Your equipment, meat and fat, and all your liquids must be cold before you begin. This is especially true when you deal with duck fat, which has a very low melting point. Once you begin, you need to keep putting things in your fridge and freezer to keep them cold, so make room ahead of time.

You want your meat and fat close to, but not actually, freezing. Why all this emphasis on temperature? The answers are sanitation and chemistry. Well-chilled meat and fat are less likely to spoil. Chemistry comes in when you grind and mix the meat and fat. If they are too warm, the fat can smear over the meat, coating it. This destroys the structure of the sausage by limiting the ability of the meat to bind to itself in the mixing stage: when you mix the ground sausage, the meat creates a bind much like gluten does when you knead bread. If your meat is too warm, the fat breaks this bind and you have made spicy cat food, crumbly and nasty.

Sausages need fat, but which fat? Duck fat, although wonderful, does not make a great charcuterie fat, at least in most cases. It is too soft, is too unsaturated, and has a melting point that is too low. Fat from a duck or goose starts to sweat at room temperature, which is disastrous in sausage making. The problem with soft fat is "smear," as already noted. Duck fat smears far more easily than pork fat does.

I recommend pork fatback for sausages and salami, as it is neither too soft like duck fat nor too hard like beef tallow. Pork fat also has a neutral taste.

Once you have several batches of sausages under your belt, you can start thinking about perfecting your craft. Here are ten tricks and tips I've learned over the years:

1. When you make fresh sausages, use fresh ingredients—fresh herbs, fresh garlic, and so on—if possible. You will notice the difference.

2. When you use dried spices, such as peppercorns, fennel seeds, or coriander seeds, toast them in a dry pan before adding them to the sausage mixture. It heightens their flavor, even weeks later. Don't toast dried herbs, however, or you will burn them.

3. After you've ground the salt, spices, and meats together, you can leave this loose mixture in the fridge for several hours, or even overnight, before you mix it with the paddle attachment of a stand mixer or with a wooden spoon. This resting period will help the mixture bind better, which will prevent crumbly sausages. You can also do this before you grind. However, don't let the mixture rest after you have mixed it, as it will become very difficult to stuff into casings.

4. Stuff your sausage fairly loosely when making the initial coil. This gives you more wiggle room to make links. If your initial coil is too taut, you won't be able to twist each link enough to keep the whole coil from unraveling. Stuffing too tightly also increases the chance that the casing will burst, which is no fun. Also, vary the length of the links according to the richness of the mixture. This is a matter of opinion, of course, but I think leaner links should be long and skinny and fatty ones should be short and plump.

5. When trimming meat, spend the time to trim off the silver skin, the whitish membrane that encases many individual muscles. This is not difficult on domestic ducks and geese, but it is on wild birds, which is why I use only breast meat when making sausages with wild ducks and geese.

6. The poorer the meat quality, the finer the grind. If I am dealing with shot-up ducks or an ancient bird, I will pass it through the fine die a second time. That second grind will greatly improve your sausage.

7. Choose your fat wisely. Use pork fatback, if possible, though there is plenty of suitable fat in pork shoulder, too. Avoid using fatty bits that are stringy or too soft.

8. The liquid you use to moisten your links matters a lot. The same sausage recipe made with red wine will taste different from one made with white wine. Vinegar will change it again, as will water, fruit juice, or liqueur; I've added ouzo to a few of my recipes. Put some thought into not only what kind of liquid you want to use but also its quality. If you won't drink it, don't use it. Also err on using less liquid rather than more, especially when the liquid is acidic, like vinegar or wine. Too much acid can break the bind in your sausage.

9. The most important thing to learn is balance. Make enough sausages, and after a while, you will develop an eye for the correct quantity of spices or herbs, the best length for links, and so on. All of the flavor elements in a good sausage are in harmony. Savory is easy, as is salty. Sour can come from vinegar, and sweet from any number of sources. Herbs need to play well with one another, as do spices.

10. My final bit of advice is to write everything down. If you don't keep accurate notes, you will never be able to tinker with your recipes, and most importantly, you will never be able to recapture those moments of perfection.

DUCK SAUSAGES, HUNTER'S STYLE

To me, "hunter's style" means coarse grained and flavored with traditional European game seasonings, such as caraway, juniper, and sage. This recipe has all three, with sage as its main seasoning.

If you are using domestic birds, use either leg or breast meat. If you are using wild birds, use only breast meat, unless you have lots of goose legs. Wild duck legs are too small to bother with for this recipe.

Before you begin this recipe, review the information on sausage making on pages 182 to 184. These sausages are perfect in Cassoulet (page 130), in the English Duck Pie that follows, or simply pan roasted or grilled.

DIFFICULTY: ✳ ✳ ✳ ✳

MAKES ABOUT 4 POUNDS
(ABOUT 16 SAUSAGES)

PREP TIME: 2 HOURS

COOK TIME: 15 MINUTES

3 pounds duck or goose meat (see headnote)

1 pound pork fat, preferably fatback

2 tablespoons (1 ounce or 30 grams) kosher salt

1 teaspoon quatre épices or five-spice powder

1 tablespoon juniper berries, ground

2 tablespoons chopped fresh sage

2 teaspoons caraway seeds

1 tablespoon freshly ground pepper

10 to 12 feet hog casings, optional

⅓ cup red wine, chilled

Put your meat grinder or stand mixer grinding attachment and coarse and fine dies in the freezer. Put a large bowl and your sausage stuffer in the refrigerator. Chop the meat and fat into chunks 1 to 2 inches across, cutting the fat a little smaller than the meat. As you work, put the pieces in a bowl set in a larger bowl filled with ice to keep the ingredients cold.

Add the salt, *quatre épices*, juniper, and half each of the sage, caraway, and pepper to the meat and fat and mix quickly to combine. Cover the bowl with plastic wrap and put it in the freezer for 30 minutes.

If you are stuffing the sausage meat into casings, put the casings in warm water to cover and set aside to soak for 30 minutes or so.

Remove your grinding equipment and bowl from the freezer and fridge and outfit the grinder with the coarse die. Working quickly, push the sausage mixture through the grinder, capturing it in the cold bowl. (If you are using the KitchenAid attachment, use it on level 4, about medium-fast.) When all of the mixture is ground, put it in the fridge and clean up the grinder and work area.

Add the remaining half of the sage, caraway, and pepper and the wine to the ground mixture. Using a stand mixer fitted with the paddle attachment on its lowest speed— or a wooden spoon or clean hands—mix the sausage well for 1 to 2 minutes. This is where cold meat matters: you get a better bind by mixing longer, but the longer you mix, the warmer the sausage gets. It's a balancing act. You want the mixture to look sticky and begin to bind to itself.

If you're making patties, you're done. You can store the sausage in bulk, tightly covered, for a day or so, or make patties, seal them, and freeze for up to 9 months.

If you are making links, put the mixture back in the fridge and clean up again. I cannot stress enough how important it is to work clean. Hot, soapy water is your friend.

continued

continued from previous page

Remove the casings from their soaking water, and run warm water through them. This flushes them and also reveals any leaks. If you find a leak, cut out that part of the casing. Remove the sausage stuffer from the fridge. Slip a casing onto the tube of your sausage stuffer, and leave about 6 inches of the casing trailing off the end of the tube. You need this to tie off later. Pack the sausage into the stuffer and start cranking it down slowly. You want to push out air from the stuffer first. This is why you don't tie off the trailing end immediately.

When the meat starts to come out, use one hand to regulate how fast the casing slips off the tube. You want it to be slow and regular. Coil the filled casing as you go, and do not be tempted to make links just yet. Remember to leave about 6 inches of the casing trailing off the other end, too. When the casing is full, tie off one end with a double knot or use kitchen twine.

Now, using both hands, start at the tied-off end of the coil and pinch off what will become 2 links. I like my links about 6 inches long, but you could go longer or shorter. Gently pinch down and wriggle the sausage back and forth until you can feel your fingers touch. Then, with a flip, roll the link you just made forward three to five times. Move down the coil and do the same thing, only this time you must flip the link backward; it's a little harder. This alternating twist will help keep your links from unraveling too easily. If all of this twisting is too much for you, tie the links off with kitchen twine. Repeat until all of the sausage mixture is in casings.

Working from both ends, gently compress the meat in each link; this should reveal any air pockets. You want the meat to be tight in the casings. Sterilize a needle by heating it in a burner's flame until it glows, then use the needle to pierce the casing wherever there is an air pocket. Gently compress the meat in the links again. Repeat this process until there are no more air pockets.

Place your hanging rack in a place where you won't mind drips on the floor. Hang your sausages on it, making sure they do not touch one another. Leave your links to dry for an hour or two.

Layer the sausages in a large storage container, separating the layers with paper towels, and place the container in the fridge. If you are making sausages in cold weather, it's even better to let them hang overnight, but the temperature needs to be no warmer than about 42°F and no colder than about 32°F. You do no want the sausages to develop bacteria or to freeze.

Eat the sausages the next day, or divide them into practical-size packets and store them in the refrigerator for up to 1 week or in the freezer for up to a year.

ENGLISH DUCK PIE

This is an absolute meat bomb of a pie. It is based on the recipe for English Pork Pie in Hugh Fearnley-Whittingstall's *The River Cottage Meat Book*. I have adapted it with my own spices—and lots and lots of duck.

DIFFICULTY: ★ ★ ★ ★

SERVES 8 TO 12

PREP TIME: 30 MINUTES

COOK TIME: 5 HOURS, INCLUDING BRAISING TIME FOR THE FILLING

Although domesticated or wild duck or goose meat works great here, I find that this is an especially good recipe to use with "off" birds, such as snow geese and diver or sea ducks, which need to be skinless and have all of the fat removed.

Know that this pie is for cold days, for people who do a lot of manual labor, or for hunters coming in from the field. If this does not apply to you, just serve thin slices. Accompany them with a good-quality mustard and lots of pickles. You need the acidity and zing of the mustard to counteract the meat and fat. Otherwise, expect a bad case of the meat sweats.

The one piece of special equipment you need to make this pie is an 8- to 10-inch springform pan. This recipe is time-consuming, but some steps can be done a day or more in advance, and when you are finished, the pie will keep, well wrapped, in the fridge for up to 2 weeks.

FILLING

2 pounds duck or goose legs

Kosher salt

2 cups Basic Duck Stock (page 222) or chicken or beef stock

1½ pounds Duck Sausages, Hunter's Style (page 185), or pork sausage, preferably Polish or bratwurst, casing removed

10 ounces pancetta or bacon, minced

12 fresh sage leaves, minced

3-inch rosemary sprig, chopped

2 teaspoons freshly ground black pepper

1 teaspoon cayenne pepper

1 teaspoon kosher salt

CRUST

4¼ cups all-purpose flour, plus more for rolling

1½ teaspoons kosher salt

7 tablespoons lard

7 tablespoons unsalted butter or duck fat

1 cup warm water

1 egg, lightly beaten

1 egg, lightly beaten, for egg wash

Start this recipe by braising the duck legs for the filling. Preheat the oven to 300°F. Salt the legs well and arrange them in a Dutch oven or other large, heavy pot with a lid. Pour in the stock, cover the pot, and put the pot in the oven. Cook for 1½ to 3 hours, until the meat is almost falling off the bones. The timing varies depending on how old the birds are.

When the legs are done, remove them from the pot, let them cool until they can be handled, and then pull the meat off the bones. Reserve the meat for the filling. (This step can be done up to a few days in advance; store the meat in an airtight container in the refrigerator.)

Now, make the crust. In a large bowl, stir together the flour and salt and make a well in the center. In a small saucepan, heat the lard and butter over low heat just until melted. Pour the melted fat, warm water, and egg into the well. Starting at the rim of the well, and using a fork, gradually draw the flour into the liquid ingredients. Continue to incorporate the flour until the ingredients come together in a shaggy mass. Knead it by hand in the bowl for 3 to 4 minutes, until a cohesive ball forms. Wrap the dough in plastic wrap and refrigerate for at least 1 hour. (The dough can be made up to 1 day in advance.)

continued

To assemble the pie, have ready an 8- to 10-inch spring-form pan. Cut off about one-fourth of the dough, re-cover, and set aside. On a floured work surface, roll out the remaining dough into a circle ¼ inch thick and large enough to cover the bottom and sides of the pan. This is a thick crust that you can manhandle, so you don't need to be too dainty. The diameter of the pan will determine how thin you roll out the dough. Carefully transfer the dough circle to the pan and press it gently into the bottom and up the sides. Ideally, it will reach all of the way to the rim.

To finish making the filling, in a bowl, combine the duck meat, sausages, pancetta, sage, rosemary, black pepper, cayenne pepper, and salt and mix well. Turn the filling into the pie crust. Preheat the oven to 350°F.

To make the top crust, roll out the reserved dough into a circle large enough to cover the top of the pie. It should be large enough to overlap the rim of the pan slightly and about the same thickness as the bottom crust. Paint the top edges of the bottom crust with some of the beaten egg, then carefully lay the top crust over

the filling. Seal the top and bottom crusts by crimping the edges together. Cut a hole in the center of the top crust about ½ inch in diameter.

Bake the pie for 30 minutes. Lower the heat to 325°F and continue to bake for 1¼ hours.

Remove the pie from the oven, let cool for 5 minutes, then carefully release the pan sides. Paint the whole pie with the remaining beaten egg and bake for another 15 to 20 minutes, until golden.

Remove the pie from the oven and let it rest. There is a chance that the meats may settle, leaving a big gap under the top crust. You can prevent this by first letting the pie cool to room temperature. Reattach the springform pan sides to the pie, then cover the top with plastic wrap. Now top it with a board or flat pot lid about the same shape and size as the top of the pie. Put a weight on the board and refrigerate the pie for at least 12 hours.

Serve the pie chilled or at room temperature.

GOOSE NECK SAUSAGES

If you have ever seen a goose, you will immediately be struck by how long its neck is. Well, that long neck makes the perfect sausage casing. Sadly, I did not invent this. I thought I had when I stuffed the neck of a Canada goose with sausage and smoked it. But then I realized that the French had been doing it since the Middle Ages. Damn. Reinvented the wheel again. Oh well, it's still good.

This is the highest use of a part of the bird that would otherwise be rendered into fat or go into the stockpot. Goose skin can be surreally tasty, a combination of crispiness and fat that a regular hog casing cannot provide. While you can do this with duck necks, especially those of pintail or Moulard, goose skin is best because it is long enough to make a proper sausage.

Look for geese and ducks with intact necks in Asian markets or a local farmers' market. You may have to ask in advance, but if you know of a farmer who raises geese and ducks in your area, it should not be too difficult to score some necks.

If you raise birds yourself, or you are a hunter, here's how you prepare the necks when you want to make these sausages:

- Pluck the bird right up to its chin. You want as much length as you can muster for the neck. Do not use necks that have skin that is torn badly or has holes in it. Push the actual neck out of the skin; it will be attached by little fibers, but these pull off easily.

- Remove the windpipe and any other organ-looking bits from the skin. Wash the neck skin thoroughly inside and out.

- Dry the neck skin well and lay it flat, or folded over once on itself. The skin retracts when removed from the neck, so you want it to be as long as possible. Wrap the skin snugly in plastic wrap or vacuum seal it and freeze it. It will keep for up to a year.

When it is time to stuff the skin, you will need a sharp knife, some fine kitchen twine, kitchen shears, and, of course, some sausage meat. Here is how you stuff it:

- Start by tying off the narrow end of each neck with the twine. Tie it well with a double knot!

- Stuff the meat into the skin by hand, with a piping bag, or with a plastic bag with a corner cut out.

- Leave at least ½ inch space between the meat and the edge of the fat end of the neck.

- Gather the fat end of the neck and gently squeeze the meat into the narrow end. You want to compress the meat into the skin to make it pretty tight. Don't overdo this, though, or you might undo the knot on the narrow end.

- Tie off the fat end well with the twine. Trim the twine, then trim the loose ends of the neck skin with kitchen shears. Don't cut too close to the twine, but make it look presentable.

The keys to cooking these sausages are getting good color on the skin and slow cooking the insides. Here are three ways to cook them:

- Gently brown the skin in a frying pan over medium heat. You will need a little fat to keep the skin from sticking to the pan. Then put the sausages in a 325°F oven for 15 to 20 minutes, depending on their size.

- Leave a loop of kitchen twine at the narrow end of each sausage and hang them in a smoker for 45 minutes to 1 hour, until the internal temperature registers 160°F. This is my preferred method, as the smokiness really adds to the sausage.

- Leave a loop of kitchen twine at the narrow end of each sausage and hang them from the top rack of an oven set at 300°F for 45 minutes to an hour. Even this method will yield more even browning than on the stove top. If you do the oven method, put a baking sheet under the sausages to catch any drips.

What to stuff them with? Well, that's up to you. You can stuff them with any regular sausage meat, or you can get as exotic as you want. At his Double Crown restaurant in New York City, chef Brad Farmerie served duck neck sausages stuffed with ground duck, foie gras, and wild mushrooms. "But my favorite was when we stuffed them with boudin noir or black pudding," he said. "I loved that contrast."

Me? I'm partial to stuffing goose neck sausages with ground giblets from the geese themselves, flavored with wild sage. It may be a bit hard core, but if you're willing to use a neck as a casing, why not fill it with seasoned ground giblets?

SMOKED GOOSE SAUSAGES, POLISH STYLE

These are deep, rich, smoky sausages that go well with lentils or other beans. They are also good with wild rice or *farro*. And, like almost any sausage, they are excellent with sauerkraut and some good mustard. This recipe works with any waterfowl, domesticated or wild. Use leg or breast meat if using domesticated birds, and use only breast meat if using wild birds, unless you have lots of goose legs. Wild duck legs are too small.

You will make these sausages exactly like the hunter's style sausages on page 185, but with the added step of smoking. If you have a smoker, just follow the directions that came with it to set it up and smoke sausages. If you don't have a smoker, you can convert a kettle grill into a smoker fairly easily (see page 43). If you don't have a smoker or a kettle grill, these sausages are perfectly good unsmoked, too. You will need to cook them, however.

As for which wood to use, Polish sausages are excellent smoked over cherry or apple wood. Oak, beech, and maple are also good choices. The dry milk helps the sausages retain moisture during smoking. If you are not smoking these links, omit the dry milk. And if you cannot find dry milk, you can still get a good result even if you do smoke them, as I explain in the method.

DIFFICULTY: ✱ ✱ ✱ ✱

MAKES 2½ POUNDS
(TEN 6-INCH SAUSAGES)

PREP TIME: 1½ HOURS

COOK TIME: 3 HOURS

2 pounds goose or duck meat

8 ounces pork fat, preferably fatback

1 tablespoon plus 1 teaspoon (20 grams) kosher salt

Heaping ½ teaspoon (4 grams) Insta Cure No. 1 (page 196)

¼ cup dry milk, optional

1 tablespoon minced fresh rosemary

5 cloves garlic, finely minced (about 2 tablespoons)

1 teaspoon dried marjoram

1 tablespoon freshly ground pepper

¼ cup red wine, chilled

10 to 20 feet hog casings

To make these sausages, follow the directions for the hunter's style sausages on page 185, adding the curing salt, the dry milk, the herbs, and the pepper with the kosher salt and adding the wine when you beat the mixture with the stand mixer.

After the links have hung to dry for 1 hour, set up your smoker and gently smoke the sausages for 3 to 4 hours, until the interior of a link registers about 160°F. Remove the sausages from the smoker and shock in an ice-water bath for 5 minutes. Pat dry and store in the fridge for up to a week, or freeze for up to a year.

If you are not using dry milk, before you put the links in the smoker, fill a stockpot or other large pot with water and heat it to 160°F. The water should be steaming, not simmering. Gently add the links and poach them for 20 minutes. Meanwhile, ready an ice-water bath. The moment the links come out of the hot water, shock them in the ice-water bath for 5 minutes. Dry them well and proceed with smoking as directed above. This combination of poaching and shocking helps the sausages retain moisture. If you fail to do this, the links will shrivel.

Because you have smoked the sausages, they are cooked, and to serve them, you need only reheat them. Make sure you do not overcook the links at this point, or they will get crumbly and sad.

If you have not smoked the sausages, my baseline method for cooking fresh sausages is to preheat the oven to 325°F, put a little oil in an ovenproof sauté pan, brown one side of the sausages, then pop the whole thing in the oven for 15 minutes.

DUCK HOT DOGS

The hot dog. An American classic. Something everyone has an opinion on, and something few people actually know how to make. A good dog is as memorable as a bad dog is horrible. And I've had some bad hot dogs, notably those made from chicken or turkey. So why would a duck hot dog be better? In a word, *fat*. In two words, *duck fat*. A duck hot dog is like eating a burger made from a ground rib-eye steak. It is a statement.

This sausage is unusual in that it is an all-duck sausage—no pork fat. You can only do this by emulsifying the sausage. Emulsify? As in salad dressing or hollandaise? Exactly. Only emulsifying meat is a little harder than emulsifying a hollandaise. Everything involved in the process must be superclean and supercold—colder even than for regular sausage. Oh, and you need a big food processor. And some dry milk doesn't hurt, either.

If all goes well, you will end up with a sausage that is light yet rich and has a very smooth texture. Ideally, it will be neither too smoky nor too heavily spiced. And when you take a bite, it will taste like what you want it to be, in this case, a hot dog—a very good, very ducky hot dog.

Before you begin this recipe, review the information on sausage making on pages 182 to 184.

I generally make these links with the breast meat from wild ducks or geese, but domesticated birds work just as well. You could use meat from goose legs or domesticated duck legs, too.

DIFFICULTY: ✱ ✱ ✱ ✱ ✱

MAKES ABOUT 2 POUNDS
(ABOUT 8 TO 10 LINKS)

PREP TIME: 1⅓ HOURS

COOK TIME: 2½ HOURS

1½ pounds duck or goose meat

8 ounces duck or goose skin

About 10 feet narrow hog or sheep casings

Scant ½ cup ice water

4 ounces rendered duck or goose fat, frozen

Scant ½ cup dry milk

1 tablespoon plus 1 teaspoon (20 grams) kosher salt

Heaping ½ teaspoon (4 grams) Insta Cure No. 1
   (see page 196)

1 tablespoon sweet paprika

1 teaspoon garlic powder

1 teaspoon dried marjoram

½ teaspoon freshly ground pepper

½ teaspoon smoked paprika

Put your meat grinder or stand mixer grinding attachment and fine die in the freezer, and a large bowl and the sausage stuffer in the refrigerator.

Chop the meat into chunks 1 to 2 inches across. Put the chunks in a bowl and put the bowl in the fridge. Chop the skin into about ½-inch pieces, put the pieces in a bowl, and put the bowl in the freezer.

I generally use hog casings, but the narrower sheep casings are more traditional for hot dogs. Put the casings in warm water to cover and set aside to soak for 30 minutes or so.

After the skin pieces have been in the freezer for about 1 hour, they should be stiff but not rock hard. Remove your grinding equipment and bowl from the freezer and outfit the grinder with the fine die. Working quickly, pass the skin through the grinder, capturing it in the bowl. Then pass the meat through grinder into the bowl. Check the temperature: if the ground mixture is below 32°F, you can proceed. If not, put it in the freezer until it is cold enough and clean up your work area.

You will now need to work fast, so have everything ready.

When the ground mixture is between 28°F and 32°F, put it into a large food processor along with the ice water and buzz for 30 to 60 seconds, until emulsified. Add the duck fat, dry milk, kosher salt, curing salt, sweet paprika, garlic powder, marjoram, pepper, and smoked paprika and buzz for 1 to 2 minutes, until emulsified. (If your food processor is not big enough to handle this job, you will need to split everything evenly into two batches. Keep the second batch of meat, skin, and fat in the freezer while you work with the first batch.)

Remove the sausage stuffer from the fridge and put the sausage mixture in it. Put the stuffer, now filled with the sausage mixture, into the fridge and clean up your work area.

Remove the casings from their soaking water, and run warm water through them. This flushes them and also reveals any leaks. If you find a leak, cut out that part of the casing. Remove the sausage stuffer from the fridge and stuff the casings as directed in Duck Sausages, Hunter's Style on page 185. Create links of any length you like; I usually make them 6 to 8 inches long. Tie them off with kitchen twine, which will prevent them from unraveling when you poach them.

When all of the links are tied, place your hanging rack in a cool place and hang the links on it while you heat a large pot of water. As the water is heating, sterilize a needle by putting the tip into a flame until it glows. Look for air bubbles in the links and prick any you find with the needle to deflate them.

When the water reaches 160°F to 170°F—it should be steaming, not simmering—gently add the links and poach for 25 minutes. Be careful that the water temperature does not go beyond 178°F, or the links may burst. Meanwhile, ready a large ice-water bath. When the links are done, shock them in the ice-water bath for 5 minutes.

Hang the links to dry again for at least 1 hour or up to overnight if you can hang them in a place between 33°F and 42°F. This will allow what is called a pellicle (membrane) to form, which helps the smoke adhere to the sausage. If you skip this step, your sausages will look sad.

If you have a smoker, follow the directions that came with it to set it up, using oak, apple, maple, or other hardwood. Smoke the sausages for 3 to 5 hours, depending on how smoky you want them. It is important that the smoker be as cool as possible—remember, you've already cooked the sausages. I turn my smoker on, but leave the heater off. If you don't have a smoker, see page 43 for how to fashion one from a kettle grill.

Remove the links from the smoker and return them to the rack. Let them cool on the rack for a couple of hours. Layer the sausages in a large storage container, separating the layers with paper towels, and place the container in the fridge overnight. Eat the links the next day, or divide them into practical-size packets and store them in the refrigerator for up to 10 days or in the freezer for up to a year.

Because you smoked the hot dogs, they are cooked, and you need only reheat them to serve them.

DUCK BRAUNSCHWEIGER

This is another emulsified sausage like the Duck Hot Dogs on page 192, but this one hinges on duck (or goose) liver. As I have already mentioned, I am not a fan of the texture of liver, but I do like its flavor. This means I spend a lot of time chopping livers or masking the texture in other ways. Here, the livers are whipped into an emulsified sausage with the texture of a hot dog.

As with all my sausage recipes, any duck or goose breast meat or any meat from goose legs (wild or domesticated) will work here. Same goes for the livers; you can use those from any sort of waterfowl.

Braunschweiger is very rich, and few people can eat more than a link or two. Serve this German sausage as part of a charcuterie plate, and be sure to have something acidic around to balance it. I recommend sauerkraut and a grainy mustard. Open a dry German Riesling or a crisp German lager to accompany it.

Before you begin this recipe, review the information on sausage making on pages 182 to 184.

DIFFICULTY: ✱ ✱ ✱ ✱

MAKES 3½ POUNDS (TWELVE TO FIFTEEN 6-INCH LINKS)

PREP TIME: 2 HOURS

COOK TIME: 3½ HOURS

1 pound duck or goose livers

About 15 to 20 feet hog casings

2 tablespoons duck fat or unsalted butter

½ cup minced yellow onion

1½ pounds duck or goose meat

12 ounces pork fat, preferably fatback

1 tablespoon plus 2 teaspoons (26 grams) kosher salt

Heaping ½ teaspoon (4 grams) Insta Cure No. 1 (see page 196)

2 teaspoons freshly ground pepper

2 teaspoons dried marjoram

1 teaspoon dry mustard

½ cup semolina flour

⅔ cup crushed ice

Put your meat grinder or stand mixer grinding attachment and fine die in the freezer, and a large bowl and sausage stuffer in the refrigerator.

Remove the livers from the refrigerator and leave at room temperature for at least 20 minutes. This helps them cook more evenly.

Put the casings in warm water to cover and set aside to soak for 30 minutes or so.

In a sauté pan, heat the duck fat over high heat. Add the onion and sauté for 6 to 8 minutes, just until the edges begin to brown. Transfer the onion to a bowl and let cool.

Fill a large saucepan with water and heat to about 170°F. The water should be steaming, not simmering. Add the livers and poach for 5 minutes. Meanwhile, ready an ice-water bath. When the livers are ready, immerse them in the ice-water bath to cool for 5 minutes, then remove and pat dry.

Chop the duck meat and pork fat into chunks 1 to 2 inches across. Put the chunks in a large bowl and add the onion, livers, kosher salt, curing salt, pepper, marjoram, and mustard and mix well.

Remove your grinding equipment and bowl from the freezer and outfit the grinder with the fine die. Working quickly, pass the liver mixture through the grinder into the bowl. Put the bowl in the freezer while you clean up your work area.

You will now need to work fast, so have everything ready. When the ground mixture is between 28°F and 32°F, put it into a large food processor, add the semolina, and pulse to combine. Add the ice and buzz for 1 to 2 minutes, until the mixture is emulsified. (If your food processor is not big enough to handle this job—most home food processors will handle about half this amount—you will need to split everything into two batches. Keep the second batch of meat in the freezer while you work with the first batch.)

Remove the sausage stuffer from the freezer and put the sausage mixture in it. Put the stuffer, now filled with the sausage mixture, into the fridge and clean up your work area.

Remove the casings from their soaking water, and run warm water through them. This flushes them and also reveals any leaks. If you find a leak, cut out that part of the casing. Remove the sausage stuffer from the fridge and stuff the casings as directed in Duck Sausages, Hunter's Style on page 185. Create links of any length you like; I usually make them 5 to 6 inches long. Tie them off with kitchen twine, which will prevent them from unraveling when you poach them.

When all of the links are tied, place your hanging rack in a cool place and hang the links on it while you heat a large pot of water. As the water is heating, sterilize a needle by putting the tip in a flame until it glows. Look for air bubbles in the links and prick any you find with the needle to deflate them.

When the water reaches 160°F to 170°F—it should be steaming, not simmering—gently add the links and poach for 25 minutes. Be careful that the water temperature does not go beyond 178°F, or the links may burst. Meanwhile, ready a large ice-water bath. When the links are done, shock them in the ice-water bath for 5 minutes.

Hang the links to dry again for at least 1 hour or up to overnight if you can hang them between 33°F and 42°F. This will allow what is called a pellicle (membrane) to form, which helps the smoke adhere to the sausage. If you skip this step, your sausages will look sad.

If you have a smoker, follow the directions that came with it to set it up, using oak, apple, maple, or other hardwood. Smoke the sausages for 3 to 5 hours, depending on how smoky you want them. It is important that the smoker be as cool as possible. I turn my smoker on, but leave the heater off. If you don't have a smoker, see page 43 for how to fashion one from a kettle grill.

Remove the links from the smoker and return them to the rack. Let them cool on the rack for a couple of hours. Layer the sausages in a large storage container, separating the layers with paper towels, and place the container in the fridge overnight. Eat the links the next day, or divide them into practical-size packets and store them in the refrigerator for up to 10 days or in the freezer for up to a year.

Because you smoked the sausages, they are cooked, and you need only reheat them to serve them. Or not; I actually prefer these cold as part of a charcuterie plate.

SALAMI

This is the most technically advanced level of sausage making, but making your own dry-cured salami is nothing short of alchemy. Raw meat made not only safe but unforgettably wonderful by the caresses of salt and time is culinary magic.

On a practical level, being able to make your own salami opens you up to a new world of convenience food: many salamis are specifically designed to be carried around in a pocket as a movable snack. Indeed, I am focusing on recipes for these sorts of salamis in this book because they make memorable snacks for the duck blind and because they are easier to make than the wider, more traditional Genoa type that you get at the deli counter.

Consider what follows as a primer to serious salami; this will get you started. If you want to go further in depth, I refer to several excellent resources in the bibliography on page 230.

At its core, making salami involves three steps:

1. You make a fresh sausage and inoculate it with nitrate and, in many cases, a bacterial starter. More on this in a moment.

2. You hang the sausage in a moist, warm environment for a day or two, which lets good bacteria defeat any bad ones that might be lurking in your meat.

3. You move the salami to a cooler, drier place to age. The goal is to allow the sausage to lose moisture slowly until it is firm throughout. Once the moisture level drops sufficiently, the meat is safe and stable at regular room temperatures.

Curing Salts and Bacterial Starters

While excellent salami can be made without sodium nitrate or a bacterial starter culture, only experts can make such salami safely. The preservatives sodium nitrite and sodium nitrate, known commercially by such brand names as Insta Cure No. 1 and No. 2, Tinted Cure Mix (TCM) No. 1 and No. 2, and Sel Rose Cure No. 1 and No. 2, and generically as Prague powder no. 1 and no. 2 or pink curing salt no. 1 and no. 2, are important safeguards against botulism and food poisoning. These additives also help the meat bind to itself and give it a pretty red color. The no. 1 cures are are a mix of salt and sodium nitrite, and the no. 2 cures combine salt, sodium nitrite, and sodium nitrate.

You can't use sodium nitrite, or a no. 1 cure, alone in long cures because it gets used up before its protection is no longer needed, which can result in dangerous consequences. That's why salami makers use no. 2 cures that contain sodium nitrate—in my case, Insta Cure No. 2. Think of the no. 2 cures, the ones with sodium *nitrate*, as time-release capsules of *nitrite*: the nitrate breaks down into nitrite over time, giving you the extended protection you need.

Specialized bacterial starter cultures, which inoculate the meat with good bacteria, are not strictly needed if you are making salami in the right conditions. But again, unless you are an experienced salami maker, I highly recommend using them. These good bacteria crowd out and kill any toxic bacteria. They are also vital to getting that distinctive tangy flavor of a good salami: the lactic acid the good bacteria gives off is what makes a salami tangy.

You can buy Insta Cure No. 1 and No. 2 or other brand-name pink curing salts at most decent butcher shops or online. Bacterial starter cultures, such as Bactoferm T-SPX, the brand I use, are available online through Butcher & Packer and The Sausage Maker.

A final note: I use weight measurements first for curing salts, kosher salt, sugar, and bacterial starter in the salami recipes for greater precision, though I do provide standard volume measurements as well. Use the weight measurements if you can.

Aging Your Charcuterie

You will need to hang your salamis (and the Goose Prosciutto on page 173) in a curing chamber. The temperature of the chamber needs to be between 50°F and 65°F—the ideal is 55°F—and the humidity must be between 60 percent and 85 percent. If you are blessed with a basement that meets these criteria, you're good to go. Most of us are not, however, and need to build a chamber.

Many people start with a wine fridge. This is great if you already have one, as they allow you to control temperature and, to some extent, humidity. But if you don't own one already, you can set up what I use. My curing rig is the following:

- An old fridge bought on Craigslist.

- A temperature regulator bought at my local brew shop. The regulator goes into the wall, the refrigerator goes into the regulator, and a probe goes into the fridge itself. You set the temperature with a dial gauge.

- A small humidifier that sits inside the fridge. I live in California, where humidity levels can drop to 10 percent. This will destroy salami in a day, so I need extra humidity. To control it, I use a humidity regulator, which I bought online. It works the same as a temperature regulator.

The whole shebang cost me less than two hundred dollars, and I can control both temperature and humidity with precision.

ITALIAN DUCK CACCIATORE SALAMI

I am a big fan of the easy-to-eat salami. Thin salamis you can carry along with you are a real treat on the road or in the field; I love to eat them in the duck blind in winter. As far as salami recipes go, this one is pretty easy. It uses standard hog casings, which can cure in as little as a couple of weeks, though a month is better. The flavorings here make a powerfully spiced salami. You can pare them back if you want, or change them any way you wish. Just don't mess with the kosher salt, curing salt, or sugar. Before you begin this recipe, review the information on sausage making on pages 182 to 184.

DIFFICULTY: ✷ ✷ ✷ ✷

MAKES 5 POUNDS
(20 TO 22 EIGHT-INCH LINKS)

PREP TIME: ABOUT 3 HOURS
TO MAKE THE SAUSAGES,
PLUS FERMENTING TIME AND
CURING TIME

COOK TIME: N/A

4 pounds duck or goose meat

1 pound pork fat, preferably fatback

38 grams (2 tablespoons plus 1 teaspoon) kosher salt

20 grams (about 2 tablespoons) sugar or dextrose

5 grams (1 teaspoon) Insta Cure No. 2 (see page 196)

3 tablespoons sweet paprika

2 tablespoons freshly ground pepper

1 tablespoon garlic powder

1 tablespoon ground coriander

2 teaspoons caraway seeds

1 teaspoon pure chile powder

10 to 15 feet hog casings

20 grams (about 2 tablespoons) T-SPX bacterial starter (see page 196)

¼ cup distilled water

¼ cup red wine

Chill the meat and fat in the freezer for about 1 hour. You want it close to frozen, even a little crispy cold. Put your meat grinder or stand mixer grinding attachment and fine die in the freezer, and a large bowl and sausage stuffer in the refrigerator.

Chop the meat into 1-inch chunks and place in a large bowl. Chop most of the fat into 1-inch chunks as well, but finely dice about ¼ pound and set in a small bowl in the freezer; add the rest of the fat to the bowl with the meat. Add the kosher salt, sugar, curing salt, paprika, pepper, garlic powder, coriander, caraway, and chile

powder to the meat mixture and mix well. Put it in the freezer to chill for 1 hour.

Put the casings in warm water to cover and set aside to soak for 30 minutes or so.

After the meat mixture has been in the freezer for 1 hour, remove your grinding equipment and bowl from the freezer and outfit the grinder with the fine die. Working quickly, pass the meat mixture through the grinder, capturing it in the cold bowl from the fridge. Put the meat mixture back in the fridge while you clean up your work area.

Remove the casings from their soaking water, and run warm water through them. This flushes them and also reveals any leaks. If you find a leak, cut out that part of the casing. Return the casings to the warm water until needed.

When the meat is 28°F to 35°F, get your bacterial starter ready: in a small bowl, gently mix the starter with the distilled water and let sit at room temperature for 5 minutes.

Take the meat mixture out of the fridge and put it in the bowl of a stand mixer fitted with the paddle attachment. Add the finely diced fat from the freezer. Add the starter solution and wine and mix on the lowest speed for 1 to 1½ minutes. You will see the meat change texture. You are looking for a good bind, where the meat is beginning to stick to itself.

Remove the sausage stuffer from the fridge and stuff the casings as directed in Duck Sausages, Hunter's Style on page 185. Twist into links 8 to 10 inches long. Tie off each link with kitchen twine.

When all of the links are tied, place your hanging rack in a cool place and hang the links on it. Find a needle and sterilize it by putting the tip in a flame until it glows. Prick the casing on each link all over with the needle to remove any air pockets; this also helps the links dry more evenly.

Now you need to ferment the links at room temperature. Tent the hanging links with black plastic, using either cut-open garbage bags or other plastic sheeting. If you have a humidifier, put it under the sausages. You need them to stay moist. If you cannot get your humidity to

85 to 95 percent, spritz the sausages every 6 to 12 hours to keep the skins moist. This is very important. Let the sausages hang for at least 24 hours or up to 48 hours. This is the fermentation stage, the stage where the starter culture you are using defeats any bad bacteria in the sausage. You will be able to smell the meat fermenting. It will be slightly sour, in a good way. The meat will also begin to darken, changing from a dull gray-red to a dense, dark, slightly shiny red.

When the sausages have finished the fermentation stage, put them in your curing chamber (see page 197) and leave them for at least 2 weeks before eating. You can let them go for as long as 6 weeks before they start to get too firm. When they are ready, store them in the fridge for up to a couple of months, or vacuum seal them and store them in the freezer for up to a year.

DUCK LANDJAEGER

Landjaeger. Such a cool name, eh? It's a German dry-cured sausage that is made small enough to fit into your coat pocket on a cold day when you are out hiking, fishing, or hunting. Traditionally made with beef and pork, this *Landjaeger* is made with duck or goose, plus pork fat. Other than seasoning, the difference between this salami and the Italian duck salami on page 198 is that you smoke *Landjaeger*.

Use hog casings or sheep casings for this salami. In essence, *Landjaeger* is a really, really good Slim Jim—a snack to be enjoyed outdoors, not sliced like a wider salami.

This sort of narrow, dry-cured smoked salami exists in many parts of the world. The Chinese equivalent follows this recipe. The method is identical; only the flavors change. Before you begin this recipe, review the information on sausage making on pages 182 to 184.

DIFFICULTY: ✶ ✶ ✶ ✶ ✶

MAKES ABOUT 5 POUNDS
(20 TO 22 EIGHT-INCH LINKS)

PREP TIME: ABOUT 3 HOURS
TO MAKE THE SAUSAGE, PLUS
HANGING AND CURING TIME

COOK TIME: 3 TO 5 HOURS
FOR SMOKING

4 pounds duck or goose meat

1 pound pork fat, preferably fatback

38 grams (2 tablespoons plus 1 teaspoon) kosher salt

15 grams (about 1 tablespoon) sugar or dextrose

5 grams (1 tablespoon) Insta Cure No. 1 (see page 196)

2 tablespoons freshly ground pepper

2 teaspoons ground allspice

1 teaspoon garlic powder

1 teaspoon caraway seeds

1 teaspoon ground coriander

½ teaspoon celery seeds

10 to 15 feet hog or sheep casings

20 grams (about 2 tablespoons) T-SPX bacterial starter (see page 196)

½ cup distilled water

Chill the meat and fat in the freezer for about 1 hour. You want it close to frozen, even a little crispy cold. Put your meat grinder or stand mixer grinding attachment and fine die in the freezer and a large bowl and sausage stuffer in the refrigerator.

Chop the meat and fat into 1-inch chunks and place in a large bowl. Add the kosher salt, sugar, curing salt, pepper, allspice, garlic powder, caraway, coriander, and celery seeds and mix well. Put the meat mixture in the freezer to chill for 1 hour.

Put the casings in warm water to cover and set aside to soak for 30 minutes or so.

After the meat mixture has been in the freezer for 1 hour, remove your grinding equipment from the freezer and bowl from the fridge and outfit the grinder with the fine die. Working quickly, pass the meat mixture through the grinder, capturing it in the cold bowl. Put the meat mixture back in the freezer while you clean up your work area.

Remove the casings from their soaking water, and run warm water through them. This flushes them and also reveals any leaks. If you find a leak, cut out that part of the casing. Return the casings to the warm water until needed.

When the meat is 28°F to 35°F, get your bacterial starter ready: in a small bowl, gently mix the starter with the distilled water and let sit at room temperature for 5 minutes.

Take the meat mixture out of the fridge and put it in the bowl of a stand mixer fitted with the paddle attachment. Add the starter solution and mix on the lowest speed for 1 to 1½ minutes. You will see the meat change texture. You are looking for a good bind, where the meat is beginning to stick to itself.

continued

continued from previous page

Remove the sausage stuffer from the fridge and stuff the casings as directed in Duck Sausages, Hunter's Style on page 185. Twist into links between 6 and 8 inches long. Tie off each link with kitchen twine.

When all of the links are tied, place your hanging rack in a cool place and hang the links on it. Find a needle and sterilize it by putting the tip in a flame until it glows. Prick the casing on each link all over with the needle to remove any air pockets; this also helps the links dry more evenly.

Now you need to ferment the links at room temperature. Tent the hanging links with black plastic, using either cut-open garbage bags or other plastic sheeting. If you have a humidifier, put it under the sausages. You need them to stay moist. If you cannot get your humidity to 85 to 95 percent, spritz the sausages every 6 to 12 hours to keep the skins moist. This is very important. Let the sausages hang for at least 24 hours or up to 48 hours. This is the fermentation stage, the stage where the starter culture you are using defeats any bad bacteria in the sausage.

When the sausages are ready, fire up the smoker. If you have a smoker, follow the directions that came with it to set it up, using oak, hickory, maple, or any fruit or nut wood. Put ice cubes in the water tray to keep the temperature as cool as possible. You are not cooking the links here; you are just giving them a good smoking. Smoke the links for 2 to 3 hours, depending on how smoky you want them, making sure the temperature stays cool. If the temperature inside the smoker goes beyond 150°F, douse the links in an ice-water bath to stop any cooking, then pat them dry. If you don't have a smoker, see page 43 for how to fashion one from a kettle grill.

Put the sausages in your curing chamber (see page 197) and leave them for at least 2 weeks and as long as 5 weeks before eating. When they are ready, store them in the fridge for up to a couple of months, or vacuum seal them and store them in the freezer for up to a year.

LAP CHEONG VARIATION

These links are made the same way the *Landjaeger* links are made but with different spices. There are many versions of this sausage, but mine is intended to be both spicy and sweet.

DIFFICULTY: ★ ★ ★ ★ ★

MAKES ABOUT 5 POUNDS
(20 TO 22 EIGHT-INCH LINKS)

PREP TIME: ABOUT 3 HOURS
TO MAKE THE SAUSAGE, PLUS
HANGING AND CURING TIME

COOK TIME: 3 TO 5 HOURS
FOR SMOKING

4 pounds duck or goose meat

1 pound pork fat, preferably fatback

75 grams (about ⅓ cup) sugar or dextrose

5 grams (1 teaspoon) Insta Cure No. 2 (see page 196)

1½ teaspoons five-spice powder

1 teaspoon ground Sichuan pepper, optional

1 tablespoon sweet paprika

1 to 2 teaspoons cayenne pepper or other hot chile powder

10 to 15 feet narrow hog or sheep casings

¼ cup Shaoxing wine or dry sherry

¼ cup soy sauce

20 grams (about 2 tablespoons) T-SPX bacterial starter (see page 196)

¼ cup distilled water

Cut, chill, season, and grind the meat mixture as directed for Duck Landjaeger on page 200. When you put the ground mixture in the bowl of a stand mixer, add the wine and soy along with the dissolved starter and mix with the paddle attachment. Proceed as directed to ferment, smoke, and cure the links.

DUCK FAT

Duck fat is one of the chief glories of working with waterfowl, and along with goose fat, it is among the most heart-healthy fats in all of nature. Although this fat is not unsaturated like olive oil is, they are the least saturated of all terrestrial animal fats.

The fat of wild ducks and geese is even less saturated than the fat of their domesticated counterparts: after rendering, straining, and pouring batches of wild duck fat into jars, nine times out of ten it will remain liquid at my wintertime room temperature, which is about 68°F. Only a highly unsaturated fat will do this. For comparison, domestic duck fat doesn't liquefy until about 70°F.

It may sound odd, but a deeply satisfying snack is duck or goose fat smeared on a piece of pumpernickel bread, then sprinkled with a little coarse salt. That and a sour dill pickle make a perfect pick-me-up between larger meals.

Rendered fat from domestic ducks is ivory and slightly ducky. Rendered goose fat is even whiter and is almost neutral tasting. Both are excellent for pastry making, if you can keep everything cold. Domestic duck fat works best for savory pastries, while goose fat will work even with sweet pastries.

Rendered fat from grain-eating wild birds has its own special power. It will be slightly more yellow—the color of pale butter—than domestic duck fat, and it most definitely tastes of duck. Holly and I render close to a half gallon of wild duck fat each year, and it is our day-to-day cooking fat. We no longer live as close to the wilderness as we once did, but we still appreciate the special gift wild duck fat represents. But not just any wild bird makes it into the rendering pot, as you shall see.

When you cook with duck or goose fat, you need to remember that it has a relatively low smoke point at 375°F. This is higher than virgin olive oil or butter and about the same as clarified butter or lard. What that means is that you should use it over medium to medium-high heat, not high heat. In other words, you don't want to stir-fry with duck fat. But the stuff is excellent for browning meats before they are braised, and it is a classic in baked foods such as potatoes.

How to Render Duck Fat

To render duck fat, you must first get the fat off the carcass. Look in the cavity of the bird: there are often large pockets of fat in the cavity of domestic ducks and geese, and often in wild birds, too. Next look for stray fat in the neck and tail. I use a sharp knife or kitchen shears to cut off the flaps of fatty skin around the cavity of the bird, the neck, and the tail. You can do this even on birds you intend to roast whole. If you are parting out your bird, trim around the breast and leg portions and save that for rendering. Next slice off the fatty skin on the back of the bird; you want this removed anyway for your stock making.

Once you have all of your fatty bits, cut them into small pieces ½ to 1 inch wide. I find that snipping off pieces with kitchen shears works best. Rinse them well under cold running water and put into a colander to drain.

Select a sauté pan just large enough to hold all of the duck fat and pour in water to a depth of about ½ inch. Add the fatty bits and turn the heat to medium-high. As the water begins to simmer, stir the fat around to keep any pieces from sticking to the pan bottom.

When the water begins to boil, turn the heat down to a bare simmer and allow the water to boil away. By this time, plenty of fat will already have rendered—enough to prevent the fat from scorching. Keep cooking the fat in its own fat over low heat so only cracklins are left. You can eat these or toss them.

Let the fat cool for a few minutes. Meanwhile, line a fine-mesh sieve with a plain paper towel and set the sieve over a bowl. Pour the slightly cooled fat into the sieve and let it drip for a few minutes. When only debris and sediment is left in the towel, remove the sieve, discard the towel, and pour the duck fat into a jar.

Screw a lid on the jar and store the fat in the fridge, where it will keep for up to 6 months, or in the freezer for up to a year.

Fat from Wild Birds

First, only render fat from those species that aren't in the habit of eating fishy things. I recommend the following, in order of preference: pintail, specklebelly goose, green-winged (or blue-winged) teal, mallard, wigeon, gadwall. Which species have the sweetest fat will vary depending on your region, but in general, seed- or grain-eating ducks and geese will taste the best. In my area, many typically "off" birds, such as gadwalls, gorge themselves on rice and get almost as fat as a domestic duck. Never render the fat from sea ducks, divers, shovelers, or other wild birds that subsist mainly on crustaceans or insects, as it will taste fishy.

If you are uncertain whether the fat from your wild bird is worth rendering, you have two means to judge: your eyes and your nose. Look for white fat. I have rarely encountered white fat on a wild bird that was not sweet. Yellow fat can often be fine, but orange fat is always a bad sign: that color comes from crustaceans, the same thing that turns salmon meat orange. Once the fat is rendering, smell it. If it smells nice and ducky, it's good. If it smells fishy or "off," toss it. And when in doubt, remember that one bird you can always count on is the pintail, which invariably has nice fat.

Most the fat on a wild bird comes from the pope's nose, or tail section. Be sure to wash it thoroughly under cold running water to remove any stray bits of intestine. Many sources say you must remove the oil gland on the back side of the tail. I've done it, and skipped it, and I have never noticed any difference in the fat's flavor. You may also find lots of fat around the gizzard of a wild bird, and like domestic duck, in the neck, back, and trimmings from the breast and legs.

Once you have secured the fat, chop it, render it, and store it as you would the fat from domestic fowl.

DUCK FAT SAFFRON AIOLI

Aioli is one of those magic sauces, equally at home with both fried foods and poached meats. It is garlic mayonnaise—aioli requires garlic to be an aioli—to which I have added some saffron for color and flavor.

Traditional aioli uses just garlic and olive oil, but warm duck fat is even better. The trick to making any aioli is to get everything to emulsify. Duck fat emulsifies more easily than olive oil does, and adding an egg yolk makes the task even easier.

Since this aioli will keep in the fridge for several days, it is good to have around when you plan on eating fried foods. I also like it with simply poached duck breast and with chicken or any white fish.

DIFFICULTY: ✱ ✱

MAKES ABOUT 1 CUP

PREP TIME: 15 MINUTES

Large pinch of saffron threads

2 tablespoons hot water

**1 or 2 cloves garlic, minced and mashed
   with the side of a knife**

1 or 2 chicken egg yolks, or 1 duck egg yolk

**1 to 2 teaspoons freshly squeezed lemon juice
   or white wine vinegar**

1 teaspoon kosher salt

**¾ cup duck fat, melted and kept warm,
   plus 2 tablespoons if needed**

In a small bowl, crumble the saffron threads into the hot water and let steep for 10 minutes.

In a blender, combine the garlic, the egg yolks, 1 teaspoon of the lemon juice, and the salt and buzz briefly on medium speed to mix. Add the saffron solution and blend until combined. Stop the blender and scrape down the sides of the canister with a rubber spatula. Turn on the speed to low, remove the lid, and slowly pour in the ¾ cup duck fat, blending until the mixture emulsifies into a mayonnaise-like consistency. You might not need all of the duck fat, or you may need a tablespoon or two more. Taste for acid and salt, adding a little more of the remaining 1 teaspoon lemon juice and some salt if needed.

Serve at once. Or, transfer to an airtight container and refrigerator for up to several days.

DUCK FAT HOLLANDAISE

Hollandaise is one of those foundational French "mother sauces" taught in cooking school. Only I never went to cooking school. My introduction to hollandaise came in the early 1980s, when my family would go out on Sunday mornings to brunch, that unloved child of breakfast and lunch. I loathed hollandaise then, and for many years afterward. Duck fat changed me. At some point, I realized that you can make a hollandaise without butter, and that you can add a little cayenne to spice things up. Done this way, hollandaise becomes a zingy, ducky, mayonnaise-like dream sauce! It's still mostly fat, so a little goes a long way.

Serve this hollandaise with Duck Eggs Benedict (page 212), poached duck breast, asparagus, or really anything else you can think of.

DIFFICULTY: ✱ ✱

MAKES ABOUT ½ CUP

PREP TIME: 5 MINUTES

3 duck egg yolks, or 4 chicken egg yolks

5 teaspoons freshly squeezed lemon juice

Pinch of kosher salt

Pinch of cayenne pepper

7 tablespoons duck or goose fat, melted

3 tablespoons unsalted butter, melted

In a blender, combine the egg yolks, lemon juice, salt, and cayenne and buzz on medium speed for about 30 seconds. Stop the blender and scrape down the sides of the canister with a rubber spatula. Turn on the speed to low, remove the lid, and slowly pour in the duck fat and butter. Re-cover, turn the speed to high, and blend for 15 seconds or so.

Serve at once. If you like, the sauce can be held for up to a few hours if put in a warm place, like on your stove top if you are cooking.

DUCK FAT PIE DOUGH

Pie dough made with duck fat? Yes, please! Pie dough made with goose fat has a long tradition in Britain and Germany, and its neutral flavor compares favorably with pie crusts made with lard, which, as many pie aficionados know, makes the flakiest crusts. And you can even use duck fat rendered from wild birds if you are making a savory pie. The duckiness of the fat adds another layer of flavor to the pie.

The recipe that follows is a dough suitable for making a dessert pie, such as the wild berry pie, opposite. If you want to make a crust for a savory potpie, make the dough as directed, using ½ cup cold duck fat and ½ cup cold unsalted butter in place of the amounts given below.

The key to a flaky pie crust is to have everything very cold: fat, water, and in the case of this duck fat pastry, a chilled marble board, if possible. Although not strictly necessary, the cold marble helps keep the ingredients cold as you work. Remember, duck fat melts at about 76°F, and your hands are 98.6°F, so you need to work fast. When in doubt, stop everything and chill the dough in the fridge for 30 minutes before continuing.

DIFFICULTY: ✳ ✳ ✳

MAKES DOUGH FOR ONE
9-INCH DOUBLE-CRUST PIE
OR TWO 9-INCH SINGLE-
CRUST PIES

PREP TIME: 1½ HOURS

COOK TIME: 30 MINUTES,
IF PREBAKING CRUST

2½ cups all-purpose flour, plus more for rolling

½ teaspoon salt

1 teaspoon sugar

¾ cup very cold unsalted butter, cut into ½-inch cubes

¼ cup very cold duck fat

3 to 4 tablespoons ice-cold vodka

2 tablespoons ice water

In a food processor, combine the flour, salt, and sugar and pulse to mix. Add the butter and duck fat and pulse 6 to 8 times, until the mixture looks like a coarse meal. Start adding the vodka, 1 tablespoon at a time, pulsing until the mixture just begins to clump together. If you compress some of the dough and it holds together, it's ready. If the dough doesn't hold together, add the water, 1 tablespoon at a time, pulsing until it does. Too much water will make the crust tough.

Take the dough out of the food processor and clump it together on a clean work surface. Divide the dough in half, and shape each half into a disk. Don't overknead the dough as you shape the disks or the pastry will be tough. You want to see little bits of butter in the dough. Sprinkle a little flour around the disks, then wrap them separately in plastic wrap and refrigerate for at least 1 hour or up to 2 days.

Remove a dough disk from the refrigerator. Let it sit at room temperature for 5 minutes, so it softens enough to roll out. Dust the work surface with flour, then roll out the dough into a 12-inch circle about 1/8 inch thick. As you roll out the dough, check to see if it is sticking to the work surface. If it is, add a bit of flour under the dough to keep it from sticking. Carefully roll the dough circle around the rolling pin, position the pin over a 9-inch pie plate, and unroll the dough, centering it on the pie plate. Gently press the dough into the bottom and up the sides of the pie plate. Using a pair of kitchen shears, trim the dough, leaving a ½-inch overhang. (If you're making an open pie, read the instructions on prebaking below.)

If making a single-crust pie, roll the overhang under itself, then pinch the dough around the rim to create a fluted edge. To prebake the crust, preheat the oven to 425°F. Line the dough with a large piece of aluminum foil or parchment paper, and fill the lined crust with pie weights or dried beans. Bake for about 15 minutes, until dry to the touch. Carefully remove the weights and foil, turn the oven down to 350°F, return the crust to the oven, and continue baking for 20 to 30 minutes, until golden brown. Pour or spoon the filling into the crust. If you have partially baked the crust and the filling needs cooking, return the pie plate to the oven and bake according to individual recipes. The second dough disk can be treated the same way, or it can reserved in the refrigerator for use later.

If making a double-crust pie, roll out the second dough disk the same way you rolled out the first disk. Pour or spoon the filling into the bottom crust, then gently place the second dough circle over the filling. Pinch the top and bottom dough circles together firmly along the rim. Using kitchen shears, trim the excess dough, leaving a ¾-inch overhang. Holding the edge of the bottom pastry away from the rim, fold the overhang of the top pastry under it, creating an edge. Flute the edge using a thumb and index finger, or crimp with a fork. Cut 3 or 4 slits in the center of the top crust to allow steam to escape during baking. Bake as directed in individual recipes.

ELDERBERRY PIE
WITH DUCK FAT CRUST

I live near Sacramento, in the heart of California's great Central Valley. Here, if you are a forager, it is the elderberry that occupies most of your attention in summer. It is our dominant berry. And if you are a hunter, few places on earth are blessed with duck hunting as good as we get several miles north of the city. So consider this pie an homage to my home.

　　If you don't have elderberries, you can use Sacramento's second-most popular wild fruit, the blackberry. Luckily, it is available throughout the country.

DIFFICULTY: *

MAKES ONE 9-INCH DOUBLE-
CRUST PIE; SERVES 6 TO 8

PREP TIME: 25 MINUTES

COOK TIME: 35 TO
45 MINUTES

1 recipe Duck Fat Pie Dough (see 209)
4 cups fresh or frozen elderberries, blackberries,
　or blueberries
¾ cup sugar
¼ cup instant tapioca
2 tablespoons freshly squeezed lemon juice,
　if using elderberries or blueberries
Pinch of kosher salt
2 tablespoons unsalted butter, cut into small pieces
1 duck or chicken egg yolk beaten with 1 tablespoon
　heavy cream, half-and-half, or milk, for egg wash

Make the pie dough and refrigerate as directed in the dough recipe.

Preheat the oven to 425°F.

To make the filling, in a bowl, combine the berries, sugar, tapioca, lemon juice, and salt and mix gently. Crush the berries a little to bring out a little more juice. Let stand for 15 minutes.

Meanwhile, roll out a dough disk and use to line a 9-inch pie plate as directed. Roll out the second dough disk the same way.

Pour the filling into the bottom crust. Scatter the butter over the filling, then lay the second dough circle on top and trim and flute the edges as directed. Paint the top crust with the egg wash.

Bake for 15 minutes. Remove the pie from the oven and tent the edges of the crust to prevent burning, or use a pie protector. Turn the oven temperature down to 350°F and return the pie to the oven. Bake for 20 to 30 minutes, until the crust is a pretty gold.

Let the pie sit for at least 30 minutes before cutting. If you cut into it too soon, the filling will spill out on everything.

DUCK ARRABBIATA PASTA SAUCE

Arrabbiata means "angry," and Italy's *arrabbiata* sauce (pictured on page 101) is named for the chiles in it. This is essentially a standard version of that great pasta sauce that's been "ducked up." It's a great recipe for when you have some extra duck fat and stock lying around, such as during the workweek after you've roasted a duck and made stock over the weekend.

DIFFICULTY: *

SERVES 4 TO 6

PREP TIME: 10 MINUTES

COOK TIME: 45 MINUTES

2 tablespoons duck fat

½ cup chopped red or yellow onion

5 cloves garlic, minced

6 fresh sage leaves, minced

2 tablespoons tomato paste

½ teaspoon cayenne pepper, or 1 small fresh hot chile (such as Thai or serrano), chopped

1 cup light red wine (such as Grenache or Pinot Noir)

1 cup Basic Duck Stock (page 222)

4 cups crushed tomatoes, canned or fresh

3 tablespoons minced fresh flat-leaf parsley

Kosher salt

1 pound spaghetti or other dried pasta

Grated Parmesan cheese, for garnish

In a large sauté pan, heat the duck fat over medium heat. Add the onion and cook, stirring occasionally, for 3 minutes, until translucent and soft. Add the garlic and sage and cook another for 2 minutes. Add the tomato paste and cayenne, stir well to combine, and cook for 3 minutes.

Add the wine, mix well, and turn the heat up to high. Boil down the mixture until it is thick. Add the stock and boil down until reduced by half.

Add the tomatoes, stir well, and turn down the heat to a simmer. Add half of the parsley and simmer for 15 to 20 minutes, until thickened. You want the sauce thick enough to coat the pasta easily without leaving a puddle at the bottom of a bowl or plate. If you want a perfectly smooth sauce, puree it in a blender. The color will lighten a bit unless you let it cool overnight.

While the sauce is cooking, bring a large pot filled with water to a boil and season generously with salt. Add the pasta and cook until al dente, according to the package directions. Drain, transfer to a large bowl, and toss with some of the sauce.

To serve, divide the pasta among individual plates, ladle a dollop of the sauce on top of each serving, and garnish with the remaining 1½ tablespoons parsley. A little grated cheese would not be out of place.

DUCK EGGS

Anyone who has ever seen a farm-fresh duck egg has been smitten by its giant, pre-ternaturally orange yolk.

In the kitchen, a few key differences distinguish duck eggs from chicken eggs. For starters, duck eggs are larger: a normal one weighs about 70 grams or 2½ ounces, roughly the size of a jumbo chicken egg. A duck egg will also have a larger yolk than a chicken egg of comparable size. I've substituted duck eggs for chicken eggs in many baking recipes (breads, cakes, and muffins mostly) and have never had a problem, but it's best to weigh them for more complicated baking recipes.

You'll also notice that the shell of a duck egg is thicker than the shell of a chicken egg. That translates into excellent keeping qualities: a fresh duck egg will keep for six weeks or more in the fridge. The inner white on a duck egg—all eggs have two layers of white, one thick, one thin—is very strong; it will stand up when you fry it. That's normal, and a sign of a fresh egg. If you are whipping the whites, know that it takes a little more work to whip them than it does chicken egg whites, but once you have them whipped, they are more stable. When a duck egg is cracked into a pan, the yolk tends to stand up higher than than the yolk of a chicken egg yolk, too.

In the kitchen, these differences generally mean that it's better to cook duck eggs at a lower temperature than you would chicken eggs. If you don't, the white can get rubbery. For the technically minded, the white of a duck egg begins to set at 131°F; that of a chicken egg starts at 135°F.

To make perfect soft-boiled duck eggs, put the eggs in a pot just large enough to hold them and add cool water to cover the eggs by 2 inches. Turn on the heat to high and bring to a simmer, not a boil. Turn off the heat, cover the pot, and let stand for 8 to 12 minutes, depending on how soft you want your egg yolks.

To fry a duck egg without getting a rubbery white, cook it over medium-low heat until the yolk is cooked to your liking. Or, you can "steam fry" it: fry it over medium-low heat just until the outer edge of the white has set, then add a splash of water to the pan and cover the pan until the yolk is cooked to your liking. The resulting steam will finish cooking the egg without the egg white becoming chewy.

It is getting easier all the time to buy duck eggs. Your best bet is always an Asian market, as Asians eat about 85 percent of all the duck eggs consumed in the world. A local farmers' market may be another good source. Many poultry farmers are raising ducks for eggs these days and selling the eggs at local markets.

DUCK EGGS BENEDICT

Eggs benny, only with duck eggs, duck fat hollandaise, and, if you want an extra kick, duck prosciutto. It is a little gonzo, but a lot of awesome. This recipe is a lot easier than it sounds, and it is sure to impress anyone who tries it. It's so good, you might want to serve it as a light dinner instead of for brunch.

DIFFICULTY: ✱ ✱ ✱

SERVES 4

PREP TIME: 15 MINUTES, MOSTLY MAKING THE HOLLANDAISE

COOK TIME: 20 MINUTES

8 slices bacon or thinly sliced duck prosciutto (page 173)

2 teaspoons distilled white vinegar

1 recipe Duck Fat Hollandaise (page 206)

4 duck eggs

2 English muffins, split

Unsalted butter

2 tablespoons chopped fresh flat-leaf parsley

If using bacon, fry it slowly in a pan until crispy, then drain on paper towels. If using prosciutto, reserve.

While the bacon is cooking, bring a large, wide saucepan two-thirds filled with water to a boil, then add the vinegar. Bring the water to a boil again, then lower the heat to a bare simmer.

Transfer the hollandaise to a container with a spout and set it on a warm—but not hot—place on or near the stove top.

Now, poach the duck eggs. Working with 1 egg at a time, crack the egg into a small bowl, then slip the egg into the barely simmering water. The moment it begins to solidify, slip in another egg. Then repeat until all 4 eggs

are cooking, making sure that they are not touching one another. Turn off the heat, cover the pan, and let sit for 4 minutes. (Remember which egg went in first, as you'll want to take it out first.) When it comes time to remove the eggs, one at a time, gently lift them out with a slotted spoon. Set them on paper towels for a moment while you construct the dish. Note that the timing is a little variable on the eggs, depending on the size of your pan, how much water, how many eggs, and how runny you like them. You might have to experiment a little with your setup to figure out what you need to do to cook the eggs exactly the way you like them.

As soon as all of the eggs are in the poaching water, toast your English muffins.

To assemble the dish, butter the cut side of each muffin half and place each half, butter side up, on a plate. Top with the bacon or prosciutto. If you like, trim the meat to fit the muffin. Put a poached egg on top of each meat slice, then pour the hollandaise evenly over the eggs. Sprinkle with the parsley and serve at once.

DUCK EGG PASTA

Tajarin (tah-ya-RIN), a specialty of the Piedmont region of Italy, is a lordly pasta, profligate in its use of egg yolks. Some recipes call for as many as thirty egg yolks for a batch to serve six. My recipe is not quite so extravagant. Even so, you will need a dozen duck eggs to make this pasta.

Serve *tajarin* simply. Traditionally, it is tossed with fresh butter; use the best you can afford. Truffles are often included, and I've used Oregon white truffles with this and can attest that they are wonderful. Another common way to dress this dish is to use some demi-glace, *glace de viande* (page 226), or other smooth meat sauce. A light dusting of grated pecorino or Parmesan cheese is a nice finishing touch.

What to do with all those whites? Well, you can make egg white omelets, clarify a batch of consommé (page 228), or do what they do in Italy: after the Sunday feast of *tajarin*, the weekday pasta is made with the whites. That pasta is called sheets and linens, and the recipe follows.

DIFFICULTY: ✳ ✳ ✳

SERVES 4 AS A MAIN
COURSE, OR 6 AS A
PASTA COURSE

PREP TIME: 2 HOURS

COOK TIME: 3 TO 5 MINUTES

4 cups Italian 00 flour or all-purpose flour

Large pinch of kosher salt

12 duck egg yolks

2 tablespoons water

Olive oil, for coating

In a large bowl, whisk together the flour and salt. Make a well in the center, and add the egg yolks and water to the well. Break up the egg yolks a bit with a fork. Then, using the fork and starting at the rim of the well, gradually draw the flour into the liquid ingredients. Once the mixture has come together into a stiff dough, knead vigorously in the bowl for 5 minutes, until the dough is smooth and elastic. Coat the dough with a little oil, then wrap in plastic wrap and let rest at room temperature for at least 30 minutes, though 1 hour is better.

Divide the dough into 4 to 6 equal portions. Keep the portions covered when you are not working with them to prevent them from drying out. You can roll out the dough with a rolling pin on a floured work surface, or with a pasta machine, following the directions that came with the machine. You want the dough sheets to be reasonably thin; I take mine to No. 7 on my Atlas machine, where No. 9 is the thinnest setting. Then, using the machine or by hand, cut the sheets into long, narrow ribbon noodles. Piedmontese pasta makers pride themselves on how narrow they cut their *tajarin* by hand, but you could cut the dough into fettuccine, linguine, or the even wider *pappardelle* and it would still be good. Make sure you have plenty of flour to keep the noodles from sticking to one another.

To cook the noodles, bring a large pot of salted water to a boil, add the noodles, and stir well to prevent them from sticking together. Cook until they float, then, once the pasta is floating on the roiling water, cook for 1 minute more. Drain the pasta and dress as suggested in the headnote.

Sheets and Linens Pasta Variation: Proceed as directed, substituting 12 egg whites for the 12 egg yolks.

DUCK EGG CAKE WITH ROSEMARY

This is an insanely easy cake to make. It goes together in just minutes and tastes awesome: a touch ducky—more so if you use wild duck fat—sweet, but not overly so, with a little hit of rosemary to even things out. I originally made this as a sort of stunt, but it's so good I've put it into the regular rotation.

If you like a sweeter cake, up the sugar to a full cup, and if you hate rosemary, skip it or sub in lemon verbena, sage, or winter savory.

Serve the cake with fruit and maybe a little whipped cream. A sweet dessert white wine, like a *vin santo* or a Sauternes, is a perfect choice.

DIFFICULTY: *

MAKES 1 LOAF CAKE;
SERVES 4 TO 6

PREP TIME: 10 MINUTES

COOK TIME: 50 MINUTES

Unsalted butter or duck fat, for greasing

4 duck eggs

¾ cup sugar

3 tablespoons olive oil

7 tablespoons duck fat, melted

2 tablespoons minced fresh rosemary

1½ cups cake flour

1 tablespoon baking powder

Healthy pinch of kosher salt

Preheat the oven to 325°F. Grease a 9-inch loaf pan with butter.

Crack the duck eggs into a large bowl, add the sugar, and beat with a whisk until well combined and slightly frothy. Drizzle in the oil and duck fat while stirring the mixture. Once the fat is well incorporated into the mixture, sprinkle the rosemary on top.

In a second bowl, whisk together the flour, baking powder, and salt. Using the whisk, stir the flour into the egg-fat mixture until combined.

Pour the batter into the prepared pan and bake for 50 minutes. Stick a toothpick into the center of the cake, and if it comes out clean, the cake is ready. If not, bake for another 10 minutes.

Let the cake cool in the pan on a cooling rack for 5 minutes, then turn it out onto the rack. Slice and eat warm or at room temperature.

STOCK, GLACE, AND CONSOMMÉ

Making your own stock will change your cooking forever, especially when it comes to waterfowl cookery. Duck stock is nearly impossible to buy, and a great many recipes in this book rely on it. Yes, you can substitute beef or chicken stock, depending on the recipe, but there is no substitute for homemade duck stock.

There are other reasons besides flavor for making your own duck stock. Consider thrift. Let's face it, ducks and geese are relatively expensive compared to chicken, beef, or pork. You want to stretch your dollar as far as it will go, right? Making your own stock will either give you a whole new meal out of your bird, or it will enrich many subsequent meals when you use it later. A simple Italian risotto using home-made duck stock instead of water is the difference between a so-so side dish and an exciting main course.

Conservation comes into play for wild birds. By making stock, you are getting more out of each duck, ducks that you killed. At the risk of getting preachy, it is our obligation as hunters to use as much of the animals we bring home as we can—down to the bones. Stocks achieve this. Do I make stock with every duck that Holly and I bring home? No, but I do make several gallons each year, freezing it or pressure canning it so I have duck stock at the ready. (For more on pressure canning, see opposite.)

More than any other type of recipe, ingredients and amounts in stocks are a guide, not dogma. Stock making is an art, with a little science tossed in just to make things interesting. I make stock every few weeks, and my stocks are seldom identical. You can add more or less meat and bones. No onions? Use leeks or green onions. Want a little more sweetness? Add more carrots, or a parsnip. Want a deeper, darker flavor? Roast or caramelize all your vegetables before you toss them in the pot. Need a light stock? Don't roast the bones or vegetables. Don't like bay leaves? Leave them out.

Although stock making is not subject to hard-and-fast rules, here are a handful of tenets that I always follow:

- I never use peppers, cabbage, or mustardy things (mustard greens, radishes, turnips, or the like) in my stocks. I find that they result in off flavors.

- I try never to let my stock boil. I like a clear stock, and extended boiling will make your stock cloudy.

- I add things in succession. Meat and bones can take the longest cooking, followed by roots and onions, spices and "hard" herbs such as rosemary, then soft things like parsley or fresh tomatoes.

- I always strain the stock twice, first through a fine-mesh sieve, then again with a plain (unprinted) paper towel or cheesecloth lining the sieve. Because the towel or cheesecloth blots up much of the fat, I end up with a clear stock.

- I use dried mushrooms in nearly every stock recipe. Why? They add color and a jolt of savory flavor that makes any stock richer. I have easy access to pounds of dried mushrooms—I am a fanatical mushroom hunter when I am not duck hunting—but even a small handful enlivens a broth.

❥ I never salt my broth until after it has been strained. The only salt that goes into it initially is from the bones; I oil and salt them before I roast them in the oven. A light hand with salt in the beginning allows me to control saltiness better later. If you don't do this, you can end up with a salty broth as it cooks down.

❥ For a thick, rich stock, add duck (or chicken, pig, or calf's) feet. You can buy bags of duck feet at Asian markets, or, if you are a hunter, save the feet from the birds you bring home.

PRESSURE CANNING STOCK

Having pressure-canned duck stock around the house will set you free. I never have less than a gallon in my pantry. Duck stock is expensive to buy—if you can find it—and if you are a hunter-gatherer like me, your freezer space is at a premium. Pressure canning is the way to go.

You will need a pressure canner, not a pressure cooker. I prefer the heavier model made by All American, but many people swear by the lighter, more inexpensive canner manufactured by Presto. Either is fine.

Have your stock strained and simmering when you get ready to can it. Your jars (I always can in quarts) should be sanitary. I do this by putting clean jars on a baking sheet in a 225°F oven for at least 20 minutes. Your lids need to be fresh; save used lids for when you don't need a perfect seal. You can use old lid rings, however.

When you are ready, take your jars from the oven and fill them, leaving about 1 inch of headspace. Make sure the jar rims are clean and dry. Put the lids on the jars, add the rings, and tighten with your fingertips. You want the rings reasonably tight but not jammed on.

Put the jars in your canner. Pour water into the canner to come one-fourth of the way up the sides of the jars. My canner requires a smear of oil around the lip to seal perfectly, so if yours does, too, do that now. Seal the canner according to its directions. Turn on the heat to high. Watch for steam to shoot out of the vent. Once this happens, count off 7 minutes.

When 7 minutes of steaming have passed, put the canning weight on the vent: if you are at 1,000 feet above sea level or below, put it on the 10 psi notch. If you are at a higher elevation, you may need the 15 psi notch. Watch the pressure gauge, and when it hits the proper psi, count off 25 minutes. Adjust the burner heat as needed for the pressure to remain where it should be, and if you find the gauge dropped below correct pressure, do not count those minutes.

Once 25 minutes have passed, turn off the burner and let the canner return to regular pressure by itself. When the gauge reads zero, open the canner, being careful not to scald yourself with steam. You can either leave your jars alone until they cool, or you can use tongs to move them to a cutting board or other work surface to cool fully.

When the jars have cooled completely, label and date them, store them in the pantry, and use within a year.

BASIC DUCK STOCK

This is my standard duck or goose stock. It is the stock that I call for in the recipes in this book. In other words, you need to make lots. Every time you get a carcass, save it for stock. If you don't have a lot of ducks around at one time, save them up for future rounds of stock making. You can chop up the carcasses before freezing, so they take up less space.

Make this stock when you have a day off, as it takes all day. The good news is that you will be rewarded with 4 quarts or more of rich stock that is a perfect base for stews, soups, or wintertime risottos or polenta—or even eaten on its own as a clear soup.

DIFFICULTY: ✱ ✱

MAKES ABOUT 6 QUARTS

PREP TIME: 20 MINUTES

COOK TIME: 6 HOURS

Carcasses of 4 to 6 wild ducks, 2 to 3 wild geese, or 1 to 2 domestic ducks or geese, including wing tips, neck, and innards (not the liver), if possible

Vegetable oil, for coating

Kosher salt

1 pig's foot or 20 duck or chicken feet (optional)

1 large yellow or white onion, chopped

1 large carrot, sliced

2 celery stalks, chopped

4 cloves garlic, chopped

½ ounce (about 1 handful) dried mushrooms (any kind)

1 tablespoon black peppercorns

1 tablespoon juniper berries (optional)

3 bay leaves

1 large sprig rosemary

Tops from 1 fennel bulb (optional)

Stems from 1 bunch flat-leaf parsley, chopped

10 fresh sage leaves, chopped

1 tablespoon dried or fresh thyme

Coat the carcasses and various bird bits with oil. Salt them well and put in a large roasting pan. Put in the oven, turn on the oven to 400°F, and roast for about 1 hour, until well browned.

Meanwhile, score the pig's foot all over, or chop the duck feet with a cleaver or other heavy knife, to break the skin and expose the joints and bones. There is collagen in the feet that will seep into the water and give the finished stock more body.

When the carcasses are ready, remove them from the oven and chop them into large pieces with heavy kitchen shears or a cleaver. This will make it possible to fit them all into your stockpot. Transfer them to a large stockpot and add the feet. Pour in cold water to cover everything by about 1 inch. Turn the heat to medium, bring to a bare simmer, and cook very gently for 2 to 8 hours. Do not let this boil.

Meanwhile, put the onion, carrot, celery, and garlic in the roasting pan and stir to coat with the fat that has rendered from the duck bits. If you are using domestic ducks or fatty wild ones, you may have too much fat: if you have a pool of fat at the bottom of the roasting pan, drain off all but about 3 tablespoons. You can strain the fat and reuse it (it's great for roasting potatoes). Put the vegetables in the oven and roast for about 45 minutes, until browned.

When the vegetables are browned, pour about 4 cups water into the roasting pan and scrape up any browned bits with a wooden spoon.

When the stock has simmered for at least 2 hours, add the vegetables, the liquid from the roasting pan, and all the remaining ingredients. Stir well and simmer, uncovered, for 1½ to 2 hours longer.

Turn off the heat and strain the stock. Set up a fine-mesh sieve over another large pot (you may need 2 pots if you don't have a second large pot). Line the sieve with a piece of plain paper towel or cheesecloth and ladle the stock through the sieve. Change the paper towel or rinse the cheesecloth once or twice. This step is vital to making a clear stock. Do not attempt to capture the last dregs of stock at the bottom of the pot, or you will have cloudy stock.

Your stock is now ready. Season to taste with salt, adding a little at a time. Skip the salting if you want to further concentrate flavors by simmering the strained stock for as long as you like. Check every 15 minutes or so to see if the flavor is as you want it.

Transfer the stock to jars, let cool, cover, and refrigerate for up to 1 week or freeze for up to 9 months. Alternatively, pressure can the stock (see page 221) and store for up to 1 year.

CHINESE DUCK STOCK

Chinese stocks are generally lighter and more aromatic than Western stocks. This is the stock I use in the Asian recipes in this book.

DIFFICULTY: ✴ ✴

MAKES ABOUT 6 QUARTS

PREP TIME: 20 MINUTES

COOK TIME: 4 HOURS

Carcasses of 4 to 6 wild ducks, 2 to 3 wild geese, or 1 to 2 domestic ducks or geese, including wing tips, neck, and innards (not the liver), if possible
1 pig's foot or 20 duck or chicken feet (optional)
1 ounce (about 1 handful) dried shiitake mushrooms
1 tablespoon black peppercorns
5 star anise pods
3-inch piece fresh ginger, sliced but not peeled
1 cup Shaoxing wine or dry sherry
1 large yellow or white onion, sliced
1 large carrot, sliced
1 celery stalk, chopped
4 cloves garlic, chopped
Soy sauce, for seasoning

Use kitchen shears or a cleaver to cut the carcasses into manageable pieces. Put them into a large stockpot. Score the pig's foot all over, or chop the duck feet with a cleaver or other heavy knife, to break the skin and expose the joints and bones. There is collagen in the feet that will seep into the water and give the finished stock more body. Add the pig's foot or duck feet to the pot, then add water to cover everything by 1 inch. Turn on the heat to medium and bring to a simmer, skimming off any scum that forms on the surface. Simmer gently, uncovered for 20 minutes.

Add the mushrooms, peppercorns, star anise, ginger, and wine and continue to simmer, uncovered, for 2 to 3 hours. Stir in the onion, carrot, celery, and garlic and continue to simmer for 1½ hours.

Turn off the heat and strain the stock. Set up a fine-mesh sieve over another large pot (you may need 2 pots if you don't have a second large pot). Line the sieve with a piece of plain paper towel or cheesecloth and ladle the stock through the sieve. Don't try to capture the last dregs of stock at the bottom of the pot, and change the paper towel or rinse the cheesecloth once or twice. These steps are vital to making a clear stock.

Your stock is now ready. Season to taste with soy sauce, adding a little at a time. Skip the soy sauce if you decide to further concentrate flavors by simmering the strained stock for as long as you like. Check every 15 minutes or so to see if the flavor is as you want it.

Transfer the stock to jars, let cool, cover, and refrigerate for up to 1 week or freeze for up to 9 months. Alternatively, pressure can the stock (see page 221) and store for up to 1 year.

MASTER STOCK

A key component of good Chinese cooking is master stock, or *lu shui*. It is not so much a recipe as a practice. You start with a good Chinese stock (see above), and as you use it to poach meats or vegetables, you strain it after each use and save it. Its complexity increases with each use. Over time you will need to replenish seasonings like the star anise, ginger, and Shaoxing wine, but in theory, you can keep a master stock forever.

It's important to boil your master stock after each use, then strain it through a fine-mesh sieve, cool it quickly, and store it in the refrigerator. If you don't plan on using it again within 4 or 5 days, freeze it. (Master stock doesn't keep as long in the fridge as regular stock because of the fine debris from meats and vegetables in it.)

DUCK GLACE DE VIANDE

Demi-glace. A spoonful can make a good sauce great or a weak soup strong. Thick, rich, and silky, a good demi-glace tastes fatty without being so. It is the essence of whatever it's made from. And while you can buy veal or beef demi-glace in places like Whole Foods or Williams-Sonoma, finding duck demi-glace is nearly impossible unless you order it online from D'Artagnan. Plus, the homemade stuff makes use of parts of the duck many people toss in the trash. It is culinary gold, conjured from garbage.

Technically, this recipe yields *glace de viande,* which is even better than demi-glace. A demi-glace is made with the roux-based *sauce espagnole,* and a *glace de viande* is a collagen-rich stock that is cooked down to the point where it will gel in the fridge. A demi-glace can never be as crystalline in pure flavor as a real *glace de viande.*

The key to a good *glace de viande* is collagen. Traditionally, it is made from a stock that contains veal bones, which are loaded with the stuff. Pig's feet are another excellent source. Chicken feet have a decent amount of collagen, and so do duck feet. Hunters actually are in the best position here, as they can merely snip off the feet of the birds they bring home and store them in the fridge for later.

The only challenge with this recipe is that it is a major undertaking. It takes all day, but you can break the process into several days, if you like. However you decide to do it, it's worth it. Either domesticated or wild ducks can be used for this recipe.

DIFFICULTY: ✶ ✶ ✶ ✶

MAKES 2 TO 4 CUPS

PREP TIME: 30 MINUTES

COOK TIME: 12 HOURS

Carcasses of 3 to 5 ducks or 2 geese, with some meat
   still attached (such as wings and necks)
Olive oil, for coating
Kosher salt
20 to 30 duck or chicken feet or 2 pig's feet
2 yellow or white onions, chopped
4 carrots, chopped
5 celery stalks, chopped
4 cloves garlic, mashed with the side of a knife
Stems from 1 bunch flat-leaf or curly parsley
1 large sprig fresh thyme or 1 tablespoon dried thyme
1 large sprig rosemary or 1 tablespoon dried rosemary
4 bay leaves
1 tablespoon juniper berries, crushed (optional)
1 tablespoon cracked peppercorns

Trim off as much fat as possible from the carcasses. Coat the carcasses with oil, salt them well, and put in a large roasting pan. Put in the oven, turn on the oven to 400°F, and roast for 45 minutes to 1 hour, until well browned. (Alternatively, grill the carcasses over a hot fire until well browned.)

Meanwhile, chop the duck feet with a cleaver or other heavy knife, or score the pig's feet all over, to break the skin and expose the joints and bones. This opens up the feet so that the collagen can come out, which is what will make the concentrated stock solidify. You cannot skip the feet in this recipe.

When the carcasses are ready, remove them from the oven and chop them into large pieces with heavy kitchen shears or a cleaver. This will make it possible to fit them all into your stockpot. Transfer them to a large stockpot and add the feet. Pour in enough cold water to cover by 1 to 2 inches.

Turn on the heat to medium-high and bring the liquid to a bare simmer, skimming off any scum that forms on the surface. Simmer gently, uncovered, for 4 to 6 hours; the longer you go, the more powerful the final product. (You can stop now if you like, refrigerate the stock, and pick up the process the next day.)

Add the onions, carrots, celery, garlic, parsley stems, thyme, rosemary, bay, juniper, and peppercorns. Resist the urge to salt the stock. Continue to simmer gently, uncovered, for 1½ hours.

Turn off the heat and strain the stock. Set up a fine-mesh sieve over another large pot (you may need 2 pots if you don't have a second large pot). Line the sieve with a piece of plain paper towel or cheesecloth and ladle the stock through the sieve. Don't try to capture the last dregs of stock at the bottom of the pot, and change the paper towel or rinse the cheesecloth once or twice. These steps are vital to making a clear stock. You should now have about 6 to 8 quarts of stock. (This is another place where you can stop, refrigerate the stock, and pick up the process later.)

When you are ready to reduce the stock to a *glace*, set the pot over low heat, but do not center the pot over the burner. By positioning the pot off center, you will concentrate the impurities on one side of the pot, where you can easily skim them off frequently. Let the stock simmer for at least 6 hours. Take your time, and the stock should reduce to about one tenth of its original volume. This final reduction process can last overnight; be sure to put the pot on a low-flame burner turned to its lowest setting. If you have a heat diffuser, use it. In the end, you should have a dark, clear, shiny stock.

Pour this concentrated stock into small storage containers and refrigerate. Once it has fully cooled, it will set up like gelatin and will keep for up to 2 weeks or longer. Or, pour it into ice-cube trays or small glass jars and freeze for up to 1 year. Remember, a little goes a long way: when you need a bomb of meaty flavor, drop just a spoonful into a sauce or soup.

"Not the cry, but the flight of the wild duck, leads the flock to fly and follow."

—CHINESE PROVERB

DUCK CONSOMMÉ

Consommé is one of those classic French preparations that anyone who attends cooking school learns to make. Perhaps because of this, I've heard all sorts of chefs describe consommé as boring or overly fussy. But at its best, consommé is a powerfully flavored stock so clear that you can read the Bible through it. A well-made consommé is also one of those dishes that is far harder to execute than it looks. Consommé shows skill and panache without shouting, like a Savile Row shirt: crisp, understated, but oozing style and class. Consommé is the Grace Kelly of soups.

Tragically, consommé died about the same time as Princess Grace, in the early 1980s. What happened? Why do we not see it on menus anymore? Probably the same reason no one wears a vest with a suit these days. Consommé is passé, like sole meunière or steak Diane. But I ask you to consider consommé with fresh eyes.

A perfectly executed consommé is almost entirely devoid of fat—though I prefer just enough fat floating on the surface to make it look like a sprinkling of gleaming jewels is adorning it. It will taste powerfully of whatever it is made from, and, of course, it will be crystal clear.

It is that clarity that is so difficult to achieve—in life, in writing, and in soup.

DIFFICULTY: ✳ ✳ ✳ ✳ ✳

MAKES ABOUT 4 QUARTS

PREP TIME: 30 MINUTES

COOK TIME: 1¼ HOURS, PLUS TIME TO MAKE THE STOCK

2 to 3 pounds lean duck or goose meat, cut into 1-inch chunks

1 large yellow or white onion, chopped

2 large carrots, chopped

2 large celery stalks, chopped

1 ounce (about 2 handfuls) dried mushrooms (any kind), soaked in hot water until soft, drained, and chopped

4 cloves garlic, chopped

10 egg whites

2-inch sprig rosemary, chopped

6 to 8 fresh sage leaves, chopped

4 bay leaves

5 quarts Basic Duck Stock (page 222)

2 tablespoons kosher salt

1½ cups tomato puree

Pass the meat, onion, carrots, celery, and mushrooms through a meat grinder fitted with the fine die, or pulse in a food processor until you have a rough mash. Do not puree the ingredients. Transfer the mixture to a bowl and mix in the garlic, egg whites, rosemary, sage, and bay. Cover and chill for at least 4 hours or up to overnight. This is called the raft.

Pour the cold stock into a stockpot and add the salt. Add the tomato puree to the raft and mix well, then add the raft to the stock. Turn the heat on to medium and bring slowly to a simmer. *Do not let the stock boil under any circumstances or you will ruin your consommé.* Stir every couple of minutes until the raft begins to float on the surface.

When the raft has formed, poke a 1-inch hole in its center, and let the consommé simmer gently for 1¼ hours, never allowing it to boil.

Put a fine-mesh sieve over a container large enough to hold the consommé, and line the sieve with a plain paper towel or cheesecloth. Turn the heat to low under the consommé, and ladle the consommé into the sieve, allowing it to drain into the container. When you get to the bottom of the stockpot, pick out the raft and discard it, then pour the remaining consommé through the sieve.

Chill the consommé or serve immediately. Taste and adjust the seasoning with salt before serving.

SELECTED BIBLIOGRAPHY

Beard, James. *Fowl & Game Cookery*. New York: Harcourt Brace, 1979.

Bellrose, Frank. *Ducks, Geese and Swans of North America*. Harrisburg, PA: Stackpole Books, 1980.

Bugialli, Giuliano. *Classic Techniques of Italian Cooking*. New York: Simon & Schuster, 1982.

Cameron, Angus, and Judith Jones. *The L. L. Bean Game & Fish Cookbook*. New York: Random House, 1983.

Child, Julia, Louisette Bertholle, and Simon Beck. *Mastering the Art of French Cooking*. Vols. I and II. New York: Knopf, 1961.

Daguin, Ariane, George Faison, and Joanna Pruess. *D'Artagnan's Glorious Game Cookbook*. New York: Little, Brown, 1999.

De Gouy, L. P. *The Derrydale Game Cookbook*. Lanham, MD: Derrydale Press, 2000.

Dickson-Wright, Clarissa. *The Game Cookbook*. Lanham, MD: Kyle Books, 2005.

Diehl, Kari Schoening. *The Everything Nordic Cookbook*. Avon, MA: Adams Media, 2012.

Dunlop, Fuchsia. *Land of Plenty*. New York: W. W. Norton, 2001.

———. *Revolutionary Chinese Cookbook*. New York: W. W. Norton, 2006.

Escoffier, Auguste. *Le Guide Culinarire*. New York: John Wiley & Sons, 2011.

Fearnley-Whittingstall, Hugh. *The River Cottage Meat Book*. London: Hodder and Stoughton, 2004.

Griffiths, Jesse. *Afield*. New York: Welcome Books, 2012.

Hasheider, Philip. *The Complete Book of Butchering, Smoking, Curing, and Sausage Making*. Minneapolis: Voyageur Press, 2010.

Herrick, Christine Terhune. *The Consolidated Library of Modern Cooking*.Vol. III. New York: R. J. Bodmer, 1905.

Keller, Thomas. *Under Pressure*. New York: Artisan, 2008.

Kutas, Rytek. *Great Sausage Recipes and Meat Curing*. Buffalo, NY: The Sausage Maker, Inc., 2008.

Livingston, A. D. *The Duck and Goose Cookbook*. Harrisburg, PA: Stackpole Books, 1997.

Marianski, Stanley, and Adam Marianski. *The Art of Making Fermented Sausages*. Denver: Outskirts Press, 2008.

———. *Home Production of Quality Meats and Sausages*. Seminole, FL: Bookmagic, 2010.

McGee, Harold. *On Food and Cooking*. New York: Scribner, 2004.

McLagan, Jennifer. *Fat*. Berkeley: Ten Speed Press, 2008.

———. *Odd Bits*. Berkeley: Ten Speed Press, 2011.

Miller, Gloria Bley. *The Thousand Recipe Chinese Cookbook*. New York: Simon & Schuster, 1984.

Nguyen, Andrea. *Into the Vietnamese Kitchen*. Berkeley: Ten Speed Press, 2006.

Page, Karen, and Andrew Dornenburg. *The Flavor Bible*. New York: Little, Brown, 2008.

Picard, Martin. *Au Pied du Cochon*. Vancouver: Douglas & McIntyre, 2006.

Ruhlman, Michael, and Brian Polcyn. *Charcuterie*. New York: W. W. Norton, 2005.

Schwabe, Calvin. *Unmentionable Cuisine*. Charlottesville, VA: University of Virginia Press, 1999.

Scripter, Sami, and Sheng Yang. *Cooking from the Heart*. Minneapolis: University of Minnesota Press, 2009.

Shaw, Hank. *Hunt, Gather, Cook*. Emmaus, PA: Rodale, 2011.

Sheraton, Mimi. *The German Cookbook*. New York, Random House, 1993.

Volokh, Anne. *The Art of Russian Cuisine*. New York: MacMillan, 1983.

Wise, Victoria. *American Charcuterie*. New York: Penguin Books, 1986.

Wolfert, Paula. *The Cooking of Southwest France*. New York: John Wiley & Sons, 2005.

Wright, Clifford. *A Mediterranean Feast*. New York: William Morrow, 1999.

ACKNOWLEDGMENTS

HANK'S ACKNOWLEDGMENTS

No book is a solo endeavor, but this one has been quite the team effort. I have benefited from so many others' expertise and advice that I feel compelled to at least attempt to thank them all in print. I am certain I will miss some people, and for that I apologize in advance.

First and foremost I'd like to thank Holly Heyser, who shot the photographs throughout this book. Holly is not solely a wonderful photographer. She is also my best friend, duck hunting buddy, and confidante; we've shared the past dozen years together, and I hope we share many more in the years to come.

Thanks also to my agent Jason Yarn and my editors Jenny Wapner and Melissa Moore, as well as the rest of the crew at Ten Speed—special shout-out to Sharon Silva, quite possibly the best copyeditor I've worked with in twenty-plus years as a writer.

A lifted glass in honor of Elise Bauer, for her overall wisdom; Jesse Griffiths, for being a sounding board for some of my crazier ducky ideas; Ariane Daguin, for being the doyenne of all things duck; and to R.J. Waldron and Charlie Peebles, for making me a better duck hunter.

This book is not just a compendium of my knowledge. I've had the privilege of tapping the creative minds of some of the best chefs in America, all of whom have made this book a bit richer: Aaron Barnett, Chris Cosentino, Romy Dorotan, Brad Farmerie, Sheamus Feeley, Bill Fuller, Matt Jennings, Liam LaCivita, Eddy LeRoux, Tony Maws, Patrick Mulvaney, Chrysa Robertson, Michael Smith, David Soohoo, Michael Tuohy, Paul Virant, and Andrew Zimmern.

Special thanks to author Paula Wolfert, the guru of duck confit, for setting me on the right path; to Kate Hill, for the schooling on cassoulet; and to Bob del Grosso, Christian Spinillo, and Scott Stegen, for making sure my charcuterie section passes muster with the "meat mafia."

For all of you who tested the recipes in this book, I thank you. There are too many to enumerate here, but you know who you are. Without you, these recipes would not be as wonderful as they turned out to be. Glad y'all got my back!

Finally, I'd like to thank the readers of *Hunter Angler Gardener Cook*. It is because of you I am here. Without your constant questions, exhortations and support, I would probably be working as a two-bit political hack somewhere dark and unpleasant. You have made my dreams come true, and for that I will be forever grateful.

HOLLY'S ACKNOWLEDGMENTS

Thanks to Carina Bassin, who generously let me pillage her family's hundred-year-old farm in Ione, California, for the authentically distressed wood that appears as tabletops in photos throughout this book; Katrina Heyser, whose keen eye for thrift store plates, bowls, and silverware is also in evidence throughout the book; Ruth Heyser, whose constantly evolving art is a source of endless inspiration to me; and Hank, whose decision to start writing about food was the reason I finally took up photography in earnest. Thank you for feeding my body, my soul, and my passion for photography, and also for reheating dinner every time it gets cold during a photo shoot.

INDEX